MADAME PRUNIER'S FISH COOKERY BOOK

*Selected, Translated and Edited, with an
Introduction and Notes, from Les Poissons,
Coquillages, Crustacés et leur Preparation
Culinaire par Michel Bouzy*

BY

AMBROSE HEATH

ADAPTED FOR AMERICA BY
CROSBY GAIGE

WITH A SPECIAL FOREWORD BY
MADAME S. B. PRUNIER

DECORATIONS BY
Mathurin Meheut

DOVER PUBLICATIONS, INC.
NEW YORK

This Dover edition, first published in 1971, is an unabridged and unaltered republication of the work originally published by Julian Messner, Inc., New York, in 1939. This work consists of material from *Les poissons, coquillages, crustacés et leur préparation culinaire par Michel Bouzy*, selected, translated and edited, with an introduction and notes, by Ambrose Heath and adapted for America by Crosby Gaige; also included is a foreword by Madame S. B. Prunier.

International Standard Book Number: 0-486-22679-4
Library of Congress Catalog Card Number: 74-143673

Manufactured in the United States of America
Dover Publications, Inc.
180 Varick Street
New York, N. Y. 10014

CONTENTS

MADAME PRUNIER COMES TO AMERICA

FOREWORD BY MADAME PRUNIER

MADAME PRUNIER COMES TO AMERICA

BY CROSBY GAIGE

AN AMERICAN GOURMET reading Madame Prunier's charming and appetite-provoking book is immediately beset by two emotions—one a sense of gratitude for her verbal ambassador herewith presented to you by The House of Messner—the other an ambition to meet the lady in person, to be able to savor of her inspired cooking, in short to have Madame as well as her book as an honored visitor to our shores. I say shores, and I mean literally our shores—the Atlantic coast from Northern Maine to the tip of Florida, around the Gulf, and up the California coast, and along Oregon's cliffs. Nor would I have her forget the reaches and rapids of our brooks and rivers and the clear blue waters of our inland lakes.

Well we have our coastal waters, and our inland lakes and streams and we are blessed with myriads of the finny delicacies that inhabit them. And now by happy chance we have Madame Prunier to tell us how to make the most of our opportunities. What the painters of Florence have meant to their art, what the glassmakers of Venice and the diamond-cutters of Holland have meant to theirs, what the practitioners of any great craft have meant in any particular field, the Prunier family have meant in their own domain. The results of their taste and knowledge are here in this book for our study, our enjoyment and our benefit.

The American housewife can well afford the time to study this book from cover to cover. The inspiration of French cookery are the sauces, the spices and the other seasonings and here they are in wise and detailed profusion. Take for example the cod, a valuable and prevalent fish. What happens to it in the average American kitchen? Cod fish balls, or *"Croquettes a l'Americaine,"* as Madame courteously calls them. It is a far cry from our own stand-by to Croquettes de Morue, and from our creamed cod fish to Morue Grand Mere. A practicing knowledge of the chapter on cod fish alone would raise the ordinary cook from the ranks of the ordinary to the exciting and unusual. And the same observation may apply to the salmon, the mackerel or the flounder.

My piscatorial memories are many and wide-spread. I shall never forget the tender succulence of a brook trout caught and fried in butter not ten feet from the rushing stream that was its home. It is a long journey from that to a dinner at Jack and Charlie's "21" this last August 25th. The host was Mac Kriendler and the occasion was in honor of the first grouse to arrive from Scotland via airplane and Ile de France. The grouse were superb but to me the great moment of the evening was the fish course. It consisted of a ten pound lake-trout and—I was going to tell you how it was prepared, but Madame Prunier has saved me the trouble. On page 13, she tells us of the court-bouillon in which it was cooked, on pages 27 and 33, she reveals the secrets of the *Maître d'hôtel* butter and the sauce Hollandaise that were served with it.

Actually, every recipe in this book can be cooked in America with American fish, and practically all of them call for fish known here and to be found in the larger coastal markets. However, where a brill is called for a turbot may be used; a butterfish or a flounder may be substituted for a gudgeon; a dace for a tench; a mullet for a gurnard. And, since Mr. Ambrose Heath was considering the English housewife in editing this book, he devotes several pages to the whiting, a fish unobtainable here. Loath to sacrifice even these few examples of Madame Prunier's talent, I suggest that the common American frost fish be used instead of whiting in these excellent recipes.

There are certain small points of terminology of really *haute cuisine* that need clarifying for the average American housewife. For instance, when you are told to "strain through a napkin," use cheesecloth; "press through a fine tammy cloth," use muslin. The "fine sieve" referred to is not an implement of our ordinary kitchen nor of the ordinary house furnishing store, but can be had from *de luxe* establishments like Lewis and Conger, etc. For bain marie, a double boiler can in most cases be used.

I should like Madame Prunier and her readers to know that in the great fish markets of our coastal cities—New York's Fulton Market where the fish auctions are colorful and exciting, in the Boston fish dock where the boats from off the New England coast meet in not always friendly rivalry for their sales, in Charleston, in New Orleans, in the California fish markets and at the Oregon docks, thousands of tons of fish, daily lose their amateur standing as citizens of the sea and become food products, a vitally important contribution to the country's commerce and a significant part of the American dietary.

Our pan fish are many, a delicious array and low in cost for housewife or gourmet who will take the time to visit the fish market and pick and choose. For this simple process there are the black bass, the crappie, calico bass, the rock bass, the Sacramento perch, the sun fishes. There are the white and yellow bass, a white perch, and the yellow perch too. All of these have white, flaky flesh, but little fat, and are so easily cooked that a child can prepare them. Preparation *a la meuniere,* page 8, is a distinct addition to most pan fish.

Another popular Atlantic and Gulf coast fish is the blue fish which is firm and sweet and one of the best food fishes in the country. Broil a small blue fish and serve with Anchovy butter, page 25.

Cat fish, those fellows with ugly faces and ugly reputations, are found in United States and Mexican waters in about thirty-four species; twelve of these are favorites with fishermen who know that the market men will take them. They are skinned before they are cooked, and are, in this country, popular for stewing and boiling and frying.

Out in the Mississippi and Wabash country the cat fish is a staple product and at road-side stands a cat fish steak ranks in popularity with the hamburger. These steaks can be improved if treated like grilled salmon steaks, page 143.

The small cat fish of our Eastern ponds, known to me in my boyhood days as a bull-head, is one of the sweetest fish on earth. Instead of just frying it, try the extra *meuniere* touch as mentioned above and see the difference it will make.

Through the middle-western part of the country the appetite is for panned fish and baked, stuffed fish, many of which come from the Great Lakes. The Cisco, or lake herring, of the Great Lakes, the New York lakes, and those of New England and Canada north to the Hudson Bay, are cooked like small trout, see page 100, and in fact are often put off on hungry restaurant diners for trout. They are sweet and delicate.

Cod and mullet are other favorites widely known. Madame Prunier deals well with both of them. Of Pompano, however, she knew naught. It is one of the great delicacies of the sea. Try it grilled with Sauce Bearnaise, page 30.

The flat fishes such as flounder, plaice, sand dabs, soles and turbots are universally popular as restaurant fish for they are simple to bone, easily cooked and easily eaten. But real sole is rare in this country—most of it is small flounder and so are sand dabs flounder. In San Francisco where they are a famous dish, I probably would get into trouble for making that statement although the U. S. fisheries experts will back me up on it. There happen to be in this present volume thirty pages of recipes devoted to sole, most of which can advantageously be used for our American flounder.

There are dozens of varieties of grouper in our markets. On both coasts mackerel is caught in several varieties and like trout, many different fish are called mackerel. Trout is a name given to members of the salmon family—rainbow, cutthroat, steelhead, speckled and Dolly Varden being among the best known and the steelhead and Dolly Varden frequently found in salt water as well as in lakes and brooks. Madame Prunier has a whole chapter on trout.

There are so many varieties of clams that when you just order clams in an American restaurant you may find yourself engaged in a half hour's conversation with the head waiter before you can make clear just what is wanted. He may ask you if you want quahogs, hard clams or round clams found from Cape Cod to Texas; or there are the long clams or soft clams, found from South Carolina up the coast to the Arctic Ocean. There are razor clams from the Pacific, from the south of Oregon to the Arctic; also there are the little necks or hard shell clams, the butter clams, and the great Washington clam which reaches a length of eight or ten inches (and is minced for cookery). These play an important role among American shell fish.

Madame Prunier tells us how to steam clams, how to prepare a clam rizotto on page 54 and on page 62 gives the recipe for a clam bisque which is excellent. Little necks or cherry stones may be used in these dishes.

I am going to take the liberty of presenting my own adaptation of a Spanish recipe using clams that is a great favorite in my household. It is called paella after the iron casserole used in Spanish kitchens.

PAELLA

Into a good-sized stew pan or casserole I pour a cup of good olive oil and into that I slice a few onions. Meanwhile, having prepared and disjointed a couple of nice broiling chickens, I consign them to the hot oil along with the onions. I saute them until the onions are a golden brown. The next contribution is Spanish or Italian rice, a demi-tasse of it for every person to be served.

On the stove I have a pot of rich chicken broth at a boil. I watch the contents of the stew pan carefully, stirring from time to time to keep the rice from burning. When the rice begins to dry out a little I add a cup of the boiling broth, and when this is absorbed, another.

At this point I add to the pot a dozen and a half tiny peanut clams, in their shells, well scrubbed. (You may have to order these diminutive clams from your fish market in advance.) I also enrich the stew with half dozen or so thin slices of Italian or Spanish sausage and two dozen cleaned shrimp.

All the essentials being thus concentrated in the stew I now prepare the seasoning. Into my mortar I put three cloves of garlic, one-half teaspoon of saffron and a small cupful of hot chicken broth. These I proceed to belabor with a pestle until all the broth is thoroughly impregnated with both the color and the flavor of the saffron and garlic. I then strain this colored and seasoned broth into the stew.

When the rice is properly cooked, enough cups of the boiling broth having been added to complete the job, each kernel should be separate and not a mushy mess. Over the top of the concoction I finally place a few strips of pimento and sprinkle some grated cheese. The whole dish I now put under the broiler for about five minutes.

I serve the paella from the pan or casserole in which it has been cooked.

Oysters have spread themselves out also. The Gulf of Mexico produces small Crystal Rivers and Apalachicolas; North Carolina bays on the Atlantic coast are full of oyster beds which are locally in favor; Virginia tidal water has been famous for its oysters since that shore was first settled.

Present day American gourmets know them as Lynnhavens and Chincoteagues and Rappahannocks among others from this district. The Chesapeake Bay of both Virginia and Maryland has long been famous as a great oyster producing area which brought forth many established favorites; the Chesapeake Bays which are small or medium and mildly salty and Choptanks, of unusual flavor and prized by the good eaters of that section.

Delaware Bay also produces oysters which have made their own reputation for flavor and of course Long Island waters, with commercial oyster farming established there as a great industry, produces the types most popular in New York restaurants and probably the best known in the country as a whole: Bluepoints, Fire Island Salts, Gardiners Bays and Gardiners Island Salts, Robbins Islands and the Seapure from deep waters, and the Oyster Bays are these favorites, with probably Bluepoints being the most commonly asked for in the fish-market and restaurants.

From Rhode Island at least four well-known oysters are widely popular; these are the Narragansett Bays, Silver Leafs, the Sea-to-Home and the Nayatt Point—that great aristocrat of the oyster world.

Many of these specialties are known best near the fishing grounds, but others are popular all over the country because of the freezing methods now employed for distant shipping and the refrigeration car facilities for handling these perishable delicacies.

There is no doubt of the truth of Madame's statement that oysters are best served raw from their shells. Personally, I prefer them without any trimmings. The English usually add a spot of vinegar and a dash of freshly ground pepper from a mill. In America we invented an excellent concoction called Cocktail Sauce. I like this sauce in which to dunk a bit of roll, but not as a ruby bath to wash away the salt sea tang that every self-respecting American oyster carries within its shell as its own proper introduction to the palate.

Our author sets forth many delicious ways of cooking oysters. Most of them are adaptable to our smaller or medium sized varieties such as Bluepoints, Oyster Bays, Nayatt Points, etc. Try her. *Huître a la Florentine* on page 229 and her own specialties—*Huître Mornay* and *Huître Poulette* on pages 231 and 232.

This is true of crabs too; hard crabbing goes on the whole year in southern waters; the soft crab season is from the first of May to the last of October. I must also mention the huge Pacific coast crabs, hardly known on our eastern shore; and the miniature oyster crabs, which live inside oyster shells and as a rule are used as garnish in other fish cookery.

If I personally were dealing with crabs, I would not go crabbing nor would I go to the fish market for live crabs, but taking the line of least resistance, hie myself to the nearest grocer for a can of good crabmeat. A mere twist of the wrist with the can opener and Madame's recipe for *Crabe a la Bretonne,* page 200 or *Crabe au Paprika,* page 201 will bring surcease from any of the minor annoyances of life.

The crawfish, which is salt water, and the crayfish, which is from fresh water, are both miniature members of the lobster family and, as in Europe, are used by American cooks for soups, bisque and garnishing. Except on the West coast where the crawfish is cooked and eaten like lobster. It is a mouth watering experience to follow the Prunier adventures with *langouste, écrevisse* and *homard.*

The true American lobster is found on the North Atlantic from North Carolina up to Labrador, with eastern Maine the source for an abundance of this superb sea food. There is a Spiny lobster of the West coast, cooked and eaten much the same but lobster from the Atlantic is responsible for the high reputation of that food in this country.

The big prawn which may be as long as seven inches and the little shrimp, of two inches or more, are also favorites but we have not been very original in our cookery of these. We have learned and can still learn from European chefs.

Madame Prunier, when you come to visit us, may I suggest that you leave Docteur Rondelet and Maitre Pierre Belon at home. Come with an open heart and a silver-lined copper frying pan. Bring an assorted wardrobe for our climate is capricious. Be well assured of your welcome and be prepared to take out citizenship papers. For nearly three hundred years there has been slowly mounting in our American kitchens a piscatorial consciousness, a sort of fish frenzy. With you at its head this movement might well, and from my point of view, very well too, replace both of the major political parties.

Caesar, I am told, conquered Britain for its oysters. Thank *le bon Dieu* he never heard of America. May I, with my hand upon my heart and with due regard for insular idiosyncrasies, assure you that there never was born a Colchester nor a Whitstable Native who, upon chance encounter with a Nayatt Point, would not raise his shell and wave his, or is it her, gills in silent ostrean salute to sheer superiority.

FOREWORD
BY MADAME S. B. PRUNIER

It is a tradition to be able to ask indulgence for a new-born child, but for this book I do not think it is absolutely necessary, since the editing and translation were entrusted to Mr. Ambrose Heath, whose culinary and gastronomical learning is so well known. And perhaps you will agree with me in thanking him for the work which he has done with so much enthusiasm and understanding, and with me hope that, thanks to him, my book will appeal to and interest you. If it does not succeed in doing so, and I shall be heart-broken if it does not, it will at any rate have the distinction of being one of those rare books dedicated entirely to the cooking of Fish and Shellfish.

Perhaps you would like to know why I made up my mind to publish this book. When I first came to England, I was very agreeably surprised to find so many people who were interested in their food, people whom I serve every day with my dishes at my restaurant and who are continually asking me for the recipes. I felt sure that a collection of those recipes would be welcomed. And then, I thought, wouldn't it be a way, by putting them within the reach of all, of popularising fish dishes, more particularly dishes demanding the use of those common fishes which people do not seem to want at any price on their tables? And this reminds me of a remark made to me by one of my clients. " Oh, Madame Prunier," she exclaimed, " you give us fishes which we wouldn't dream of eating anywhere ; you call them by a funny French name, and we all adore them ! " . . . Yes, why should not people get out of the usual rut in serving fish ? All fish are excellent, I assure you, if they are well prepared.

Perhaps you know the old French saying : *C'est la sauce qui fait manger le poisson.*" In this book you will find recipes for a good number of sauces, some of them simple ones to encourage the housewife who has a prejudice against fish (first, because she may be suspicious of its freshness ; and, second, because of the difficulty she has in buying any but certain usual sorts; and, third, because she may find its preparation too complicated), other sauces, more elaborate, for the Cordon Bleus, as we call the first-rate cooks, and then several original and unusual ones for the *blasés.* But of whatever kind they are, all are practicable.

If this book is the kind of thing my friends and clients want to have, I must confess that its compilation is not recent, nor is it my own personal work. Actually the original inspiration was my Father, Emile Prunier, twelve years ago. Being as anxious as I am to encourage people to eat fish and at the same time to gather together the result of twenty-five years' work and research, a month before he died he explained to his chef and old collaborator, M. Michel Bouzy, and to me the manner in which he would like to see his fish cookery book planned. Unhappily he was never able to finish it, and that is why M. Bouzy published in 1929 his *Les Poissons, Crustacés et Coquillages,* in which he collected principally the Prunier recipes and on which this present book is founded.

In memory of my Father, to whom the book was dedicated, I agreed to become its Godmother, and the famous Maître Escoffier its Godfather, and perhaps you will be interested to see the menu which was composed for the book's christening.   Here it is :

A Luncheon
given
on the appearance of the book
Les Poissons, Coquillages et Crustacés
by Michel Bouzy

———

Les Fruits de Mer
Crabes diablés
Filets de Sole Emile Prunier
Le Bar farci et accomodé à la manière Angevine
Faisans rôtis et flanqués de Cailles aux Marrons
Salade de Saison
Fromages
Les Pêches Melba
(as created by Maître Escoffier)
Une Corbeille garnie de Friandises

———

Les grands Anjou de côteau de Layon
(Clos de l'Aiglerie)
Gevrey Chambertin 1915
Champagnes Perrier-Jouet et Lanson

Café spécial Malgache
Liqueur Cointreau

You yourself will, with the aid of this book, be able to prepare the fish recipes in this menu, and you will agree with me that my chef didn't treat us badly—far from it !

So it is this Godchild, revised, corrected and augmented by new recipes, of which I owe a good number to my collaborator and chef in London, M. Maurice Cochois, that I have the honour to offer you today. If its success results in increasing the sale of fish, and in particular of those fishes which have hitherto been ignored, and so helps the fishing industry, I shall have done a very little towards paying a debt to a country where I have been welcomed with such warmth and courtesy. It is not too much to say that it was this welcome that finally decided me to offer this book to my friends.

72 St. James Street,
London, S.W.1
June 1938.

Chapter *1*

Advice on Buying Fish—Elementary Rules for Cooking Fish

IN a country where fish is hardly ever served in any other way than boiled, fried or grilled, this chapter should be of the very greatest use, and every word should be read and digested carefully. Apart from the somewhat exotic fashion *au bleu*, the cooking of fishes by braising, *au gratin* and *à la meunière* will to a great many be a revelation of deliciousness and simplicity. The *gratins* in particular afford an admirable way of imparting often to quite a dull fish an interest which transforms it into a first-class dish, and in those fishes of which we have tired because of their insipidness we shall see a remarkable change if we turn to the *court-bouillon* for their "poaching."

This, by the way, is a word which should never be forgotten. Fish should never be *boiled*, unless it is to make a soup of some kind, in which case the flavour must be boiled out into the liquid in which it is cooked. To *poach* a fish, however, is a very different matter and produces a very different result.

The frying of fish *à la meunière* is another fashion to which I should like to draw special attention. It is simple, it is quick, and it is delicious ; and yet how many times have we encountered fish cooked in this way on the tables of our friends ?

The instructions in this chapter demand serious attention, and once their simple procedure is mastered, the cooking of fish in all its possible ways need have no terrors even for the mistress when the cook is out !

ADVICE ON BUYING FISH AND SHELLFISH

Absolute freshness and good quality are essential. Freshness in fish can be recognised by the lively brilliance of the eyes, by the rosy colour of the gills, and by the stiffness of the flesh. If the eyes are dull and the fish limp, it is not fresh, as the limpness comes from the fibres relaxing. This lack of freshness can also be recognised by the smell.

Lobsters, Crawfish (*Langouste*), Crayfish and so on ought to be taken alive. The flesh of these shellfish when dead is soft, and has lost the best of its qualities. Mollusca and Shellfish such as Oysters, Clams, Cockles, Mussels, etc., ought to feel heavy in the hand and have their shells tightly shut. If the shells are open, the shellfish should be rejected.

As far as is possible, fresh-water fish ought to be alive, and only killed when the time comes for cooking them. All the same, these fish will keep better than sea-fish, and they can be kept for a day or two by wrapping them in a good covering of fresh grass.

According to their kind, fish weighing from five to seven ounces will do for one person : and those of half a pound to three-quarters for two persons. Two pounds gross of Salmon and Salmon Trout should be allowed for five people, but if a cut piece is bought, two pounds will be enough for six.

Taken by the whole fish, about half a pound of Turbot or large Brill should be allowed per head.

A Lobster weighing a pound or just over is enough for two.

A Crawfish (*Langouste*) of two pounds is enough for four.

According to their size, two or three Crayfish (*Écrevisses*) are allowed per head.

THE GRILLING OF FISH

All fish that is to be grilled should first be cleaned, scaled or well scraped, dried or well wiped with a clean cloth (especially if the fish has been washed first), and if the fish is thick-fleshed, scored here and there. By scoring I mean making little slits in the flesh on each side, the reason for this being that these help to hasten the cooking of the fish.

Flat fish, such as Soles, have their heads cut off diagonally. The end of the tail is trimmed with scissors, and the black skin is removed. The white skin is left on, but it should be well scraped, and the fins cut off. For other fish of this kind, it is usual to make an incision on the black side and in the middle of the fish, penetrating to the backbone, and from head to tail.

When the fish are prepared in this way, brush them over with oil and put them on a *very hot* grill. If it is not hot enough, they may catch, stick to the bars and break when they are turned over. During their cooking, continue to brush them over with oil from time to time.

The heat of the grill must naturally be governed by the thickness of the fish you are grilling. The smaller the fish, the fiercer the heat should be : if it is a large and thick one, the cooking should be conducted more gently so that the heat will gradually penetrate the flesh.

Very large fish, which would be cumbersome to grill whole, can be cut across into slices of about an inch to an inch and a half thick. These can then be treated in the same manner as small whole fish.

THE FRYING OF FISH

DEEP FAT FRYING

The best fish for frying, in general, are the flat fish, Soles, Turbot, Plaice, Lemon Soles, and so on ; and after them the other white-fleshed fish such as Whiting, Saithe and Cod, the last two being cut into fillets or cutlets (steaks).

The best frying medium to use is oil, for this can be heated up to 280° Fahr. without burning, whereas the best beef kidney fat cannot exceed 175° Fahr.

Fat used for frying fish should never be used for any other purpose, for the repeated frying of fish will leave its flavour in the fat.

It should be remembered that any fat before being used should be strained, for it is sure to contain some of the burnt flour or breadcrumbs of food which has been fried in it, and these will burn and speck whatever is fried in it next.

It must be carefully noted in frying fish in deep fat that—

(1) The proportion of fat to fish is correct. There should always be plenty of it, for the more there is, the quicker it will heat up and the longer hold its heat, and you will be sure (which is most important) that the fish are completely submerged in the fat.

(2) If you are frying a certain number of fish, or pieces of fish, at the same time, you must remember that they will considerably reduce the heat of the fat when they are plunged into it, and you must counteract this by putting the pan at once on to a strong heat, so that it will recapture its original temperature as quickly as possible.

(3) The frying fat must be very hot (slightly smoking) when the fish is plunged into it, so that it " seizes " at once.

That is to say, it must be hot enough to form a fried envelope, as it were, round the fish, which will prevent the fat from penetrating into the fish, and so making it indigestible.

All thick-fleshed fish should be scored, as has been explained already.

Whatever sort the fish is, whether whole or in fillets or in cutlets, it should first be rolled in slightly salted milk, or in beer, then rolled in flour and shaken to remove the flour which does not stick to it. Having been plunged into the fat, the fish will be found to be cooked when it rises to the surface. It should then be drained on a clean cloth, dried and slightly salted, and served on a dish with a grid or on a napkin or doyley.

A heap of very green fried parsley should be put at each end of the dish, and the fish may be surrounded with quarters of lemon.

At the same time there should be handed separately some such sauce as Béarnaise, Tartare, Rémoulade, etc.

COOKING FISH À LA MEUNIERE

SHALLOW FRYING

The cooking of fish in this particularly attractive manner seems to be little known in the majority of English kitchens. It is extremely simple, but needs some care. It is only suited to small fish or the slices of larger ones.

The method is this. The fish (whole, in fillets or in slices) are simply seasoned with salt and pepper, and fried in a frying-pan in very hot butter. When they are golden on each side, they are taken out and dished, a little lemon juice is squeezed over them, and a few pinches of roughly chopped fresh parsley are added. A piece of butter is then put into the pan in which they were cooked, and when this has become *noisette*, that is, slightly browned and giving out a nutty flavour, it is quickly poured over the fish, which is served immediately while the butter is still foaming.

There are a number of variations on this method, by which the fish, after being cooked, is garnished with certain things, *e.g.* slices of oranges, or of mushrooms, or shrimps : in which case the dish, while still *à la meunière*, takes its name from the added ingredient. For example, *Sole Meunière à l'orange, aux champignons, aux crevettes*, and so on. But the plain *meunière* is the best, and it is pleasant to think that it might have originated in the Miller's Wife (La Meunière) taking the little trout from her husband's hands, her own large and floury from baking, throwing the fish into fresh butter, and then when they were cooked, sprinkling a little parsley over them : the lemon, I am sure, came later.

By the way, if the fish are simply fried golden in this way, and the parsley, lemon and nut-brown butter are dispensed with, they are simply called *dorées*, and not *à la meunière* at all.

THE COOKING OF FISH AU BLEU

The important point in this method of cooking is that the fish should be alive. It should be taken from the water, stunned, cleaned through the gills, and trimmed. Be careful to handle it as little as possible, and do not scale or scrape it or even wash it, so as to leave on it the natural slime which plays an important part in making it look blue.

Put the fish on the grid of a fish kettle, sprinkle them with boiling vinegar, and cover them with a *court-bouillon* prepared beforehand. If the fish is fairly large, the *court-bouillon* should only be warm ; but if they are small, such as River Trout, Tench, and so on, they should be plunged into the *court-bouillon* while it is boiling.

Cook them in the usual manner, keeping the liquid just trembling, and serve them on a napkin, surrounded by parsley, removing the scales at the time of serving.

Fish cooked in this way can be served either hot or cold. If hot, they should be accompanied by a slightly salted melted butter and steamed or boiled potatoes. If cold, a Ravigote Sauce or a Gribiche Sauce may be offered.

THE BRAISING OF FISH

Only large fish such as Salmon, Turbot, Trout, Brill, etc., are suitable for braising, either whole or in large pieces, and for the cooking of these, special utensils of special shapes are necessary. These are the long fish kettle for Salmon, Trout, Bass, Grey Mullet, and so on ; and the turbot kettle for fish of the same shape as the Turbot. Both these utensils are furnished with a grid, on which the fish is placed, and this makes it easier to lift it out when it is being dished, and to slip it off on to the serving-dish. If these large fish are cooked in an unsuitable utensil, grave risk is run of breaking them when they are being dished.

To braise the fish, butter the bottom of the pan well, scatter on it some carrot and onion cut in rounds, and add a *bouquet garni* (page 13). Season the fish with salt and pepper, and let it stew very gently in the oven with the lid on for a quarter of an hour. Then moisten with fish fumet (page 15) and red or white wine according to the recipe

being followed. If red wine is used in the moistening
liquor, increase the proportion of thyme in the *bouquet garni*
a little. The liquor ought to come nearly half-way up the
fish. Bring to the boil, and continue to cook in the oven,
gently and evenly as is necessary in all braises, basting frequently. When the fish is cooked, the liquor is strained
then properly reduced and added to the sauce accompanying
the fish.

THE POACHING OF FISH

The fish is placed in the fish kettle or turbot kettle, according to its shape, and covered with the *court-bouillon* (page
13), which has been prepared beforehand. In the case of
Salmon, Trout, Bass, Grey Mullet, etc., this *court-bouillon*
should be cold. The *court-bouillon* for Turbot and Brill (see
page 13) should be prepared only just as it is wanted. In
either case, the fish should be completely immersed. For a
fish weighing four pounds, Salmon, Trout, etc., about six
quarts of *court-bouillon* will be needed. For a slice weighing
about half a pound or so, a pint and three-quarters.

As soon as the *court-bouillon* comes to the boil, draw the
utensil to the side of the fire, and keep the liquid just gently
trembling so that cooking proceeds by a gradual penetration
of heat into the fish ; that is to say, simply *poach* it. Uncon-
trolled boiling will not help matters in the least, and will
risk the fish being broken. The times for the fish mentioned
above are : ten minutes for two pounds, fifteen minutes for
four pounds, twenty minutes for six pounds, and thirty
minutes for fish weighing from eight to ten pounds.

White fish like Turbot, Brill, Sole, etc., take seven to ten
minutes for every two pounds. For fish weighing from
eight to ten pounds the poaching time as calculated above

must be lessened by four or five minutes for every two pounds. For a fish weighing a pound and a half to two pounds three quarts of *court-bouillon* will be needed, and the time of poaching should be from eight to ten minutes.

(NOTE.—The time of poaching is calculated from the moment the liquid comes to the boil.)

It is better to use vinegar in court-bouillons intended for oily fish, Herring, Mackerel, Gurnard, whole Salmon, and so on, as well as for court-bouillon intended for Lobster, Langouste, and Crab : in short, for those cases where the court-bouillon is not afterwards used to make a sauce. The proportion of vinegar is half a teacupful to a quart of water.

GLAZING

In the case of certain fish cooked whole or in pieces, and of cold fish cooked again in a border or in scallop shells, the procedure known as Glazing (*Glaçage*) is demanded.

This is usually done in the case of fish masked with a very buttery sauce, and it consists in obtaining very rapidly a thin golden coating on the surface of the sauce. This can be obtained by fierce heat, either in the oven or by a salamander. Glazing must be done very quickly, because if it is done too slowly, the sauce may curdle.

A type of sauce for glazing is *Sauce Vin Blanc* (page 37).

LIGHT GRATINS

These are of two sorts. The first is obtained on a fish nearing the completion of its cooking, by sprinkling it with fine browned breadcrumbs, and dotting it with pieces of butter or pouring some melted butter over.

The second is by the use of Mornay Sauce (page 34), or in some cases White Wine Sauce. This form of *Gratin* can be used—

(1) for whole fish poached and masked with Mornay Sauce ; for cooked fish heated up in scallop shells or in a border of Duchesse potatoes or rice. The reduced cooking liquor of the fish is generally added to the sauce ;

(2) for various white meats ;

(3) for certain vegetables. Mornay Sauce, which is to be used with vegetables, is sometimes combined with a certain amount of Duxelles Sauce (page 13).

The operation of the *Gratin* consists in sprinkling the objects with grated cheese, which is then sprinkled with melted butter. The melted cheese then forms a light crust over the sauce. As in glazing, the objects should be exposed to a fierce heat, a very hot oven or a salamander. In certain cases, a little fine browned breadcrumbs may be mixed with the cheese.

RAPID GRATINS

Fish treated in this way is always cooked fish, and as far as possible should be cut in small regular slices. It is usually prepared in a border or in scallop shells. The agent of the Rapid *Gratin* is the same as in the case of the Complete *Gratin* (see below), that is, a Gratin Sauce or a fairly thick Duxelles Sauce. The operation consists in warming up the fish and covering it with just the necessary amount of sauce. This is then sprinkled with brown breadcrumbs and melted butter. Here the only object is to obtain the formation of a browned surface, and since the fish is already cooked, all there is to be done is to brown the top under fierce heat.

COMPLETE GRATINS

In the case of this *Gratin*, the fish and its garnish are raw. The agent is a fairly thick Duxelles Sauce (page 13). In the cooking of a Complete *Gratin*, three points must be borne in mind—(1) the size of the fish, (2) the amount of sauce to be used, and (3) the degree of heat to be applied. Whatever the fish, the aim of this form of cooking is at the same time to cook the fish, reduce the sauce to its proper thickness, and to produce a browned top, all at the same time.

The larger the fish, the larger the quantity of sauce, and the gentler the heat should be.

If there is not enough sauce in proportion to the size of the fish, the sauce will reduce and the *Gratin* form before the fish is cooked : if, on the other hand, too much sauce has been used, it will be cooked and the *Gratin* will have formed before the sauce will have thickened properly.

The smaller the fish, the less sauce it will need, and the greater the heat applied to it should be : the fish should cook, the sauce reduce and the *Gratin* form, all at the same time.

To make a Complete *Gratin* requires a good deal of attention. It is really a matter of experience, but that experience is easily acquired.

Chapter II

Auxiliary Preparations for Fish Dishes—A few Garnishes

THERE are always a number of basic and auxiliary preparations which must inevitably enter into the composition of other dishes. The simplest way of dealing with these would, of course, be to repeat the recipe with every dish for which it was needed. This would be convenient to those to whom these auxiliary recipes are unfamiliar ; but it would take up much too much space.

These recipes have been collected together in this chapter so as to be easily found, more especially for the sake of the housewife or mistress who has discovered, for one reason or another, that the business of the kitchen devolves more and more upon herself, and will not be so used to these recipes as is the professional chef or cook.

At the end of the chapter has also been added a short selection of the better-known garnishes for various fish dishes, which will be found useful in the kitchens of large houses where entertaining is often on a grander and more lavish scale than in the ordinary household. But these garnishes will, in most cases, be found quite simple and by no means beyond the scope of the ordinary kitchen.

AUXILIARY PREPARATIONS FOR FISH DISHES

Aspic.—Aspic is very clear fish jelly flavoured with some wine or other. The preparation of a *maigre* Aspic is the same as that of all others, namely this. Line a broder mould

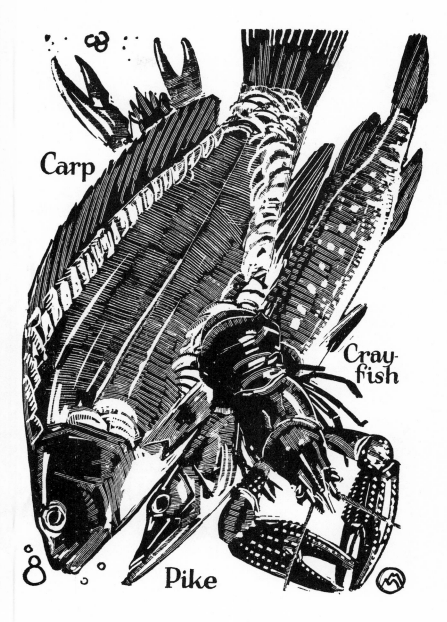

Carp

Cray-
fish

Pike

with jelly, and decorate the bottom and sides with truffle, hard-boiled egg-white, gherkins, capers, tarragon leaves, etc. Set this decoration with a little more jelly, and also set a layer of jelly in the bottom of the mould. On this arrange the ingredients of which the Aspic is to be composed, either fillets of sole, roes, slices of lobster or crawfish (*langouste*), and so on. Fill up the mould with jelly, and let it set. Turn it out when you are ready to serve it, and not before. It can be served on a dish or on a base of some kind.

Bouquet garni.—This is made of folded parsley stalks containing bayleaf, thyme and celery in quantities proportionate to the size of the bouquet. It is then tied up with cotton or thread. In certain cases, where specially described, chervil, tarragon or fennel may also be included.

Court-bouillon for Salmon, Trout, etc.—Proportions : seven quarts of water, four ounces of coarse salt, not quite half a pint of vinegar, five ounces of carrot and the same of onion cut in round slices, half an ounce of parsley stalks, half a bayleaf, a sprig of thyme and not quite half an ounce of coarsely ground peppercorns. Bring to the boil, and boil gently for three-quarters of an hour. Strain and leave to get cold.

(NOTE.—Bass, grey mullet and other fish of that kind can be cooked in water salted in the proportion of half an ounce of salt to every quart of water.)

White Court-bouillon for Turbot and Brill.—Proportions : six quarts of water, a quart of milk, five ounces of salt, and five slices of lemon without rind or pips.

This *court-bouillon* is prepared in the turbot kettle in which the fish will be cooked.

Duxelles.—Chop up finely half a pound of mushroom stalks and trimmings, and squeeze them in a cloth by twisting it, so that as much of their moisture as possible is extracted. Lightly brown half a chopped onion in an ounce of butter and three dessertspoonfuls of olive-oil, add two chopped shallots, the mushrooms, salt, pepper and grated nutmeg. Stir on a hot fire until all the moisture in the mushrooms has evaporated, then pour the Duxelles into a basin, press it lightly down, and keep it covered with a buttered paper.

(NOTE.—This Duxelles is in frequent use in the kitchen. In the preparation of fish it is the basis of the Gratin Sauce, whether for Complete or Rapid *Gratins*. (See pages 10 and 11.)

Farce de Poisson (Fish Forcemeat).—Proportions : one pound net of the flesh of pike, whiting or other fish ; nine ounces of cold panada (see below, page 17), half a pound of butter, two whole eggs and two yolks of eggs, half an ounce of salt, a very good pinch of white pepper and a tiny pinch of grated nutmeg.

METHOD.—Pound the fish finely with the seasoning in a mortar, and keep it aside. Then pound the panada, mix the two together, and add the butter. When these are well mixed, add the eggs and the yolks of eggs, one after the other, pass through a very fine sieve or tammy-cloth, and put the forcemeat in a basin. Work it there for a few moments with a spatula to make it smooth, then put it aside in a cool place, covered with a buttered paper.

Farce pour Poisson à braiser (Forcemeat for Braised Fish).— Mix together half a pound of raw soft roes and the chopped flesh of four whitings ; a quarter of a pound of bread-crumbs first soaked in milk and then pressed as dry as possible ; a quarter of a pound of raw mushrooms chopped up and pressed dry ; two ounces of chopped onion and one ounce of chopped shallot, both lightly fried in butter and left to get cold ; two whole eggs ; a dessertspoonful of chopped parsley, a small piece of crushed garlic, salt, pepper and grated nutmeg. Mix to a paste with a spatula.

Farce mousseline (Mousseline Forcemeat).—Pound finely a pound of fish or shellfish meat with nearly half an ounce of salt, a pinch of white pepper and the whites of three small eggs added by degrees. Pass through a fine tammy-cloth, put the forcemeat into a basin, and keep it on ice for an hour. Then, still on the ice, work into it by small degrees a pint of good cream.

(NOTE.—This forcemeat is principally used for mousses and very fine quenelles.)

Fumet de Poisson (Fish Fumet).—For two quarts of fumet, put two pounds of chopped up raw fish bones and trimmings in a buttered pan with two ounces of minced onion, several parsley stalks and a dozen peppercorns. Let this stew for a while with the lid on, then add a quart of white wine and a little over two and a half pints of water. Add a pinch of salt and boil gently for twenty-five minutes. Then strain through a fine conical sieve, and keep for your use.

Gelée de Poisson blanche (White Fish Jelly).—Make a fish fumet as above. Then add, for a pint and three-quarters of fumet, nine ounces of chopped or pounded whiting flesh ; the white part of a leek and a few parsley stalks cut in small pieces ; a white of an egg, and about three-quarters of an ounce of gelatine softened in cold water. Clarify in the usual way, and strain through a napkin.

Gelée de Poisson au vin rouge (Red Fish Jelly).—This jelly is usually prepared with a red wine *court-bouillon* in which the fish itself has been cooked.

Or :—Prepare a fish fumet, substituting red wine for

white, and follow the directions given above for White Fish Jelly.

Glace de Poisson (Fish Glaze).—Fish glaze is obtained by the reduction of fish fumet. If desired, a special fumet can be prepared, as follows : stew in butter two pounds of fish bones and trimmings with half a minced onion, a small bouquet of parsley stalks and two ounces of mushroom peelings. Add a glass of white wine, reduce it almost completely, then moisten with a quart of well-strained ordinary fumet. Boil gently for twenty-five minutes, strain through a very fine sieve, decant after it has been left to settle, and then reduce to the consistence of syrup.

Herbes à Tortue (Herbs for Turtle Soup).—These herbs comprise basil, sage, marjoram, savory, rosemary (this in lesser quantity than the others), thyme, bayleaf, coriander, peppercorns and, according to taste, a little mint.

Marinade au vin blanc (White Wine Marinade).—Fry lightly in three dessertspoonfuls of olive-oil half a carrot, an onion, the white part of a leek and two shallots, all minced up, two whole cloves of garlic, a sprig of thyme and a third of a bayleaf, parsley stalks, several peppercorns and a clove. Moisten with just over three pints of white wine and not quite half a pint of vinegar. Boil gently for thirty to thirty-five minutes.

Marinade au vin rouge (Red Wine Marinade).—The same ingredients as for the White Wine Marinade, but moisten only with three and a half pints of red wine instead of white, and add no vinegar.

(NOTE.—These marinades are generally used cold, but they may sometimes be used hot, if the fish under treatment only need a short time in the marinade.)

Mirepoix ordinaire (Mirepoix).—Stew in butter equal

amounts of onion and carrot, and celery in lesser quantity, all cut in little dice. Add a fragment of thyme and a small bit of bayleaf.

(NOTE.—The mirepoix used for fish does not contain ham or bacon as does that for use with meat.)

Mirepoix Bordelaise.—Cut in small dice two ounces of the red part of a carrot, the same of onion, two small shallots and two parsley stalks. Add a pinch of powdered thyme and bayleaf. Stew in butter until the vegetables are quite cooked, then turn out into a basin, and keep for use.

Nage, ou Court-bouillon pour Crustacés (Court-bouillon for Shellfish).—Stew in butter a large carrot and two onions minced up. Moisten with a pint and three-quarters of white wine, and the same of water. Add a bouquet garni and a few peppercorns tied up in butter muslin. Bring to the boil, and cook gently for half an hour. Serve hot.

Panade au pain (Bread Panada).—Soak as much bread-crumbs as you want in boiling milk, seasoning with a little salt. When the milk has been completely absorbed, stir the mixture over a hot fire until it ceases to stick to the spatula or wooden spoon. Then spread it out on a plate or dish in a thin layer, and let it get cold before using.

Panade à la farine (Flour Panada).—Put in a saucepan eight tablespoonfuls of water, an ounce of butter and a pinch of salt. Bring to the boil, and then add, off the fire, three ounces of sieved flour. Stir this over the fire until the mixture no longer sticks to the spatula, spread it on a dish in a thin layer, and let it get cold.

Panade à la Frangipane (Frangipane Panada).—Mix in a saucepan three ounces of flour, three yolks of eggs, two dessertspoonfuls of melted butter and a pinch of salt. Moisten with a pint and three-quarters of boiling milk,

bring to the boil and stir over the fire until the right thickness is reached. Let it get quite cold before using it.

Pâte pour Coulibiac (Paste for a Coulibiac).—This is ordinary
brioche paste without sugar, which is made as follows : a
pound of sieved flour, half an ounce of salt, six ounces of
butter, four eggs, half an ounce of yeast and four scant
tablespoonfuls of warm water.

(1) With a quarter of the flour, the water and the yeast,
make your leaven. Roll it into a ball, cut the top in the
form of a cross, and keep it in a warm place until it has
doubled its size.

(2) Mix the rest of the flour with the butter, the eggs
and the salt dissolved in a few drops of water. Work the
paste with the hands, pulling it about and kneading it so as
to make it elastic. Finally, mix in the leaven, put it in a
basin, cover it, and leave it to ferment for five or six hours.

Pâte à choux commune (Choux Paste).—Put in a saucepan
three-quarters of a pint of water, a pinch of salt and three
ounces of butter. Bring to the boil, and add. off the fire,
nine ounces of flour. Stir this paste on a hot fire until
it no longer sticks to the spatula, and finish it, off the
fire, with six large eggs added one after the other.

Pâte feuilletée, or *Feuilletage* (Puff Paste).—Sieve a pound
of fine wheat flour ; make a hollow in it and put in the
middle a third of an ounce of salt and half a pint of cold
water. Mix together, and be careful that, in winter or in
summer, its consistence should be exactly that of the butter
you will use with it, in order to make certain of the perfect
blending of the two ingredients when the paste is rolled
out. When mixed, leave it for a quarter of an hour. Spread
out the paste on your board in a square, and spread on it a
pound of butter, which in winter should be well kneaded

and softened. Bring the edges of the paste together in such a way as to enclose the butter completely and to form a perfect square. Leave this for ten to fifteen minutes before beginning to roll it out, then roll it out twice. This means rolling out the paste in a band about eighteen inches long, and then folding it in three. Put the paste in a cool place for ten or fifteen minutes, then roll it out four more times, twice at a time, leaving it ten minutes between each.

(NOTE.—It is important to let the paste rest, as has been described, because if it is rolled too quickly it may become elastic, and so tend to shrink in cooking. The trimmings of puff paste can be used in the kitchen for making bar-quettes, croustades, tartlets, and so on.)

Pâte à foncer (Cold Water Paste).—Make a hollow in the middle of a pound of sieved flour, and in it put nine ounces of well-kneaded butter, a third of an ounce of salt and eight tablespoonfuls of water. Mix the flour in by degrees, knead twice and wrap the paste up in a cloth, leaving it for an hour at least before you want to use it.

(NOTE.—If you have no puff-paste trimmings, this paste can be used for barquettes and croustades served as hot hors-d'œuvre.)

Pâte à frire (Frying Batter).—Mix in a bowl a quarter of a pound of flour sieved with a pinch of salt, two dessert-spoonfuls of olive-oil or melted butter and eight table-spoonfuls of lukewarm water or beer. When needed for cooking, add two small egg-whites stiffly whisked.

(NOTE.—As far as possible, frying batter ought to be made a little in advance. The batter made with beer is used principally for fruit fritters.)

Pâte à Pannequets (Pancake Batter) (for hors-d'œuvre).— As in the case of ordinary pancake batter, mix a pound of flour with half an ounce of salt, four eggs, a pint and three-quarters of milk, and three ounces of melted butter.

Pomme de terre Duchesse (Duchesse Potato Mixture).—This composition is used for various croquettes and for bordering dishes, as described in the recipe sections that follow. Cook quickly in salted water your potatoes cut in quarters, keeping them fairly firm. Drain them thoroughly, pass them through a fine sieve, put the purée into a pan, and dry it over a quick fire. Season it with salt, pepper and grated nutmeg, and add for every two pounds of the purée three ounces of butter and six egg-yolks, or four yolks and one whole egg. Spread it out on a dish, and let it get cold before using it.

Pomme de terre Dauphine.—Make a purée of potatoes as described above. Dry it, and add to it, for every two pounds, two ounces of butter, three or four egg-yolks and half a pound of ordinary choux paste made without sugar (see page 18). Let it get cold before using.

Purée de Champignons (Mushroom Purée).—To two-thirds of a pint of Béchamel Sauce add four tablespoonfuls of cream, and reduce it to eight tablespoonfuls. Pass through a coarse tammy-cloth a pound of fresh mushrooms. Put this purée into a sauté-pan, add an ounce of butter, and stir over a hot fire until all evaporation has ceased. Mix this purée with the Béchamel Sauce, season with salt, pepper and grated nutmeg, simmer for five minutes, and finish, off the fire, with just over an ounce of butter.

Cuisson de Champignons (Mushroom Cooking Liquor).— When mushrooms are stewed in butter for a garnish, the cooking liquor which comes from them should be carefully kept, as it provides a fine flavouring agent, which is referred to in the course of the following recipes.

Roux brun (Dark Roux).—This is the binding element in the brown sauce called Espagnole. Mix four ounces of flour with just under four ounces of clarified butter. Cook gently on a low fire until the mixture is a deep brown.

Roux blond (Light Roux).—The binding element in Velouté. Mix flour and butter in the above proportions, and cook gently until the mixture is a golden brown.

RICE (RIZ)

Riz à l'Indienne.—Cook half a pound of Patna rice in a quart of salted water, stirring it from time to time. It will take a quarter of an hour to cook, and you must then drain it and wash it under the cold tap. The best way to do this is to drain it in a sieve and let the cold water run over it. Let it drain again, then spread it out on a napkin stretched on a board or tin. Then let it dry in a very cool oven.

This rice is generally used as an accompaniment to *Lobster à l'Américaine* and to poached fish.

Riz Pilaff maigre (Pilaff) (without meat stock).—Lightly brown half a chopped onion in butter, and add half a pound of Carolina rice. Stir it over the fire until the rice gets very white, then moisten it a little more than twice its height in the pan (just under a pint) with clear fish fumet (see page 15). Season it with a small bouquet of thyme, parsley and bayleaf, put on the lid, and cook in the oven for eighteen to twenty minutes. When it is cooked, each grain should be separate. When you take it from the oven, stir it lightly and mix in an ounce and a half of butter.

Rizotto maigre (Rizotto) (without meat stock).—Proceed exactly as for the Pilaff above, but when it comes to adding the fish fumet, do not do so all at once, but by degrees,

adding it three or four times as it is absorbed by the rice.
After it is cooked, mix in two ounces of grated Parmesan
and an ounce of fresh butter. Truffle, tomato pulp or
tomato purée can be added, when desired, to the Rizotto.

SOME GARNISHES FOR FISH

Américaine.—Slices of lobster tails prepared *à l'Améri-caine*; button mushrooms. Sauce Américaine.

Batelière.—Glazed button onions; button mushrooms; crayfish cooked in *court-bouillon*; fried eggs. Sauce Marinière.

Cancalaise.—Poached oysters; shelled prawns. White Wine Sauce.

Cardinal.—Slices of lobster tails; slices of truffles. Cardinal Sauce.

Chambord.—Quenelles of fish forcemeat, decorated; button mushrooms; truffles cut in olive shape; gudgeons egg-and-breadcrumbed and fried; crayfish cooked in *court-bouillon*; slices of soft roe fried *à la meunière*. A sauce made with the cooking liquor of the fish.

Chauchat.—Thick rounds of hot boiled potato, arranged overlapping one another round the fish. Mornay Sauce.

Commodore.—Large quenelles of fish forcemeat decorated with truffles and crayfish tails. Sauce Normande finished with crayfish butter.

Daumont.—Large mushrooms stewed in butter, garnished with a salpicon of crayfish bound with Sauce Nantua; little quenelles of creamy fish forcemeat; slices of soft roes egg-and-breadcrumbed and fried. Sauce Nantua.

Dieppoise.—Poached and bearded mussels; shelled shrimps' tails. White Wine Sauce.

Doria.—Cucumbers cut olive-shaped and stewed in butter, arranged round the fish cooked *à la meunière.*

Florentine.—The fish is set on a bed of blanched leaf spinach stewed in butter. It is then covered with a Mornay Sauce.

Grand Duc.—Asparagus tips bound with butter ; slices of truffle. Mornay Sauce.

Indienne.—Rice prepared *à l'Indienne* (see page 21). Curry Sauce.

Joinville.—Julienne strips of mushrooms and truffles ; crayfish tails. Sauce Joinville. (On the fish itself, slices of truffles and large prawns with their tails shelled.)

Marinière.—Poached mussels and shrimps. Sauce Marinière.

Matelote.—Glazed button onions ; button mushrooms ; crayfish cooked in *court-bouillon* ; heart-shaped croûtons fried in butter. Matelote Sauce.

Montreuil.—Olive-shaped boiled or steamed potatoes arranged round the fish. White Wine Sauce on the fish and Shrimp Sauce on the potatoes.

Nantua.—Crayfish tails and slices of truffle. Sauce Nantua.

Niçoise.—Peeled, pressed and roughly chopped tomatoes stewed in olive-oil, with a touch of garlic, fillets of anchovy, little olives and capers. Finish with chopped tarragon.

Normande.—Poached oysters and mussels ; prawns' or shrimps' tails ; mushrooms, gudgeons* egg-and-bread-crumbed and fried ; crayfish cooked in *court-bouillon* ; little croûtons fried in butter. Sauce Normande.

Trouvillaise.—Little poached mussels ; shrimps' tails ; minced mushrooms. Shrimp Sauce.

Walewska.—Tails of Dublin Bay prawns or thin slices of lobster tails ; slices of truffle. Mornay Sauce.

* SUBSTITUTE BUTTERFISH

Chapter *III*

Savoury Butters and Sauces

THIS, of course, is one of the most important chapters in the book. A sauce cannot always make a dish, but it can do wonders with it. I often think that we neglect sauces in this country, where you will find many people who think that because a dish is sauced it means that the fish is of inferior quality, and the flavour of the sauce is there to disguise it. White Sauce (with or without bits of hard-boiled egg), Anchovy Sauce and Cheese Sauce, these are about all we enjoy (?) with fish, and then generally to use up cold fish that has been left over.

The French are a nation of sauce-makers, while we prefer our roasting and grilling. There is a French saying that while one can achieve success in roasting, one has to be born a sauce-maker. That no doubt is true of such Masters as Carême, whose sauces were so marvellous that someone said, " we should wish Carême to prepare the sauce, were we under the necessity of eating an elephant, or our grand-father ! "

Nowadays I believe that sauces might even come into their own in this country, and a study of this chapter will tell you all there is to know about them. You may not be able in your own kitchen to make such a finely flavoured sauce as you get at Prunier's, but that will only be because you cannot possibly expect to have at your command the flavoured stock of a large restaurant, where so many trimmings of fish and shellfish are always available. But at any rate the simpler sauces are at your command, if you will take the trouble to make them, and here are all the recipes assembled.

For making sauces, lemon juice can be used instead of white wine for moistening the fish when it is cooking. This is better when the lemon juice is combined with mushroom. This applies to sauces used to mask such fish as sole, turbot, John Dory, cod, halibut, rock salmon, as well as scallops.

Vinegar may also be used in sauces, but only in very small quantities. A dessertspoonful per person is quite enough, and it must be used only on condition that it is entirely reduced, as in the following sauces : Béarnaise, White Butter (Beurre blanc), and in the reduction for making Hollandaise Sauce for fish. Actually vinegar can be used for all " condiment " sauces, replacing mustard, piccalilli, etc.

SAVOURY BUTTERS

(NOTE.—These butters should be used within twenty-four hours of being made.)

Beurre d'ail (Garlic Butter).—Blanched garlic well pounded and mixed with an equal quantity of butter. Pass through a fine sieve.

Beurre d'anchois (Anchovy Butter).—Two ounces of fillets of salted anchovies, washed, pounded with three ounces of butter. Pass through a fine sieve.

Beurre d'amandes (Almond Butter).—Four ounces of almonds freshly skinned and pounded into a fine paste with a few drops of water. Mix with six ounces of butter, and pass through a fine sieve.

Beurre blanc (White Butter).—(1) Reduce a good glass of white wine vinegar to which you have added a chopped shallot. Before the reduction is complete, draw the pan from the fire, and add by degrees half a pound of softened butter, stirring continuously. Finish with a little freshly ground pepper from the mill. Certain amateurs are in favour of adding roughly chopped parsley to this butter.

(2) Proceed as above, substituting very dry white wine for the vinegar.

(3) As above, using Muscadet instead of vinegar. This is called *Beurre blanc Nantaise.*

Beurre de Caviar (Caviar Butter).—Two ounces of caviar pounded very well indeed ; add six ounces of butter, and pass through a fine sieve.

Beurre Colbert.—This is a Maître-d'hôtel Butter (see page 27) to which is added a dessertspoonful of melted meat glaze for every four ounces of butter. If a *maigre* butter is wanted, the meat glaze can be replaced by fish glaze or fish fumet reduced until it is a syrup.

Beurre de Crevettes (Prawn Butter).—Prawns pounded with an equal weight of butter. Add a few drops of carmine. Pass through a sieve.

Beurre d'Échalote (Shallot Butter).—Blanch some chopped shallot quickly, squeeze it in the corner of a cloth, pound it in a mortar, and add an equal weight of butter. Pass through a sieve.

Beurre d'Écrevisses (Crayfish Butter).—The heads and shells of crayfish cooked in an ordinary mirepoix (see page 16), pounded finely with an equal weight of butter, and passed through a sieve.

Beurre d'Estragon (Tarragon Butter).—Blanched leaves of tarragon, plunged into cold water, pressed dry, and pounded with an equal quantity of butter. Pass through a sieve.

Beurre Fondu.—Put two tablespoonfuls of milk into a saucepan on a quick fire. Add about half a pound of salted butter by dropping it in in small pieces. Bring to the boil and strain as soon as the mixture has boiled. The melted butter will now have been thickened.

Beurre de Hareng (Herring Butter).—Skinned fillets of herring pounded and mixed with twice as much butter as herring. Pass through a sieve.

Beurre de Homard (Lobster Butter).—(1) Eggs, coral and the creamy inside parts of the lobster are pounded with an equal quantity of butter. Pass through a sieve.

(2) Lobster shells dried and pounded very fine. Add an equal quantity of butter, melt in a *bain-marie,* stirring now and again, and pass through a sieve.

Beurre de Laitance (Soft Roe Butter).—Poach some soft roes with butter and lemon juice, let them get cold, squash them to a paste, and add twice their weight of butter and a teaspoonful of mustard for every four ounces of roes.

Beurre à la Maître-d'hôtel (Maître-d'hôtel Butter).—Soften five ounces of butter, and add a dessertspoonful of chopped parsley, salt, pepper and a few drops of lemon juice.

Beurre manié (Kneaded Butter).—This butter is used for binding sauces, etc., at the last moment. It is made with five parts of butter and three parts of flour, and they are mixed and pounded together by means of a fork.

Beurre Meunière.—Butter cooked to the *noisette* stage, that is to say, until light brown and smelling of nuts, and completed with lemon juice and chopped parsley.

Beurre de Montpellier.—Blanch some watercress, tarragon, parsley and chervil in equal quantities, as well as rather more young spinach leaves. Drain them, plunge them into cold water, and press them dry. Pound them, adding, in proportion to their amount, chopped and blanched shallots, gherkins, capers, fillets of anchovy and a touch of garlic. To each two ounces of this purée add three hard-boiled egg-yolks, salt, pepper, three-quarters of a pound of butter and four dessertspoonfuls of olive-oil. Pass through a sieve. The colour of this butter should be a tender green.

Beurre de Moutarde (Mustard Butter).—Softened butter to which mustard is added in proportion according to taste or the purpose for which the butter is to be used. When this butter is prepared as an accompaniment to a fish, the mustard is mixed with melted clarified butter.

Beurre Noir (Black Butter).—Cook the butter in a frying-pan until it just begins to turn brown. Finish it with a few drops of vinegar swilled in the pan.

Beurre Noisette (Noisette Butter).—Butter cooked in a frying-pan until it browns lightly and begins to smell of nuts.

Beurre de Noisettes (Hazel Nut Butter).—Some sauces need to be completed with this butter, which is made by pounding slightly dried hazel nuts with a few drops of water and double their weight in butter. Pass through a sieve.

Beurre de Paprika (Paprika Butter).—Fry half a chopped onion in butter with a pinch of paprika pepper. When it is cold, mix with five ounces of softened butter, and pass through a sieve.

Beurre de Piment (Pimento Butter).—Pound up four little cooked sweet peppers. Add five ounces of butter and pass through a sieve. (Tinned red peppers might be used for this butter, if fresh ones are unobtainable.)

Beurre de Raifort (Horseradish Butter).—Add a dessert-spoonful of finely grated horseradish to five ounces of softened butter.

Beurre de Saumon fumé (Smoked Salmon Butter).—Pound two ounces of smoked salmon, and add to it five ounces of butter. Pass through a sieve.

Beurre de Tomate (Tomato Butter).—This consists of very reduced tomato pulp mixed with double its weight in butter. Pass through a sieve.

Beurre de Truffe (Truffle Butter).—Cooked truffle pounded with a little Fish Velouté (see below). Add twice its weight in butter, and pass through a sieve.

Beurre Vert (Green Butter). See *Beurre de Montpellier* (page 27).

SAUCES

HOT SAUCES—THE BASIC SAUCES

Béchamel Sauce.—Mix together four ounces of butter and five of flour, and cook this for a few seconds only, just to rid it of the flavour of uncooked flour. Moisten it with three and a half pints of boiled milk, and season it with not quite half an ounce of salt, a pinch of mignonette pepper and grated nutmeg, and bring it gently to the boil, stirring all the time. Now add an onion stuck with a clove, a bouquet of parsley, thyme and bayleaf, and let it boil gently for twenty minutes. Then strain it into a bowl, covering the surface with melted butter to prevent a scum from forming.

Velouté de Poissons (Fish Velouté).—Make half a pound of slightly browned *roux* (flour and butter), and moisten it with three and a half pints of fish stock. Bring to the boil, and boil gently for fifteen to eighteen minutes. Pour into a bowl, and stir until it is quite cold.

The preparation of this Velouté is the same as that for fish soups, save that it is rather thicker. The secret of the flavour of this sauce lies entirely in the flavour of the stock used.

THE SMALL SAUCES

Sauce Américaine.—This is the cooking liquor of *Lobster à l'Américaine*, lightly bound with kneaded butter. The sauce is finished with butter, and at the last chopped chervil and tarragon are added to it.

Sauce Anchois (Anchovy Sauce).—(1) Mix an ounce of flour with two ounces of melted butter, moisten with three-quarters of a pint of fresh cream, season with salt and pepper, and bring to the boil. Finish at the last moment with two ounces of Anchovy Butter or a dessertspoonful of Anchovy Essence.

(2) To three-quarters of a pint of White Wine Sauce add two and a half ounces of Anchovy Butter and the fillets of three salted anchovies cut in small dice.

(3) More simply still, add Anchovy Butter or Anchovy Essence to Melted Butter Sauce in whatever proportion you like.

Sauce Armoricaine.—This is *Sauce Américaine* bound with egg-yolk and cream, and flavoured with curry.

Sauce Aurore.—To just over half a pint of Fish Velouté or White Wine Sauce add four tablespoonfuls of very red and much reduced tomato purée. Finish with two ounces of butter.

Sauce Béarnaise.—Put six tablespoonfuls of tarragon vinegar into a saucepan with an ounce of chopped shallot and a pinch of coarsely ground pepper. Reduce this to about four dessertspoonfuls. Let it get nearly cold, stir in four yolks of eggs, and thicken the sauce by adding over a low heat half a pound of melted butter by small degrees. Pass the sauce through a muslin, correct the seasoning, and finish with a dessertspoonful of chopped chervil and tarragon.

Sauce Bercy.—Put four tablespoonfuls of white wine and the same of fish fumet in a saucepan with a dessertspoonful of chopped shallot, and reduce it by a third. Add not quite half a pint of Fish Velouté, bring to the boil, and finish with two ounces of butter and a teaspoonful of chopped parsley.

Sauce Blanche, dite Sauce Bâtarde (White Sauce).—This is particularly a household sauce. Mix an ounce of flour with an ounce of melted butter, and pour *all at once* into the saucepan a little over half a pint of slightly salted *boiling* water. Mix quickly by stirring with a whisk. Add a binding of three egg-yolks mixed with a little cream or milk. Keep the sauce just moving, but not boiling, on the side of the fire, then pass through a sieve, and finish with five ounces of butter and a little lemon juice.

Sauce Bourguignonne (Burgundy Sauce).—In an ounce of butter and two dessertspoonfuls of oil (nut oil, if you want to preserve the local touch), fry without browning four ounces of mirepoix composed of carrot, onion and celery. Drain off the fat, moisten with a pint of good red wine (Burgundy), add salt, pepper, a tiny bit of crushed garlic, a bouquet of parsley, thyme and bayleaf, and some mushroom trimmings, and boil gently for twenty minutes. Pass it through a conical sieve, and bind it with Kneaded Butter. Finish with a couple of ounces of butter. (If liked, you can add a little burnt Brandy.)

Sauce Canotière.—Bind three-quarters of a pint of stock, made from fresh-water fish cooked in a white wine *court-bouillon,* with two ounces of Kneaded Butter. Boil for a few seconds, and bind with three egg-yolks. Finish with two ounces of butter and a few drops of lemon juice.

Sauce Cardinal.—To just over half a pint of Fish Velouté add four dessertspoonfuls of very good fumet of sole, a dessertspoonful of essence of truffles and two ounces of Lobster Butter. This sauce should be bright red in colour.

Sauce Crème (Cream Sauce).—To a little over half a pint of Béchamel Sauce add four tablespoonfuls of double cream.

Sauce Crevettes (Shrimp Sauce).—This sauce can be made, as desired, either with White Wine Sauce or a Hollandaise. In either case, finish the sauce chosen with two ounces of Shrimp Butter (for each three-quarters of a pint of the sauce) and an ounce of small shelled shrimps. The colour of the sauce should be a fresh pale pink.

Sauce Currie (Curry Sauce).—Chop up an onion finely, and cook it in butter without colouration, with a sprig of thyme, a piece of a bayleaf and a blade of mace. Add a pinch of curry powder, four tablespoonfuls of good fish fumet and just over half a pint of Fish Velouté. Boil gently for ten minutes, then pass through a sieve, and finish with several spoonfuls of cream or coconut milk.

Sauce Diplomate.—This is a fine White Wine Sauce, to which has been added a lobster cullis, in the proportion of one-third cullis and two-thirds sauce. Add a dessertspoonful of tiny dice of truffle for each three-quarters of a pint of the mixture.

Sauce au Fenouil (Fennel Sauce).—Boil two ounces of fennel in salted water for three minutes. Drain it, plunge it in cold water, and press it dry. Add it then to three-quarters of a pint of Melted Butter Sauce (*Sauce Blanche*). This sauce is used principally with salmon and mackerel.

Sauce Genevoise.—To a mirepoix with a salmon's head or bones, and a bouquet of parsley, thyme and bayleaf, add white wine from the Geneva district. Reduce to about half, bind with a creamed butter, and add a little Hollandaise Sauce or egg-yolk.

Sauce Genoise.—This is the same as Sauce Bourguignonne, except that a red wine from Genoa is used instead of Burgundy.

Sauce Gratin.—Put four tablespoonfuls of white wine and the same of fish fumet into a saucepan with a dessertspoonful of chopped shallot, and reduce by a half. Add four dessertspoonfuls of Duxelles (see page 13) and eight tablespoonfuls of Fish Velouté. Finish with butter and chopped parsley.

Sauce Hollandaise (enough for twelve people).—Put into a saucepan two soupspoonfuls of water and a pinch of mignonette pepper, and let it reduce. Then add six egg-yolks, and on a very low heat, or in a *bain-marie*, stir in by small degrees half a pound of clarified butter. Correct the seasoning, finish with a few drops of lemon juice, and pass through a sieve.

Or :—Mix six egg-yolks with a few spoonfuls of water. Heat up slowly, whipping all the time until the eggs are foamy; then add as above half a pound of butter, season, and sieve.

If the sauce seems to be getting too thick as the butter is added, you can dilute it by adding a few drops of water.

Sauce Homard (Lobster Sauce).—To three-quarters of a pint of Cream Sauce add two ounces of Lobster Butter made with the coral or the pounded eggs. Season with a few drops of Anchovy Essence, and garnish with little dice of lobster meat.

Sauce aux Huîtres (Oyster Sauce).—To three-quarters of a pint of White Wine Sauce add a dozen poached and bearded oysters, as well as their cooking liquor reduced and passed through a fine cloth.

Sauce Joinville.—A White Wine Sauce finished with shrimp or prawn cullis, and garnished with small shrimps.

Sauce Laguipierre.—This is made in the same way as Sauce Canotiere (see page 31).

Sauce Livonienne.—With three-quarters of a pint of White Wine Sauce mix two good dessertspoonfuls of fine *julienne* strips of the red part of carrot stewed in butter, a dessertspoonful of truffle cut in the same fashion, and a little chopped parsley.

Sauce Marinière.—This is a Sauce Bercy (see page 31) to which have been added the reduced cooking liquor of mussels. It is garnished with little poached and bearded mussels.

Sauce Matelote.—This is made with a chopped up salmon head and a *maigre* mirepoix (page 16) fried in butter without colouration. This is *flambé* with brandy, moistened with red wine, and the following ingredients are added : a piece of celery, crushed garlic, mushroom trimmings, salt, coarsely ground pepper, thyme and bayleaf. This is all boiled until reduced to half, then strained, bound with Kneaded Butter and finished with fresh butter. The fish which this sauce accompanies is always garnished with button mushrooms, glazed button onions and heart-shaped croûtons of bread fried in butter.

Sauce Mornay.—To three-quarters of a pint of Béchamel Sauce add, while it is still boiling, a binding of two egg-yolks and two ounces of grated Parmesan and Gruyère mixed. Finish with the much reduced cooking liquor of the fish for which the sauce is intended, several spoonfuls of cream and two ounces of butter.

Sauce Nantua.—This is a very creamy Béchamel Sauce (page 29), finished with two ounces of very red *Beurre d'Écrevisses* (Crayfish Butter : page 26) for every three-quarters of a pint of the sauce. It is garnished with the shelled tails of very small crayfish.

Sauce Newburg.—Fry lightly in butter a lobster cut across in pieces. Swill the pan with sherry, then add enough cream to cover the pieces of lobster, and cook for twenty minutes. Strain the sauce and add a few spoonfuls of Béchamel Sauce to which you have added the lobster coral kept back for that purpose. Add some more cream, and finish with a little Hollandaise Sauce.

Sauce Normande.—This is a *Sauce Vin Blanc* (page 37) to which have been added some oyster cooking liquor and the reduced liquor in which the fish in question has been cooked.

Sauce aux Œufs (Egg Sauce).—Mix a dessertspoonful of flour with two ounces of melted butter, and moisten with enough milk to make a slightly thick sauce. Season with salt and a little grated nutmeg. Bring to the boil, and boil for several minutes ; then add, while hot, three small hard-boiled eggs cut in large dice.

This sauce is served in particular with boiled salt cod (*Morue pochée*).

Sauce Persil (Parsley Sauce).—This is either a Béchamel or, more simply, a White Sauce (*Sauce Blanche*), well buttered, to which have been added the juice of a lemon and plenty of parsley, chopped, blanched and pressed dry. It is served frequently with salmon, mackerel, trout, and so on.

Sauce Poulette.—To three-quarters of a pint of Fish Velouté add several dessertspoonfuls of reduced mushroom cooking liquor (see page 20) and a binding of three egg-yolks beaten with a little cream. Finish with two ounces of butter and a few drops of lemon juice.

Sauce Régence.—This is a Sauce Normande (above) to which have been added the reduced cooking liquor of mushrooms and a little essence of truffle.

Sauce Riche.—This is made in the same way as Sauce Diplomate (page 32).

Sauce Soubise (Onion Sauce).—Finely chop four large onions, and stew them in butter. Add three-quarters of a pint of Béchamel Sauce, finish cooking slowly, and pass through a sieve. Season, and finish with butter and cream according to the use for which the sauce is intended. (In the autumn the onions ought first of all to be well blanched.)

Sauce Suchet.—Cut up equal portions of the red part of carrot, the white of leeks and celery into fine *julienne* strips so that there are four ounces in all. Stew these in butter, and finish their cooking with a little light fish fumet. When they are cooked, reduce the liquid completely, and mix the *julienne* with three-quarters of a pint of White Wine Sauce.

Sauce Tomate (Tomato Sauce).—Make a mirepoix without bacon (see page 16), and fry it, without colouration, in four ounces of butter. Stir in three dessertspoonfuls of flour, let this brown a little, and then add eight pounds of tomatoes with the seeds and juice pressed out, three and a half pints of tomato purée, salt, pepper, sugar, a bouquet of parsley, thyme and bayleaf, not quite half an ounce of crushed garlic, and a pint and three-quarters of stock. Cook very gently, pass through a sieve, and keep for use when wanted.

Sauce Vénitienne.—Put into a saucepan eight tablespoonfuls of tarragon vinegar and a good dessertspoonful of finely chopped shallot. Reduce by a good half, and add this reduction to three-quarters of a pint of White Wine Sauce. Pass through a sieve, and finish with two ounces of Green Butter (see page 29) and chopped chervil and tarragon.

Sauce Victoria.—This is a White Wine Sauce made with Fish Velouté, and finished with a Shrimp or Lobster Butter.

In the dish *Sole Victoria* (page 181) a Lobster Butter should be used.

Sauce Villeroy.—To three-quarters of a pint of Fish Velouté or ordinary Velouté add several dessertspoonfuls of mushroom cooking liquor and three yolks of eggs. Stir over the flame until the sauce reaches the consistence of a thick mash. (It should always be prepared at the time when it is wanted, and is only used for coating various objects which are to be served *à la Villeroy.*)

Sauce Vin Blanc (White Wine Sauce).—To three-quarters of a pint of Fish Velouté add four tablespoonfuls of fish fumet, and bind with two egg-yolks. Butter the sauce, and finish it with a little fresh cream.

The reduced poaching liquor of the fish which it will accompany should always be added to this sauce.

COLD SAUCES

Aïoli.—For four people you want eight little cloves of garlic, a pinch of salt, a yolk of an egg and half a pint of olive-oil. Pound the garlic in a mortar to a fine paste, add the egg and the salt, and mix them together. Then continue pounding while you add the oil drop by drop, as in making a Mayonnaise, afterwards pouring it in more freely. When the Aïoli gets too thick, thin it with a few drops of lemon juice and warm water. If it curdles, thicken it again in the same way as Mayonnaise (see page 39).

(Some like to add to the Aïoli a small proportion of mashed baked potato.)

Sauce Andalouse.—To just over half a pint of Mayonnaise Sauce add four tablespoonfuls of thick and very red tomato purée, and two small sweet red peppers cut in *julienne* strips.

Sauce Bohémienne.—Take two good dessertspoonfuls of cold thick Béchamel Sauce, and mix with them two yolks of eggs, salt, pepper and a few drops of vinegar. Then add about three-quarters of a pint of olive-oil in the same manner as in making Mayonnaise Sauce, and finish it with a little finely chopped tarragon.

Sauce Chaudfroid blanche (White Chaudfroid Sauce).—In certain cases, for coating slices of lobster, fillets of fish, etc., Chaudfroid Sauce is used instead of Mayonnaise thickened with jelly. This sauce is made as follows : put into a sauté-pan three-quarters of a pint of Fish Velouté and, stirring it over the flame, add by degrees just over half a pint of good white fish jelly and six tablespoonfuls of cream. Let the sauce reduce by a third, and proceed in the same way as for an ordinary Chaudfroid Sauce.

Sauce Chaudfroid à l'aurore.—With three-quarters of a pint of Sauce Aurore (see page 30), proceed as with the Fish Velouté above.

Sauce Gribiche.—Boil six eggs hard, and pound the yolks into a fine paste ; add half a dessertspoonful of French mustard, salt and pepper, and finish with oil and vinegar in the same way as in making a Mayonnaise. Finish the sauce with gherkins, capers, chervil, tarragon and parsley, all chopped, and several hard-boiled whites of eggs cut in thin *julienne* strips.

Sauce Escoffier.—This is a Mayonnaise to which have been added grated horseradish and chopped chervil and parsley.

Sauce Mayonnaise.—There is no professional secret for making Mayonnaise. It is, indeed, one of the easiest sauces to make, and in three minutes a Mayonnaise for fifteen people can be made. No mechanical whisk or spatula is needed, simply one of those small wire whisks generally used for making sauces. Mayonnaise is more easily made in summer than in winter, and the oil used for it should never be too cold, but rather at the temperature of the kitchen. It may even be slightly warmed. The coldness of the oil is likely to make it curdle, as is also the too rapid addition of the oil when the mixing is beginning.

This is the way to make it. The proportions are : for eight yolks of eggs, one tablespoonful of Dijon mustard, salt and pepper to taste, two dessertspoonfuls of vinegar and two pints of olive-oil. Put in a salad bowl the eggs, mustard, salt, pepper and a dash of vinegar. Mix them with your little whisk, and add the oil drop by drop to begin with and until the mixture of egg and oil is effected. Then pour the oil in a little uninterrupted stream, stirring quickly from right to left or left to right, whichever you like. As the oil is added, the sauce will become thick, and then a few drops of the vinegar can be added to dilute it.

Sauce Mayonnaise liée à la gelée (Jellied Mayonnaise).—To three-quarters of a pint of Mayonnaise add, little by little, eight tablespoonfuls of cold melted thick jelly.

(NOTE.—If, in spite of all, your Mayonnaise curdles, all you have to do is to start again with a little mustard, adding the curdled Mayonnaise by degrees, if there is a small quantity of the sauce ; but if a larger quantity, start with another yolk of egg.)

Mayonnaise Sauce will keep quite well for several days, but in winter see that it is kept in a warmish place. When you want to use Mayonnaise Sauce that has been made the day before or some days before, simply add a few drops of vinegar and stir vigorously.

Sauce Niçoise.—This is a Mayonnaise to which is added a

quarter of its volume of much reduced tomato purée, pounded sweet red pepper and chopped tarragon.

Sauce Ravigote.—This is a vinaigrette made with five parts of olive-oil and two of vinegar, a little French mustard, very finely chopped onion, washed and pressed dry, chopped parsley, chervil and tarragon and pepper and salt.

Sauce Rémoulade.—To three-quarters of a pint of Mayonnaise Sauce add a good dessertspoonful of French mustard and two dessertspoonfuls of chopped gherkins, capers, parsley, chervil and tarragon mixed together. Finish with a few drops of Anchovy Essence.

Sauce Russe.—Add to a Mayonnaise some of the creamy parts of a lobster and some caviar both passed through a fine sieve. Season lightly with French mustard.

Sauce Tartare.—Mayonnaise Sauce to which are added finely chopped gherkins, capers, olives, parsley and chives. Season with pepper.

Sauce Verte (Green Sauce).—Blanch in boiling salted water for ten minutes, watercress leaves, young spinach leaves, chervil, tarragon, parsley and chives, about two or three ounces in all. Drain these herbs, plunge them in cold water, and squeeze them in a cloth so as to extract as much moisture as possible from them. Now pound them in a mortar, pass them through a very fine sieve or tammy-cloth, and add this purée to three-quarters of a pint of Mayonnaise.

Sauce Vincent.—Take the herbs needed for Sauce Verte above and add to them twenty leaves of sorrel. Blanch them, plunge them into cold water, dry and pound them as above, but add when pounding three hard-boiled egg-yolks. Pass through a fine sieve or cloth, add two raw egg-yolks, and use this as a basis for a Mayonnaise, adding oil and vinegar as directed above. Season with salt and pepper.

Chapter IV

Hors-d'œuvre

THIS chapter really needs no preface, except to say how much more delightful many luncheon parties would be if the hostesses and their cooks would take a leaf out of Madame Prunier's book. And not only is this collection of hors-d'œuvre of use for luncheons, but givers of sherry parties and cocktail parties will find here many hints of supreme value.

The section of Hot Hors-d'œuvre may really be treated as a section on Savouries. There is no savoury course in France, and you will find in this selection of dishes many that fall into the category of Savouries in this country, and others, such as the *beignets*, *bouchées*, *coquilles*, *cromesquis*, *croquettes* and the delicious *Sausselis*, are what we generally know as "entrées," and particularly suitable either as a main dish at luncheon or a single course at dinner.

By the way, hors-d'œuvre is gastronomically correct only at luncheon ; never at dinner, except in the case of oysters or caviar.

COLD HORS-D'ŒUVRE

Anchois en paupiettes.—The anchovy fillets are washed, and very slightly flattened. The inside is then masked with a purée of cooked fish bound with Mayonnaise. They are then rolled up, and served surrounded with a little thread of Anchovy Butter (page 25).

Anchois aux Poivrons (Anchovies with Sweet Peppers).—
Cut up the anchovy fillets in thin strips, and let them lie
for a while in olive-oil. Arrange them criss-cross on the
dish, alternating the anchovy strips with strips of sweet
peppers. Surround them with a border of yolk and white
of hard-boiled egg, capers and parsley, all finely chopped.

Anchois des Tamarins.—Prepare the anchovies as for
Anchois en paupiettes (page 41), and after dishing them, surround the dish with a border of potato cooked in salted
water, grated while still warm, and lightly seasoned with
vinaigrette.

Anguille fumée (Smoked Eel).—This can be bought ready
for use. Cut it in very fine strips, and arrange them on a
dish surrounded by parsley.

Anguille au Paprika (Eel with Paprika, or Eel *à l'Hongroise*).—Cut the eel in fairly long sections, and cook it
with white wine and herbs (*aromates*) with the addition of a
pinch of paprika pepper. When it is cold, remove the backbone, and cut the flesh in fillets lengthwise. Arrange them
on a dish, and cover them with the clarified cooking liquor
to which a very little gelatine has been added. Leave the
dish in a cool place to set.

BARQUETTES

Barquettes are a kind of croustade, fashioned in the shape
of a little boat, and usually made from scraps of puff-paste
or short-crust. They are garnished with fish mousses or
cooked shellfish, with a salpicon, or a purée of some sort.
They are always welcome as cold hors-d'œuvres. Their
garnish can of course be varied according to the materials
at hand, and this variety, and the attractiveness of the

little boats, depends of course entirely on the imagination and taste of the cook.

CANAPÉS

These " toasts " are made with crumb of bread cut a little more than a quarter of an inch thick, lightly toasted and spread with butter while still hot. They are then cut out into whatever shape is preferred, square, rectangular, round, oval, lozenge-shape, and so on. As in the case of the barquettes, their garnishes may be widely varied according to taste. A few examples are given here.

Canapés aux Anchois (Anchovy Toasts).—Spread the toasts with Anchovy Butter, and garnish them with crisscrossed fillets of anchovy. Surround each with a little border of finely chopped hard-boiled egg and parsley.

Canapés au Caviar (Caviar Toasts).—Spread the toasts with Caviar Butter. Garnish with fresh or pressed caviar, and surround with a border of fresh butter.

Canapés aux Crevettes (Prawn Toasts).—Spread the toasts with Prawn Butter. Garnish them either with chopped prawns or with halves of prawns arranged according to taste.

Canapés Danois (Danish Toasts).—These are made with plain untoasted brown bread, cut in squares. These are then spread with Horseradish Butter. A surround of fresh caviar is placed on them, and in the middle is set a thin slice of smoked salmon in the form of a cornet, sprinkled with very finely grated horseradish.

Canapés de Homard (Lobster Toasts).—Spread the toasts with Lobster Butter. Put in the middle a slice from a lobster tail, and surround it with chopped hard-boiled egg bound with Mayonnaise.

Canapés au Poisson (Fish Toasts).—Spread the toasts with
Soft Roe Butter. Garnish them with a salpicon of cold
white fish, bound either with a thick Mayonnaise flavoured
with tomato or with a Chaudfroid Sauce *à l'aurore* (see
page 38).

Canapés Rochelaise (Rochelle Toasts).—Spread the toasts
with Soft Roe Butter. In the middle put a fine poached
oyster, and surround it with Crayfish Butter.

Carolines.—These are made with ordinary choux paste.
They are half-moon in shape, but may be shaped like little
éclairs. They are stuffed with a purée of roes or of fish,
and covered with a pink or white Chaudfroid Sauce or
glazed with white jelly.

Caviar.—The best cold hors-d'œuvre of all. Fresh caviar
is served in a timbale surrounded by ice, and it is accompanied by finely minced onion, lemon and brown bread
and butter.

Crèmes (Creams as Hors-d'œuvre).—These can be made
with the remains of white fish, shellfish, tunny-fish, caviar,
soft roes, and so on. The remains chosen are pounded with
a little thin Béchamel Sauce. They are then passed through
a fine sieve. Enough jelly is then added to make the cream
set, and at the last whipped cream is added. The creams are
usually prepared in little oiled moulds. Mussels and other
shells can be used instead, if desired.

Crevettes en Aspic (Prawns in Aspic).—Halves of fine
prawns are placed in very small ornamental moulds,
decorated or not, set in them between two layers of clear
white jelly.

To cook Prawns.—In order to preserve their fine
flavour, prawns should be cooked alive in sea-water, or at
any rate in water strongly salted. One minute's boiling is

enough. You must never try to cool them by plunging them into cold water ; let them get cold gradually. When they are served plainly (*en bouquet*), a decoration of very green parsley is liked by some.

Croûtes d'anchois.—Cut some very thin slices of bread, trim off the crusts, and cut into rather long rectangles. Fry these in clarified butter, and let them get cold. Then spread them with fresh butter, and arrange fillets of anchovy symmetrically upon them.

Duchesses.—These, like the Carolines, are made with ordinary choux paste, but in the shape of a cream bun the size of a small apricot. Take care that they are well dried. Stuff them with a purée of fish or shellfish. Glaze them thickly with white jelly, and sprinkle on them a pinch of chopped pistachio or truffle, or chopped lobster eggs, if the stuffing is of shellfish. Here again variety is the cook's prerogative.

Éperlans marinés (Marinated Smelts). See *Escabèche* (below).

Escabèche.—Only very small fishes are treated in this fashion, such as smelts, fresh anchovies and sardines, fillets of sole, small red mullet, and so on, the name of the fish being added in the name of the dish, e.g. *Escabèche* of Red Mullet.

Whatever the fish, the procedure is the same. Flour them, plunge them in smoking oil, leaving them there for an instant or two according to their size. Take them out, drain them, and arrange them in a shallow dish. Heat the oil again, and add, for each three-quarters of a pint of oil, a third of a carrot and an onion finely minced and six large whole cloves of garlic. Fry these for a few minutes, and then add half a pint of good vinegar, half a wineglassful of water, two red peppers and salt, a sprig of thyme and a bayleaf. Boil gently for a short fifteen minutes, pour it over the fish, and leave them to lie in it for twenty-four hours. Serve them then in the dish, as they are.

Fruits de Mer.—An hors-d'œuvre consisting of any small shellfish, with the exception of oysters. They are served on ice, and brown bread-and-butter is handed with them.

Goujons à la Russe (Gudgeons*à la Russe).—Cook the gudgeons in a *court-bouillon* with white wine (see page 13). When cold, drain them, wipe them, and brush them over with Mayonnaise bound with jelly. Sprinkle them with finely chopped parsley, and keep them in a cool place until the jelly sets.

Grondins à l'Orientale (Gurnards*à l'Orientale). See *Rougets à l'Orientale* (page 49).

Harengs marinés (Soused Herrings).—For twenty herrings prepare a marinade as follows : a pint and three-quarters of white wine, a pint of vinegar, three-quarters of an ounce of salt, two medium-sized carrots cut in thin rings and knotched at the edge, three medium-sized onions cut in thin rings, three minced shallots, a sprig of thyme and half a bayleaf, a pinch each of sage and basil, parsley stalks and several peppercorns. Boil this mixture gently until the carrot and onion are cooked. While the marinade still is boiling, pour it over the herrings, which you have cleaned and arranged in a sauté-pan or other shallow pan, and let them poach there for twelve minutes, without the liquid coming to the boil. Then put them into a dish, cover them with the marinade, and let them get cold.

Serve them very cold, with rounds of carrot, rings of onion, thin slices of lemon, and the marinade.

* SUBSTITUTE BUTTERFISH
* SUBSTITUTE MULLET

Harengs Mesnil - Val.—This interesting dish was discovered by M. Jean Barnagaud-Prunier on a fishing expedi-
tion to the little village of Mesnil-Val, which is near Dieppe
and Le Treport. Put four fresh herrings into a long dish
with twelve cloves, two ounces of juniper berries, half an
ounce of dried red pepper (*piment sec*), half an ounce of
mace, two ounces of black peppercorns, a wineglassful of
vinegar, salt, a little celery, thyme and a bayleaf. Add a
wineglassful of water, cover and poach gently for eight
minutes. Let the fish get cold in the liquid, and serve
them in it.

Harengs Livonienne (Livonian Herrings).—Fillet some fine
red herrings, remove the skin and bones, and keep the heads
and tails. Cut the fillets in dice, and cut in dice the same
amount of cold boiled potato and rather sharp raw apples.
Add chopped parsley, chervil, tarragon and fennel, season
with oil and vinegar, mix together, and add a pinch of
cayenne. With this salad make imitation herrings, putting
back the head and the tail on each.

Harengs saurs à la Chalutière.—Fillet some soft-roed red
herrings, skin them and cut them in strips. Soak them in
milk to remove the saltiness. Pass the roes through a fine
sieve, and moisten this purée with enough vinegar to make
a cullis. To this add onion, chervil, tarragon, chives and
the white of celery, all finely chopped. Season with salt
and pepper and a light touch of cayenne. Drain the fillets,
arrange them on a dish, and cover them with the cullis.

If preferred, the covering may consist of a mixture of
two-thirds Mayonnaise and one-third of the cullis described
above.

Huîtres (Oysters).—These can be served either at luncheon
or dinner, and should always be very cold. There are served

at the same time, lemons, thin slices of buttered brown bread and mignonette vinegar.

A special section on Oysters will be found on page 226.

Maquereaux Marinés (Soused Mackerel).—Small mackerel are best for this, and they are treated in the same way as Herrings (see page 46).

Moules (Mussels).—The smaller, the better. Open them in the usual manner over the fire (see page 223), take them from their shells, remove their beards, and bind them either with a Mustard Sauce with cream or a Mayonnaise, Rémoulade (page 40) or vinaigrette, etc. They can also, if liked, be flavoured with saffron. If you wish, you can add to the sauce chosen a little of the reduced cooking liquor of the mussels.

Œufs farcis (Stuffed Eggs).—Cut some hard-boiled eggs in half, take out the yolks and keep them for sprinkling on the stuffed halves, or use them to add to the stuffing. Any sort of purée of fish or shellfish can be used, and it should be stiffened with a little jelly. The egg-halves can also be garnished with Salade Russe bound with thick Mayonnaise, and numberless other garnishes can of course be thought of.

Olives farcies (Stuffed Olives).—Stone them, and fill them by means of a forcing-bag with Fish or Shellfish Butter.

Poutargue.—An Eastern preparation made with the dried eggs of the grey mullet or tunny-fish. It should be cut in thin slices, and dressed with olive-oil, pepper and lemon juice. Or it can be grated and used to garnish buttered toasts.

Roll-Mops.—Soak in milk, for at least five hours, some soft-roed salt herrings. Fillet them then, and spread the inside of each fillet with mustard mixed with very finely chopped onion. Roll them round in paupiettes and tie them. Arrange them in a shallow vessel, put their roes on top of them, and cover them with vinegar which has been boiled with minced onion, a bouquet of parsley, thyme and bayleaf, peppercorns, cloves, still boiling and strained through a conical sieve. When cold, pass the roes through a sieve, and moisten the purée thus obtained with the vinegar and eight tablespoonfuls of oil for each pint and three-quarters of vinegar. Pour this over the paupiettes, and let them lie in it for three days before eating.

Rougets à l'Orientale (Red Mullet à l'Orientale).—Fry the mullet in butter or oil. When they are cold, arrange them in a dish, leaving the heads and tails bare, and cover them with *Tomates à l'Orientale*, much reduced and very cold. Add rounds of lemon with the pips removed.

Tomates à l'Orientale.—Warm a little olive-oil, and put in some finely minced onions and shallots. Add, according to taste, a little finely chopped garlic and some saffron. Make some tomato pulp, removing skin and pips, add this to the onions, etc., mix well together, and then reduce until it gets like a thick jam.

Salades au Riz (Various Rice Salads).—Rice salads are made in the proportion of two-thirds of the cooked rice and one-third of the other ingredients. The rice is cooked in salted water, well drained, and dressed with vinaigrette dressing while it is still warm. Other ingredients used in these salads are : prawns or crayfish (*écrevisses*), thin strips of lobster or crawfish (*langouste*), strips or small pieces of fish remains, truffle, sweet peppers, onion, etc. ; in a word, whatever mixtures you consider good. The vinaigrette used for dressing the rice is usually made with a little mustard.

Sardines à l'huile (Sardines in Oil).—Commercial product.

Saumon fumé (Smoked Salmon).—English or Dutch. Cut in very thin slices, arrange on a dish, and surround with parsley. (Lemon juice and black pepper freshly ground from a pepper-mill will be demanded by the wise.)

Tartelettes.—The same remarks apply as to barquettes (see page 42).

Tartelettes au Thon (Tunny Tartlets).—Cover the bottom of the tartlets with Mayonnaise, and then put in each a fairly thick round of tinned tunny-fish. Surround with a little border of chopped hard-boiled egg and parsley.

Or :—garnish the tartlets with chopped tinned tunny-fish bound with Mayonnaise, sprinkling on top chopped hard-boiled egg-yolk and parsley mixed together.

Thon à l'huile (Tunny in Oil).—A commercial product. It should be arranged on a dish and surrounded with chopped hard-boiled egg.

Tomates farcies au poisson (Stuffed Tomatoes).—The tomatoes should be of the size of an apricot, opened at the stalk end and gently pressed to exclude the juice and seeds. Season the inside with salt, pepper and a few drops of vinegar, and fill them with a forcing-bag with a fine mince of cold white fish. Serve surrounded with parsley.

Tomates à la Monaco.—Prepare some little tomatoes as above, and fill them with a mince of tunny in oil mixed with onion finely chopped, washed and pressed, chopped hard-boiled eggs, parsley, chervil and tarragon, all bound with Mayonnaise.

Tomates en quartiers (Quartered Tomatoes).—Medium-sized and very red tomatoes should be used for this. Open them at the stalk end, press out the juice and pips, and lightly crush the divisions inside. Fill the tomatoes up, either with a fine salpicon, or a purée or mince of fish bound with jelly, or a Salade Russe bound with jelly or with thick Mayonnaise. Keep the stuffed tomatoes on ice for an hour, then cut them in quarters, and serve them with parsley round them.

HOT HORS-D'ŒUVRE

Anchoyade Provençale.—This is how Reboul, the author of the *Cuisinière Provençale*, describes *Anchoyade* :—

" After having washed seven or eight anchovies, soak them for some minutes to remove their saltiness, then wash the fillets, put them on a plate with several spoonfuls of olive-oil, a pinch of pepper and two or three cloves of garlic cut in little dice. You can also add a few drops of vinegar. Cut off the bottom of a loaf to the thickness of about an inch and a half, and divide this in pieces, one for each guest. Put on each several anchovy fillets, and put each piece of bread on a plate. Cut some more pieces of bread in squares. Each person takes one of these pieces, dips it in the oil on the plate and uses it to crush the anchovy on the bread. This dipping is done several times, and when all the oil is used up, the small pieces of bread are eaten, and the crust with the crushed anchovies on it is toasted before the fire."

Attereaux de Homard Pahlen (Lobster on Skewers à la Pahlen).—Fill some skewers with alternate slices of lobster tail, large mussels and oysters, both poached, and slices of truffle. Cover these filled skewers with Villeroy Sauce (see page 37), and let them get cold. Then egg-and-bread-crumb them, giving them a cylindrical shape. Fry them at once, pull out the skewers, and serve the pieces on a napkin, with fried parsley.

Barquettes and Tartelettes.—These, described already on page 42, can be served hot.

Barquettes aux Écrevisses (Crayfish Barquettes).—Fry the crayfish in a little butter, *flambez* them with brandy, cook them with fish fumet and white wine, and remove the shells from the tails. Garnish the bottom of each barquette with mushroom purée, arrange six to eight crayfish tails in each, and at each end put a crayfish's head.

Barquettes aux Huîtres (Oyster Barquettes).—Garnish the barquettes with poached oysters, cover them with Cream Sauce, sprinkling this with chopped truffle.

Barquettes Joinville (Barquettes of Prawns).—Garnish the bottom of the barquettes with small pieces of prawns bound with a creamy Fish Velouté finished with Prawn Butter. Cover with Hollandaise Sauce ; in the middle put a thread of Velouté finished with Lobster Butter, and at the end of each barquette set a prawn with the tail-shell removed.

Barquettes de Laitance Florentine (Soft Roe Barquettes à la Florentine).—Garnish the bottom of the barquettes with a little leaf spinach stewed in butter, arrange on this the soft roe, poached and cut in slices, cover with Mornay Sauce, sprinkle with grated cheese, and brown quickly under a salamander or a gas grill.

Barquettes de Filets de Sole (Barquettes of Sole).—Garnish the bottom of the barquette with small pieces of fillets of sole and mushrooms bound with a Fish Velouté made with a fumet of shellfish (*Fruits de Mer*). Cover with this sauce, and arrange on top very small poached fillets of sole alternating with slices of truffle.

Beignets d'Anchois à la Niçoise (Anchovy Fritters à la Niçoise).—Take some fine anchovies, soak them to rid them of their salt, then drain them on a plate, and wipe them dry. Fillet them with care. Dip these fillets in a light frying-batter, and plunge them, one by one, in very hot deep fat. A very few minutes will cook them. Drain them, and serve them on a napkin with fried parsley.

Beignets à la Bénédictine (Bénédictine Fritters).—Mix two-thirds Brandade of salt cod (see page 112) and a third potato purée. Add two yolks of eggs per pound of the mixture, and shape in the form of quoits. When the time comes to serve them, dip these quoits in a light frying-batter, and fry them in deep fat.

Beignets de Laitances (Soft Roe Fritters).—Poach the soft roes with white wine, drain them, wipe them dry, and dip them in a thick Béchamel Sauce mixed with lobster cullis. Arrange them on a dish and let them get cold, and when wanted dip them in frying-batter and fry them in very hot deep fat.

Beignets Mathurine (Salmon and Herring Fritters).—With a pound of ordinary choux paste mix four ounces of cold salmon flaked up and the same amount of herring fillets cut in dice. Take up the paste in teaspoonfuls, pushing it off with the finger into deep hot fat. These fritters should be treated in the same way as beignets soufflés.

Bouchées.—Bouchées for use as hors-d'œuvre should be only two-thirds the size of ordinary bouchées : they are named after the principal ingredient of their garnish, or by some other distinctive name, as these that follow.

Bouchées Hollandaise.—Garnish the bouchées with small pieces of smoked salmon bound with Hollandaise Sauce, and on the top of each place a fine poached oyster.

Bouchées Joinville.—Garnish the bouchées with cut-up crayfish tails, mushrooms and truffles bound with Joinville Sauce (see page 33). A slice of truffle surmounts each.

Bouchées Montglas.—Garnish the bouchées with poached and bearded oysters, mussels, mushrooms, crayfish tails and truffles, all bound with a white wine sauce to which has been added the reduced liquor from the oysters.

Bouchées Victoria.—Garnish the bouchées with pieces of lobster tail and truffles, bound with a Mayonnaise finished with a lobster cullis.

Clams à la Marinière.   See Mussels (page 225).

Clams Vapeur (Steamed Clams).—Open the clams in a large pan with very little water and a trifle of pepper.   Serve them as they are, handing melted butter separately.

Rizotto de Clams au Safran (Clam Rizotto).—Open the clams, and keep aside the liquor.   Prepare a rizotto (see page 21), adding to it a little saffron.   With some Fish Velouté and the liquor from the clams make a sauce, and flavour it with saffron.   Bind the shelled clams with this sauce, and serve them with the Rizotto.

Coquillages: clams, palourde, etc. (Shellfish: clams, cockles, etc.).—The best manner of appreciating these shellfish is to eat them raw, and they will be found in the cold hors-d'œuvre under the name of *Fruits de Mer*.   They can, however, be eaten hot, as has been shown in the recipes for Clams (above), which apply equally well to the other shellfish of this kind.

Coquilles de Crevettes (Coquilles of Prawns).—As an hors-d'œuvre, these coquilles should be half the size of those ordinarily served as a dish.

Coquilles de Crevettes au Currie (Coquilles of Curried Prawns).—Have ready a Curry Sauce (see page 32).   Shell the prawns, warm them without cooking them in butter, take them out, swill the pan with white wine, and mix this with the sauce.   Put into coquilles, and brown under a salamander or a gas grill. Serve rice (for curry) separately. (See *Rice à l'Indienne*, page 21.)

Coquilles de Crevettes Dieppoise.—Mix the shelled prawns with cooked mushrooms cut in dice, bind with Dieppoise Sauce, and garnish the coquilles with this mixture. Cover with the same sauce, and brown lightly.

Coquilles de Crevettes crème gratin.—Bind the prawns with Cream Sauce (see page 32), and fill the coquilles with the mixture. Cover with a light Mornay Sauce, sprinkle with grated cheese, and brown.

Côtelettes (Cutlets).—These cutlets are made in the same way as the croquettes which are described on the next page. The only difference lies in their shape. They are egg-and-bread-crumbed, but instead of being fried in deep fat they are fried in clarified butter. Their shape is self-explanatory, and a small piece of macaroni or spaghetti is inserted in the end of each to imitate the cutlet bone. They are dressed in the same way as croquettes, and served with the same sauces.

Crêpes aux Huîtres, Crevettes, etc. (Oyster Pancakes).—Make an ordinary pancake batter without sugar, and slightly flavoured with pepper. If a shellfish is used for the filling, it must be poached, drained, and its liquor, reduced, added to the batter. Pour some of the batter into the frying-pan, scatter six to eight of the oysters, or prawns, etc., over it, and fry the pancake in the usual way, tossing it. Keep them hot as they are made, and serve them as hot as possible.

Cromesquis.—These are made of the same preparation as Croquettes (see below), but they have a different wrapping.

Cromesquis à la Française.—Divide the preparation chosen into pieces weighing three to four ounces, put them on a floured board and give them a rectangular shape. When the time comes, dip them in frying-batter, and plunge them into very hot deep fat. When the batter is golden and quite dry, drain the cromesquis, and serve them on a napkin with fried parsley.

(In England it is usual to wrap the cromesqui in a very thin slice of bacon or ham before plunging it into the batter, and then frying it.)

Cromesquis à la Polonaise.—Prepare them as above, but wrap each in a very thin unsweetened pancake. Before frying, dip in the frying-batter the side of the pancake where the join is, so as to make sure that it sticks together when cooking.

Croquettes de Poissons et Crustacés (Croquettes of Fish and Shellfish).—These can be made of cold cooked fish or shellfish, with various additions, the principal ingredient being half the mixture, and the additions the other half. The various ingredients are cut into little dice, and are technically called a *Salpicon*. The sauce which binds them together is generally a Fish Velouté, very much reduced, and bound with egg-yolks ; but other sauces are also used. The proper proportion is just over half a pint for every pound of the salpicon.

METHOD.—Mix the salpicon with the sauce, spread it out on a plate and let it get cold. Then divide it in portions weighing from three to four ounces each, shape them as you like (but they are usually cork-shaped), flour them lightly, roll them in egg and then in fine white breadcrumbs. They must be fried in very hot deep fat, so that the covering of egg and breadcrumbs solidifies at once and so prevents the sauce inside from escaping. Serve them on a napkin with fried parsley, and hand the appropriate sauce separately.

Croquettes à la Dieppoise.—Mix together equal quantities of small mussels poached and bearded, prawns' tails and *cèpes* previously fried in oil, and bind them with a very much reduced Béchamel Sauce flavoured with paprika pepper. Shape, egg-and-breadcrumb, and fry. Hand a White Wine Sauce separately. (As *cèpes* are generally unprocurable in this country, ordinary mushrooms may be used ; but the flavour will not of course be quite the same.)

Croquettes Dominicaine.—In these the ingredients are two-thirds poached oysters (at least ten oysters for each croquette) and one-third mushrooms cut in dice. Mix them with a Béchamel Sauce flavoured with onion and finished with Lobster Butter. Shape in oval form, egg-and-breadcrumb, and fry. Hand separately a White Wine Sauce to which has been added the liquor from the oysters, and the whole afterwards reduced.

Croquettes de Homard (Lobster Cutlets).—Make a salpicon of lobster, truffles and mushrooms, bound with yolks of eggs and Lobster Butter. Shape as you will, egg-and-breadcrumb, and fry, and serve with a Cardinal Sauce (see page 31).

Croquettes de Merlan à l'Indienne (Curried Whiting* Croquettes).—Mix in equal parts rice cooked in fish stock and the flesh of whitings poached with white wine, allowed to get cold, and then cut in dice. Bind with a much reduced Béchamel Sauce flavoured with curry. Make the croquettes cork-shaped, egg-and-breadcrumb them, and fry them. Hand a Curry Sauce.

Croquettes de Saumon Gastronome.—Make a salpicon with three-quarters salmon flesh and a quarter truffle, and bind them with a much reduced Newburg Sauce (see page 35). Shape in rectangles, egg-and-breadcrumb them, fry them

* SUBSTITUTE FROST FISH

in clarified butter, and serve them with Newburg Sauce handed separately.

Croquettes de Sole Nantua.—A salpicon of poached fillets of sole and crayfish tails mixed with nearly the same weight of Duchesse potato mixture (see page 20), and one part reduced Béchamel Sauce. Shape in cork-shapes, egg-and-breadcrumb, and fry in clarified butter. Hand Nantua Sauce (see page 34).

Croquettes de Turbot à la Parisienne.—Equal parts of turbot and Duchesse potato mixture (see page 20), enlivened by a little chopped truffle. Shape in the form of a pear, egg-and-breadcrumb, fry, and stick a small piece of truffle in the end in imitation of the stalk. Hand a thick Fish Velouté separately.

Croquettes de Morue (Salt Cod Croquettes). See under *Croquettes à l'Américaine* (page 114).

Croquettes Nantaise.—Make a salpicon of the remains of cold fish and an equal amount of mushrooms. Mix them with a thick reduced Fish Velouté, shape them into rather long rectangles, egg-and-breadcrumb them, and fry them in deep fat. Serve separately a thin well-buttered Tomato Sauce.

Croustades Joinville.—Make some croustades, and fill them with a salpicon of fish quenelles, mushrooms, prawns' tails or crawfish (*langouste*) bound with Prawn or Shrimp Sauce.

Croustilles Saint-Michel.—Cut a slice of bread, and trim off the crusts. Garnish this with a salpicon of white fish bound with White Wine Sauce flavoured with paprika pepper. Cover with another slice of bread, dip this sandwich in beaten egg, and fry it golden in foaming butter in a frying-pan. Serve very hot indeed.

Huîtres (Oysters). See Hot Oyster Dishes in Chapter VIII (pages 226-232).

Pains de Poisson (Fish Rolls).—Make a forcemeat with well-seasoned white fish, and mix with it a third of its weight of a purée of mushrooms stewed in butter. Shape the forcemeat the size of a bridge roll, in the middle of each of which you must put a few rounds of hard-boiled egg. Wrap each in a brioche paste made without sugar, giving them the shape of a small long roll. Bake in a hot oven, and serve hot.

Piroguis au Poisson.—Flake up finely some cooked fish, add to it chopped hard-boiled eggs and well-cooked rice, and bind the mixture lightly with Fish Velouté. Roll out some puff-paste a quarter of an inch thick, and cut out scalloped rounds with a circular cutter, four inches in diameter. Put these on a baking-sheet, garnish the middle of each with a little of the fish mixture, moisten the edges a little, cover with another round of paste, pinch the edges well together, gild with yolk of egg, and bake in a hot oven.

Rastegaïs (a kind of small *Coulibiac de poisson*) (see page 139).—Roll out some ordinary brioche paste in a piece six inches by eight inches, and garnish it in the same way as a Coulibiac (see page 139), with the following ingredients : hard-boiled eggs cut in rounds, then dipped in melted butter and sprinkled with parsley ; minced mushrooms cooked in butter ; chopped onion first cooked in butter and then bound with Fish Velouté ; cooked and chopped Vésiga ; rice *à la créole*, and whatever fish is chosen cut in slices and stiffened in butter, all well-seasoned. For the actual garnishing, proceed as follows : in the middle of the pastry put successive layers of rice, eggs, mushrooms, Vésiga, fish, then begin again backwards, Vésiga, mushrooms, eggs, rice. Moisten lightly the edges of the paste, and fold them together in such a way as to enclose the contents tightly, and pinch them well together. The Rastegaïs will then have the shape of an elongated shoe. Make a little slit in the top, and bake it in a hot oven. Serve separately some melted butter containing chopped parsley.

(NOTE.—Vésiga is the dried spine marrow of the sturgeon.)

Rissoles.—These are made, usually with trimmings, either of pastry or of ordinary unsweetened brioche paste, in the latter case being called *Rissoles à la Dauphine.* Their garnish can be a salpicon of prawns, or crayfish tails, or lobster meat as principal ingredient, with mushrooms and truffles as additions. They are always fried in deep fat, and at the last possible moment before serving.

Sausselis.—With puff-paste, or puff-paste trimmings, roll out a rectangular piece as long as you wish, but three or four inches wide. Garnish the middle with a thickish layer of whiting forcemeat (see page 14) to which you may have added, if you like, some prawns or shrimps or crayfish tails, lobster meat or fillets of anchovies cut in dice. Moisten the edges of the paste, cover the garnish with a second piece of paste, pinch the edges together, gild with egg-yolk, and mark the top into divisions for helping. Cook in a hot oven, and cut the *Sausselis* up before serving immediately.

(NOTE.—The preparation of the *Sausselis* is exactly the same as that of the pastry-cook's *Dartois,* the only difference being that the contents of the former are invariably some sort of fish forcemeat.)

Petits Soufflés de Poissons (Little Fish Soufflés).—Little soufflés for hors-d'œuvre are made in little buttered porcelain cases, and always from cold fish. And whatever fish is used, it must always be first stewed in butter and then passed through a sieve. To half a pound of this purée add five or six dessertspoonfuls of very much reduced Fish Velouté ; warm it up without letting it boil, correct the seasoning, and then add three egg-yolks and four whites stiffly beaten. Put the mixture into the cases, and cook them in a slow oven. (In describing these little soufflés, the name of the fish from which they are made is usually indicated : e.g. *soufflés de merlan, d'eperlans,* and so on.)

Various little Timbales.—These timbales are made in little dariole moulds, and in various ways. The method of their preparation is as follows : butter the moulds well, and put them for an instant on ice. Put, if you like, a slice of truffle in the bottom of each, and line the bottom and sides with a layer of forcemeat about an eighth of an inch thick. Fill up the inside with a salpicon of some kind, cover with a layer of the forcemeat, and poach the moulds in a *bain-marie.* They should be accompanied by a sauce appropriate to the garnish inside them.

Chapter V

Soups

FISH SOUPS are delicious, as everyone knows who has tasted *Bisque de Homard*, for instance. But how seldom we ever come across them, except in restaurants. The simpler soups like bouillabaisse are excellent fare : conger soup, mussel soup, how cheap and satisfying they are ! But with the exception perhaps of oyster soup and in poorer homes a broth made with a cod's head, what do we know of them ?

In this chapter will be found the soups which are made from fish and shellfish. Turtle Soup, that solace of aldermen, is dealt with fully in Chapter IX.

POTAGES

Potage Bisque de Clams (Clam Bisque).—There are two sorts of clam : the soft clam and the hard clam. This soup is made with the hard clams. First of all prepare three and a half pints of Fish Velouté, which has been well cooked and skimmed. Then open three dozen hard clams, reserving their liquor. Chop them up, toss them for a few seconds in Noisette Butter (see page 28). Add them to the Velouté with the liquor strained and decanted through a cloth, and add as well half a glass of white wine. Cook gently for fifteen to twenty minutes, pass through a sieve, heat up again without boiling, and finish, off the fire, with three ounces of butter, a touch of cayenne pepper and three dessertspoonfuls of Sherry or Madeira.

Potage Bisque de Crabes (Crab Bisque).—Take two large crabs, crack their claws, remove the meat from them, flake it up with two forks, and keep it aside. Remove all the meat and creamy substance from the bodies of the crabs, pound this in a mortar, and moisten the purée thus obtained with three and a half pints of light fish fumet, add four ounces of rice, and cook gently for half an hour. Now pass through a sieve, heat up without boiling, and finish with a cupful of fresh cream lightly boiled beforehand. Season with a touch of paprika pepper. At the last minute add the flesh from the claws which have meanwhile been heated up in a little consommé.

Potage Bisque de Crevettes (Prawn, or Shrimp, Bisque).— For three and a half pints of this soup, fry in a mirepoix (see page 16) a pound and a half of live prawns, or shrimps. Proceed then as for the *Bisque d'Écrevisses* (below), and finish at the last moment with about three ounces of Prawn or Shrimp Butter. Garnish with three dessertspoonfuls of small shelled prawns or shrimps.

Potage Bisque d'Écrevisses (Crayfish Bisque).—(1) Fry lightly in butter a finely cut mirepoix consisting of half a carrot, half an onion, parsley stalks and a little thyme and bayleaf. Add the crayfish washed and cleaned, allowing four or five to each person, according to their size. Toss these over a flame until their shells are very red, then moisten with a few dessertspoonfuls of burnt brandy, four tablespoonfuls of white wine and the same of light fish fumet. Season with salt and pepper, cover, and cook from ten to twelve minutes, according to the size of the crayfish. At the same time cook four ounces of rice in white consommé. This rice must be well cooked, or, if preferred, it can be replaced by the best quality cream of rice.

(2) Shell the crayfish, keeping aside the tails and a dozen heads. Drain and well pound the broken shells, the rest of the crayfish and the mirepoix, keeping back the cooking liquor. Add the rice, then the liquor, and pass through a sieve. Moisten this purée with enough consommé to bring it to the right thickness, and heat it up just to boiling point. At the moment of serving, finish the soup with a few spoonfuls of cream, a few drops of good brandy and five ounces of butter. It should be garnished with the crayfish tails cut in small dice, and the heads stuffed with creamy fish forcemeat or with mousseline forcemeat made with lobster.

(NOTE.—The operation of cleaning the crayfish should never be neglected, in whatever way they are prepared. It consists in drawing out the intestinal tube, the end of which can be found in an opening under the middle phalanx of the tail.)

Potage Bisque de Homard (Lobster Bisque).—Cut up in small slices across the body three small live lobsters, season them with salt and pepper, fry them in a mirepoix in the same way as the crayfish (above), and finish in exactly the same way as in that recipe. This soup is garnished by dice of the lobster flesh which has been kept back for the purpose.

Potage Bisque d'Huîtres à l'Américaine (American Oyster Bisque).—Open three dozen Portuguese oysters, and poach them in their own liquor. Drain, pound them in a mortar, moisten this with the strained oyster liquor decanted through a cloth, and add three and a half pints of light Fish Velouté. Heat up, pass through a sieve, and finish with butter and a few drops of Madeira. Heighten the seasoning with a touch of cayenne. A garnish of two small poached and bearded oysters for each person can be added.

Potage Bisque de Langouste (Crawfish Bisque).—Proceed exactly as for Lobster Bisque, using live crawfish instead.

Potage Bisque de Langoustines (Dublin Bay Prawn Bisque).— Make a bisque in the same way as the *Bisque d'Écrevisses*, using live Dublin Bay prawns instead of crayfish.

Potage Fruits de Mer.—For four people you will want twelve flat oysters, twelve little clams, one quart of mussels, a few shrimps, three yolks of eggs, half a pint of cream, a pint of milk, four ounces of butter, some cream crackers, two leeks, one medium-sized onion, one stick of celery, twelve ounces of potatoes. Cut the leeks, onions, celery into small dice, and let them stew gently in the butter. Moisten them with the liquor from the shellfish and with the milk, and add the potatoes cut in little pieces. Cook for twenty minutes, and then pass through a fine conical sieve (*chinois*). Bind with the egg and cream at the moment of serving. (This is done by boiling the cream and pouring it gently on the egg-yolks, whipping hard all the time so that the egg does not curdle.) Put the bearded shellfish into the soup tureen and pour the soup over them. Hand the cream crackers separately.

Potage Ouka.—(1) With two pounds of a fish like salmon or sturgeon and the same amount of fish bones and trimmings, adding a large bouquet of parsley stalks, celery and fennel and salt, and moistening with five pints of water and three-quarters of a pint of white wine, make some fish stock. Cut in fine *julienne* strips six ounces of the white of leeks, the same of celery and two ounces of parsley roots. Stew these in butter, and finish cooking them with a little fish stock.

(2) Clarify the fish stock with chopped whiting[*] flesh (about a pound and a quarter) and five ounces of caviar.

[*] SUBSTITUTE FROST FISH

Pass through a cloth. Mix the *julienne* with the stock, and add also dice of the fish used in making the stock. Serve separately some *Rastegaïs* (see page 59), or *Kâche de Sarrasin*.

(NOTE.—The following recipe for *Kâche de Sarrasin* is taken from Escoffier's *Guide to Modern Cookery* :

" Moisten one lb. of roughly chopped buckwheat with enough tepid water to make a stiff paste ; add the necessary salt, and put this paste into a large charlotte mould. Bake in a hot oven for two hours. Then remove the thick crust which has formed upon the preparation, and transfer what remains, by means of a spoon, to a basin. Mix therewith two oz. of butter while it is still hot. Kâche prepared in this way may be served in a special timbale. But it is more often spread in a thin layer on a buttered tray and left to cool. It is then cut into roundels one in. in diameter, and these are rolled in flour and coloured on both sides in very hot, clarified butter.")

Oyster and Okra Soup.—Blanch a large chopped onion with two ounces of chopped and melted pork fat. Add three tomatoes, peeled, pressed and chopped, a few okra and two minced sweet peppers. Moisten with three and a half pints of white stock, season with a pinch of curry powder, and cook gently for a quarter of an hour. Then bind very lightly with arrowroot. A few seconds before serving, add two dozen oysters and the liquor in which they have that minute been poached.

Potage Rossolnick au poisson (Rossolnick with Fish).—Make a very light Fish Velouté to which you have added half a wineglassful of cucumber juice. After it has been cooking for twenty minutes, add a dozen bits of parsley root and the same amount of celery root cut in the shape of a clove of garlic and well blanched ; twenty pieces of *agoursis*

(Russian salted cucumber) shaped and blanched in the same way. Let it cook gently for twenty-five minutes, and then finish with a binding of two egg-yolks mixed with a little cucumber juice. The garnish consists of very small quenelles of fish forcemeat and dice of cucumber cooked in salted water.

Potage Vermicelle à la Granvillaise.—Open three and a half pints of well-cleaned mussels, adding an onion and a piece of celery both well minced, a few parsley stalks and about a pint and a quarter of water. When the mussels are opened, strain the water through a cloth, let it settle, and then decant it. Bring this water to the boil again, and in it poach five ounces of vermicelli, and add enough boiling cream (about a pint and a quarter) to make the proper quantity of soup.

VELOUTÉS

To prepare Velouté for Fish Soups.—Take a pound and a half of fish which do not have too pronounced a flavour, such as whiting,* sole, John Dory, etc., and make a fish stock with them. Avoid using fish like salmon, tunny, sturgeon, mackerel, etc. Mix four ounces of butter with five ounces of flour, brown it very lightly indeed on a low fire (it should be golden brown), and moisten it with four and three-quarter pints of the fish stock. Bring to the boil, and add a small handful of fresh mushroom peelings and a bouquet of parsley, and cook for a quarter of an hour, skimming it. This Velouté has to be made very quickly because the flavour of the fish would be too strong if the cooking were prolonged. Nor must it have the consistence of ordinary Velouté: it must be quite light. Pass it

* SUBSTITUTE FROST FISH

through a sieve, and finish it as directed in the various recipes.

In any case a Fish Velouté, as a soup, is always finished by a binding of five egg-yolks, eight tablespoonfuls of cream and five or six ounces of butter for every three and a half pints of the Velouté. This particular instruction will not be repeated in the recipes that follow.

Velouté Bagration.—A very light Velouté of smelts, to which are added three ounces of raw mushroom purée for each pint and three-quarters. Cook the Velouté for six or seven minutes, pass through a sieve, heat up, and add the binding and butter. It is garnished with thin strips of fillets of sole and slices of crayfish tails.

Velouté Carmelite.—Fish Velouté flavoured rather strongly with celery. Usual binding and buttering. Garnish : little quenelles of whiting forcemeat.

Velouté Chanoinesse. See *Velouté Cardinal* (below). It differs in the garnish, which in this case consists of small slices of soft roes poached in butter.

Velouté Cardinal.—A light Fish Velouté finished with the usual binding and five ounces of very red Lobster Butter. The garnish is a *royale* made with lobster stamped out with a cutter.

Velouté de Crevettes.—Prawns or shrimps. Fry in butter with a mirepoix, as in the case of the *Bisque de Crevettes* (page 63), a pound and a quarter of live prawns or shrimps. Pound them finely, mix them with a Fish Velouté, and pass them through a sieve. Heat up, add the usual binding, and five or six ounces of Prawn or Shrimp Butter. Garnish with small shrimps' tails and little " pearls " of truffle.

Velouté de Crevettes Cancalaise.—The same as above, but

add the oyster liquor from the garnish, which consists of three poached and bearded oysters per head.

Velouté Dieppoise.—Make the Velouté in the usual way (page 67), keeping it rather thick, and adding to it the white part of three small leeks finely minced and stewed in butter. Pass through a sieve, and finish with the decanted cooking liquor of mussels, remembering that this liquor is salted. Add the binding and butter as usual. The garnish is small shrimps' tails and poached and bearded mussels.

Velouté d'Écrevisses (Crayfish).—Cook the crayfish in a mirepoix, as for the *Bisque d'Écrevisses* (page 63), allowing three for each person. Pound the crayfish finely with the mirepoix, and mix the purée with about two and a half pints of light Velouté. Pass through a sieve, bring nearly to the boil but not quite, and finish with the usual binding and butter. The garnish consists of crayfish tails cut in half, these tails having been kept back for the purpose.

(NOTE.—The garnish of this soup admits of variation according to the ideas or whim of the cook. It may consist of either crayfish tails, little quenelles of whiting*forcemeat or of sole *à la crème*, with or without truffles ; a *julienne* of truffles, mushrooms or fillet of sole ; asparagus tips, and so on. These garnishes may consist of one or more of these ingredients. But of course any change in the garnish will imply a change in the name of the dish.)

Velouté d'Eperlans.—To three pints of Fish Velouté add three or four ounces of the flesh of smelts, chopped up and stewed in butter. Be careful of the very pronounced flavour of this little fish. Pass through a sieve, adjust to the right consistence with a very clear fumet of sole, and add the binding and the butter. Choose whatever garnish you like, so long as it suits this sort of soup.

* SUBSTITUTE FROST FISH

Velouté de Homard.—Make a *Lobster à l'Américaine* with a small live lobster. Keep back part of the flesh of the tail for the garnish, and finely pound the rest with the cooking liquor (sauce) from the lobster, and mix this purée with two and a half pints of Fish Velouté. Pass through a sieve, adjust to the right thickness with a very light fish stock, heat up, and finish with the usual binding and butter. Garnish with the reserved lobster meat cut in small dice.

Velouté Mathurine.—A Fish Velouté finished with a fumet of sole. Bound and buttered in the usual way, and garnished with small creamy quenelles of salmon.

SOUPS

Soupe aux Clams à l'Américaine (American Clam Soup).— Open four dozen clams, remove the hard parts, and keep the " nuts " in a stewpan. Add to the clam juice enough water to make just over a quart, and add too the trimmings of the clams. Boil gently for ten minutes, then pass this liquid through a conical sieve on to the clam " nuts," and let them poach in it without coming to the boil. Finish with a little over a pint of boiling cream, three ounces of butter and about three ounces of water biscuits crushed with a rolling-pin.

Soupe aux Clams (Clam Chowder).—Fry in butter five ounces of streaky bacon cut in small dice, two leeks, five ounces of onions, celery, one sweet pepper, two tomatoes skinned and roughly chopped, four ounces of potatoes, all these cut in small pieces. Add a pinch of thyme. Also poach separately three dozen clams, strain their liquor, keep back the " nuts," and moisten the vegetables with this fumet. Cook them for an hour, and add, at the moment of serving, the bearded clams and a few crushed water biscuits. Season lightly.

Soupe au Congre (Conger Soup).—Fry a large onion and the white part of two leeks, both minced, in olive-oil until they are a golden brown. Add three pressed and chopped tomatoes, four cloves of garlic, several parsley stalks roughly chopped, and two pounds of small conger cut in little cutlets. Stew thus for a quarter of an hour, moisten with five pints of boiling water, and add two cloves, half a bay-leaf, a little fennel and a small pimento. Bring to the boil, and boil gently for three-quarters of an hour. At the end of this time, pass the soup through a tammy-cloth, bring it to the boil again, and then poach in it half a pound of rather thick vermicelli.

(NOTE.—This soup should be very thick.)

Soupe aux Huîtres à l'Américaine (American Oyster Soup). —This is made in the same way as the Clam Chowder, using oysters instead of clams.

Soupe aux Moules (Mussel Soup).—This soup is made in various ways, the method differing according to the locality.

(1) It can be prepared *à la crème* in the same way as the Clam Chowder.

(2) *À la Marseillaise.*—Open three and a half pints of small and very clean mussels, together with a large minced onion, several parsley stalks, a small bayleaf and two and three-quarter pints of water, turn them on to a sieve or tammy-cloth, and keep the liquor in a basin. Remove the shells from the mussels, which you must keep warm.

With four tablespoonfuls of olive-oil fry a very light golden the finely minced whites of three small leeks, and moisten them with the carefully decanted liquor from the mussels. Bring to the boil, and add six ounces of rather large vermicelli and a pinch of saffron and of pepper. Cook gently for twenty minutes, and put the mussels back into the soup when you serve it.

(NOTE.—If you like, you can substitute seven ounces of rice for the vermicelli. Do not forget that the liquor from the mussels is salted, when you come to verify the seasoning of the soup.)

Soupe aux Moules à la Menagère (Household Mussel Soup). —Open three pints of medium-sized mussels, with an onion, a bit of celery, some parsley stalks and a glass of white wine. Take them from the shells and keep them back. Pass the liquor through a fine cloth. Stew in butter, without colouration, an onion, the white part of two leeks and an ounce of the white part of celery, all minced up, sprinkle with two dessertspoonfuls of flour, cook for a minute, and then moisten with a pint and three-quarters of boiled milk. Season with salt, white pepper and grated nutmeg, add a small bouquet of parsley, and cook gently for twenty-five minutes. Add now the liquor from the mussels well decanted, and pass the whole thing through a fine conical sieve. Bring to the boil again, boil for a few seconds, then throw in the mussels, and finish the soup with a teacupful of cream and two ounces of butter.

Soupe de Poisson à la Rochelaise.—Lightly brown a large onion and the white part of two leeks, both minced, in olive-oil. Add four tomatoes pressed and chopped and two crushed cloves of garlic. Let these " melt " for a few minutes, then moisten them with two quarts of water, season with salt and pepper, bring to the boil, and add a *bouquet garni* (page 13) and two pounds of small fish, such as weevers, gurnets, whiting, several conger cutlets, a few small crabs and fifteen mussels or so. Let the soup cook quickly for twenty minutes, then pass it through a tammy-cloth, pressing the pieces of fish lightly, so as to get their flavour. Bring the ensuing stock to the boil, and poach in it gently for twenty-five minutes seven ounces of large vermicelli.

(NOTE.—These Fish Soups vary a little according to the locality in which they are found, this being partly due to the various fishes found in those parts and also to the seasoning. For instance, in the south of France they are always flavoured with saffron.)

BOUILLABAISSES

Bouillabaisse à la Marseillaise.—The *Bouillabaisse* of Marseilles is not a fish dish : it is a soup in every accepted meaning of the word. The fishes which have been used in its preparation have left all their flavour in the stock. It must be admitted that the gastronomical value of this soup rests in the variety of fishes, large and small, which have contributed to its preparation. In any case, if it is not possible to include in it all those enumerated below, there should be five or six kinds, not including the shellfish. For as the characteristic flavour of the bouillabaisse is due to each of its ingredients, it is obvious that the more those ingredients are, the more authentic will that flavour be. Unfortunately, the fish which is the most prominent and most essential in the bouillabaisse is the *Rascasse*, a Mediterranean fish unknown on these shores. The fishes which should be included among these are : *Rascasse*, gurnet, weever (*vive*), John Dory, rock fish, conger, bass, whiting,* small crawfish (*langoustes*) and Dublin Bay prawns. For twelve persons allow eight to ten pounds of fish and five pounds of shellfish.

* SUBSTITUTE FROST FISH

METHOD.—Put into a stewpan two medium-sized onions and the whites of two leeks both chopped up ; four skinned, pressed and chopped tomatoes ; an ounce of crushed garlic, a dessertspoonful of roughly chopped parsley, a pinch of fennel, a bayleaf, a tiny pinch of saffron, the fish cut in pieces across, the *langouste* cut in sections across or the Dublin Bay prawns cut in half lengthwise, and four table-spoonfuls of olive-oil. The fishes with tender flesh, such as red mullet, bass, whiting, etc., should only be put in later. They should also be cut in slices across.

A quarter of an hour in advance cover the whole thing with *boiling* water. Salt and pepper it, and cook *very rapidly* (which will prevent the oil from keeping on the surface). After seven minutes, add the tender-fleshed fish, and continue to cook for another eight minutes, still boiling rapidly. Now pour the liquor of the bouillabaisse into a soup tureen containing thick slices of the special bread called " Navette," in sufficient quantity to make the soup very thick after it has been absorbed by the bread. (It should be remembered here that the great cooks of Marseilles, of whom Caillat is the accepted master, have declared that it is a mistake to toast or fry the slices of bread.) Turn into a shallow dish the pieces of fish, sprinkle them with a little chopped parsley, and surround them with the slices of *langouste* or the halved Dublin Bay prawns. Serve this fish at the same time as the soup.

Bouillabaisse à la Parisienne.—For ten to twelve persons : eight pounds of fish, taken from among red mullet, gurnet, weevers, small congers, rock salmon, John Dory, very small turbot and a medium-sized crawfish (*langouste*) or lobster. Fry lightly in olive-oil two medium-sized onions and the white part of three leeks chopped up. Moisten with just over a quart of light fish fumet, and about a pint and a quarter of white wine. Add three large skinned, pressed and chopped tomatoes, salt, pepper, a pinch of saffron, an ounce of crushed garlic and a *bouquet garni*. Bring to the boil, and boil for ten minutes. Add the firm-fleshed fish cut in slices across, and the crawfish (*langouste*) cut up in the same way. Six minutes after, add the tender-fleshed fish with a good dessertspoonful of roughly chopped parsley. Then let the whole thing boil as hard as it can for a quarter of an hour. At the end, bind the soup lightly with Kneaded Butter. Serve in a timbale or shallow dish the pieces of fish and *langouste*, surround them with mussels and other opened shellfish. At the same time, serve in a dish some slices of bread fried in olive-oil, and soaked in the liquor of the bouillabaisse.

Bouillabaisse du pays de Cornouailles (Cornish Bouillabaisse).—For ten to twelve people. Cut up in fairly thick rounds four or five leeks (the white part only), two pounds of medium-sized waxy potatoes, five tomatoes skinned and with their juice and pips removed, three hearts of celery cut in little quarters. Put all these into an earthenware stewpan with three and a half pints of water, salt, pepper, thyme, bayleaf and roughly chopped parsley. Cook for twenty-five minutes, and then add four pounds of fish, cleaned and cut in small slices across. These fish will have been chosen from among the following : red mullet, gurnet, whiting,* mackerel, little turbot, small rock salmon or fresh tunny-fish. Cook then for a quarter of an hour. At the end of the cooking add to the bouillabaisse a binding of three egg-yolks and four tablespoonfuls of cream. Mix delicately. At the moment of serving, scatter over the soup three dessertspoonfuls of small breadcrumb dice which have been fried in foaming butter.

* SUBSTITUTE FROST FISH

Chapter VI

Fresh-Water Fish

WHEN I was engaged in editing this book, I wondered whether this chapter would not perhaps be the most popular of all. There are so many fishermen in this country, and so few books, if indeed any, that specialise in the cooking of river fish. It is a sad moment for the amateur disciple of Izaak Walton to find his precious catch destined for a grave under a rose-bush in the garden, because his wife does not know how to cook it—a fate which did indeed befall the catch of a friend of mine. It is true that the fish was a tench (not a very promising subject for culinary skill), and the rose-bush grew and multiplied exceedingly afterwards ; but if this book had then been printed, with what pride could they have eaten their tench in the manner of Anjou, which will be found on a later page of this chapter.

A matelote of river fish is a charming dish, too, and as far as I am aware almost unknown in this country ; but then we live so near the sea and our rivers are midgets when compared with those on the Continent, that we rely more on the fishmonger's supply than our own piscatorial skill. But I think there are a great many recipes in the following pages of which old Izaak would have approved.

BARBEL (*BARBEAU*)

The best barbel come from fast-flowing rivers. Its flesh is somewhat tasteless and it has the disadvantage of a large number of bones. It should always have a well-seasoned accompaniment.

Two Ways of preparing a Barbel of Four Pounds

It is unusual for barbel to be larger than this.

(1) Cook the fish in a strongly flavoured *court-bouillon*, and serve it either *au beurre blanc* (page 25) or with a Caper Sauce or a Béchamel Sauce with egg.

(2) Skin the fish, stick pieces of anchovy fillets into it here and there, bake it with plentiful bastings of melted butter, and serve it either with Nut Butter or Mustard Butter, or if the fish has a roe, with a sauce made from the roe in a purée, thinned down to the consistence of a cullis by the addition of melted butter.

Barbeau de la Treille verte.—This recipe comes from a riverside inn which used to exist on the banks of the Yonne. It is for a barbel weighing about three pounds.

Fry lightly in butter, without colouration, two medium-sized onions and two shallots, both chopped up. Spread them in a long earthenware dish deep enough to hold the fish, which will be served in it ; add three dessertspoonfuls of chopped dried nuts and five ounces of roughly chopped mushrooms. Lay on this bed the fish well seasoned on each side, moisten with two glasses of good red wine, add four ounces of butter divided in little bits, bring to the boil, and continue cooking in a very hot oven for thirty-five minutes, basting often. When the fish is cooked the liquid ought to be practically reduced to nothing. Ten minutes before serving, sprinkle the fish with fine browned breadcrumbs and with plenty of melted butter, and let it brown. At the moment of serving, sprinkle over a little chopped parsley.

Barbeau au beurre rouge (Barbel with Red Butter).　See Carp with Red Butter (below).

Barbillons (Small Barbel) weighing from twelve ounces to a pound or so, can be

(1) used in a mixed matelote ;

(2) grilled, and accompanied by a Mustard Butter, a Shallot Butter or a simple Maître-d'hôtel Butter ; or

(3) treated *à la meunière, à la Bercy, au gratin,* etc.

CARP (*CARPE*)

Carpe au Beurre rouge (Carp with Red Butter).—Whether the carp is cooked whole or in slices, it must be cooked in a *court-bouillon*.　The fish for this dish should weigh between two and three pounds.　After it is cooked skin it and trim it.

In the long dish, or in the timbale (if it is in pieces), in which it will be served, heat some butter to the *noisette* stage, put in the carp, sprinkle with a glass of brandy, set it alight and baste the fish with it, then put on the lid and keep it hot.

For the red butter : reduce a glass of good red wine until it has almost disappeared, having added at the beginning a good dessertspoonful of finely chopped shallot, salt, pepper and a pinch of sugar to correct the acidity of the wine.　Add then, by degrees and while shaking the pan on the fire, five ounces of butter so that you get a thick and unctuous sauce.　Mask the fish with this sauce, sprinkle it with chopped parsley, and serve it.

(NOTE.—This fashion can be applied to all dark-fleshed fish, such as eels, tench, barbel, and so on.)

Carpe à la Bière.—Scale and clean a medium-sized roed carp, and keep aside the roe. Raise the two fillets, one from each side, leaving half the head adhering to each fillet. Be careful to remove the little bitter sac in the head. Now melt in butter, without colouration, two finely minced onions. Spread this onion on a dish and add a sprig of thyme, a bit of a bayleaf, a piece of celery, several peppercorns, a clove and three ounces of *pain d'épice* (which can be bought in most Continental grocers' shops in this country). Cut in dice. Season the fillets of carp with salt and pepper, moisten with just enough dark beer to cover them, and cook for twenty-five minutes. Meanwhile poach the roe in salted water with a touch of lemon juice. Drain the fillets and arrange them on a dish. Pass the cooking liquor through a sieve. It will be thick enough owing to the *pain d'épice*. Heat it up, butter it lightly, pour it over the carp fillets and surround them with the roe cut in slices.

(A light gingerbread might be used instead of the *pain d'épice*.)

Carpe au Bleu. See *Brochet au Bleu* (page 91), and proceed in the same manner.

Carpe farcie à la Bourguignonne (Stuffed Carp à la Bourguignonne).—Take a carp of four or five pounds, as heavily roed as possible. Stuff it with a forcemeat composed of breadcrumbs soaked and pressed dry, shallots tossed in butter, the roe passed through a sieve, *fines herbes* (parsley, chervil, chives and tarragon) and butter. Bind with six egg-yolks, and mix the forcemeat well together. Sew up the opening in the fish, and put the carp in a deep fish kettle. Moisten it with Beaujolais, season it, and add, if possible, a little fish glaze. Then poach it gently. When it is cooked, drain it and surround it with a matelote garnish (see page 23). Reduce the cooking liquor, and bind it. Finish like a Sauce Matelote (page 34), and pour it over the carp.

Carpe à la Canotière.—This recipe was invented during a holiday of young cooks, and executed by one of them.

Little carp, weighing about twelve ounces, should be used for it. Score them down each side, season them, and lay them on a dish which has first been well buttered and then sprinkled with shallot. Surround them with little fresh mushrooms, peeled, moisten them with white wine, and add about an ounce of butter for each carp. Cook in the oven, basting frequently.

Ten minutes before the cooking is finished, sprinkle them with fine browned breadcrumbs and melted butter, and let this brown. Surround them with trussed crayfish cooked in a *court-bouillon*, and with gudgeon*which have been egg-and-breadcrumbed and fried. The carp are, of course, served in the dish in which they were cooked.

Carpe à la Chambord.—For this first-class dish take, if possible, a Golden carp weighing about four pounds. Remove the skin and stick all over each side (*piquer*) truffles and raw mushrooms cut in the shape of little *lardons*. Season it and put it in a dish with very good red wine, brandy, thyme and bayleaf. Leave it there to marinate for several hours, or let it marinate overnight. Then drain it, and put it in a thickly buttered dish, add the wine of the marinade, and braise the fish very gently, with frequent bastings. When it is cooked, drain it thoroughly, arrange it on the serving-dish, and surround it with decorated

* SUBSTITUTE BUTTERFISH

quenelles, peeled and cooked mushrooms, olive-shaped truffles, little gudgeon* egg-and-breadcrumbed and fried, trussed crayfish cooked in a *court-bouillon*, and if the carp has a roe, the roe cut in slices and cooked *à la meunière*. Pass the cooking liquor through a sieve, and reduce it quickly by half, then bind it with Kneaded Butter, and finish with more butter. Hand this sauce separately.

Carpe à la Juive.—This Jewish dish is prepared in various ways, but the only difference between them lies in variation of seasonings. This is the usual recipe.

Cut some medium-sized carp in slices about half an inch thick. For two carp weighing about two and a half pounds each, fry lightly in eight tablespoonfuls of olive-oil, in a large sauté-pan or turbot kettle, two large onions and five shallots chopped up. Add two ounces of flour, cook it for a few seconds, and moisten it with a pint and three-quarters of white wine and the same of fish stock or water. Season with salt and a good pinch of cayenne, add a large *bouquet garni* and three crushed cloves of garlic, and bring to the boil. In this sauce put the slices of carp, with their heads. Cook gently for twenty-five minutes, then take them out and arrange them on a dish in such a way as to reconstruct the fishes' original shape. Remove the bouquet from the sauce, reduce it by two-thirds, and mix with it, off the fire, half a pint or a little more of olive-oil, in exactly the same way as you would in making a Mayonnaise. Pour this sauce over the carp after you have corrected its seasoning, sprinkle with parsley, and let them get cold. The sauce will become a jelly.

Laitance de Carpe (Carp's Roe).—The roe of the carp is

---

* SUBSTITUTE BUTTERFISH

very delicate and much sought after. It is usually employed
as a garnish, but it can be prepared by itself in the following
ways : poached in butter, as a garnish for bouchées and
omelettes ; in little porcelain cases with shrimps' or crayfish tails added, and a Shrimp Sauce or Sauce Nantua ; in
fritters and coquilles ; in a border of Duchesse potato or
rice, with a Mornay Sauce ; in a soufflé and in little timbales
of the kind called *royale* ; cooked *à la meunière*, etc.

Tourte de Laitances (Soft Roe Tart).—If carp's roe cannot
be had, the roes of shad or other fish can be used. Whatever they are, they must first be poached with butter and
lemon juice, just enough to stiffen them. Make a forcemeat
of sufficient quantity of the size of the tart you are making.
For this, chop up finely the flesh of some perch, carp
or tench with salt, pepper and grated nutmeg. Mix this
with almost the same quantity of quenelle forcemeat made
with pike (see page 94). If this forcemeat is not available, then substitute the same amount of breadcrumbs
soaked in milk and pressed dry, a few spoonfuls of cream
and a little egg to bind it. Now take a pie-dish, butter the
bottom and sides, and line it with puff-paste. Put on the
bottom a layer of half the forcemeat, then on top the
prepared roes and an ounce and a half of butter in small
pieces. Cover this with the rest of the forcemeat, and put
on a lid of pastry about a quarter of an inch thick. Join it
well on the edges of the dish, gild it with egg-yolk, decorate
it if you like, make a hole in the top, and put it into a pretty
hot oven. In forty minutes it should be done. On taking
the tart out of the oven, pour inside a few spoonfuls of
melted butter mixed with an equal quantity of fresh cream
to which a few drops of lemon juice have been added.

(NOTE.—There should be plenty of roes in this tart, and

only a small quantity of forcemeat ; and this last should be light and spongy enough to absorb the butter and cream added at the end.)

Carpe en Matelote.—Very small carp cut in slices across and treated in a *Matelote Batelière* or *Matelote Marinière* (see pages 85 and 86, under Eel). These fish are also used in a mixed matelote.

Carpe à la Polonaise.—The recipe generally used in France for this dish differs slightly from that given by certain authors, in particular from that given by Petit in his *Cuisine Russe*, in which he specifies honey where we use caramel.

(1) Chop up a large onion and four shallots, and sprinkle them on the bottom of the fish kettle, also five ounces of *pain d'épice* cut in dice. Clean a medium-sized carp, season it, put it on the drainer of the fish kettle, and nearly cover it with two-thirds red wine and one-third fish stock. Braise gently, basting from time to time.

(2) Make a light caramel with two dessertspoonfuls of powdered sugar, and dissolve it with a few spoonfuls of wine. When the carp is cooked, arrange it, after draining it, on the serving-dish. Pass the cooking liquor through a sieve, reduce it to make about three-quarters of a pint, and add it to the dissolved caramel. Heat up, butter lightly, and add a dozen shredded grilled almonds. This sauce should be handed separately.

Quenelles de Carpe.—Make these in exactly the same way as Quenelles of Pike (see page 95), substituting carp flesh for pike.

EEL (*ANGUILLE*)

Anguille grillée à la Pêcheuse (Grilled Eel à la Pêcheuse).— Or as it might be called, Fisherwoman's Grilled Eel. Cut the eel up into pieces three inches long, and cut diagonally. Score them finely, season them with salt and plenty of pepper, brush them over with olive-oil, and grill them very gently. Serve on a Bercy Butter, rather strong in shallot, to which have also been added a little mustard and some finely chopped nuts.

Anguille de Bray (Somme) à ma façon.—A recipe executed not half a mile from Cléry, during the battle of the Somme in 1916.

Medium-sized eels boned, cut in little pieces, and fried in butter. Fresh *cèpes* gathered not far from there by artillery-men, cut in slices and fried in olive-oil with chopped shallot and crushed garlic (but no parsley, for the simple reason that none was to be had). Eels and *cèpes* were finally mixed together, and finished with a drop of vinegar.

(NOTE.—This dish was much appreciated at the regimental mess, of which I had the honour to be the cook.— M. BOUZY.)

Coulibiac d'Anguille.—Make in the same way as Coulibiac of Salmon (page 139), using slices of fillets of large eels instead of salmon.

Anguille grillée Robinson (Grilled Eel Robinson).—Whether the eel is cooked whole, tied in a ring, finely scored and brushed over with oil, or cut up in pieces, it must first be gently grilled. Put ten tablespoonfuls of good red wine into a saucepan with two dessertspoonfuls of chopped shallot. Reduce to a few dessertspoonfuls, and thicken this with butter, finishing with a dessertspoonful of chopped parsley. Arrange the eel on a dish, surround it with very small new potatoes cooked in butter, or with little *Pommes Château*. Hand the sauce separately.

Hure d'Anguille persillée (Eel Mould).—Make some fish jelly with a *court-bouillon* of the trimmings of gelatinous fish and some good white braising liquor. Cut up in pieces the requisite number of eels, and let them marinate with finely chopped carrot and onion, garlic, parsley stalks, thyme and bayleaf, lemon juice, White Port and a little brandy, for an hour. Then cook them in the prepared jelly to which you add the marinade. Cook very gently for an hour. Drain the pieces of eel, remove the bones and any uneatable parts. Pass the cooking liquor through a sieve, and reduce it. Now take a rectangular mould, and arrange in it the eel fillets in layers, alternating them with layers of a large amount of chopped parsley, which has been blanched, plunged in cold water, and then pressed dry, so that between each layer of eel there is a strip of green. Finally pour the reduced cooking liquor into the mould, and let it get cold in a cool place. (All grease will of course have first been removed from the cooking liquor.) To serve, turn the mould out, cut it in slices, and serve them on a napkin with green salad round them.

MATELOTES OF EEL

Anguille en Matelote à la Batelière.—Cut the eel into small pieces, and fry them lightly in butter with minced onion. Moisten just to cover them with red wine, season them, add a *bouquet garni* and an ounce of mushroom peelings, and cook quickly. Drain the pieces, and put them into a sauté-pan. Add a dozen glazed button onions, the same number of cooked button mushrooms, and the sauce bound with Kneaded Butter. Simmer for a few seconds, and dish in a timbale or shallow dish. Surround with little heart-shaped croûtons of bread fried in butter, and with trussed crayfish cooked in a *court-bouillon.*

Anguille en Matelote des Canotiers.—This matelote can be made only with eel, but it is more usually made with other fish as well, such as perch, tench or small carp.

The preparation and the garnish is the same as that for *Matelote Batelière* (page 85), except that the moistening is made with white wine with burnt brandy, and the sauce is more heavily buttered. At the same time, there are served some fried gudgeon,* or a mixture of those little fishes known, when cooked, generically in France as " *blanchaille.*" They are usually gudgeon, bleak, roach, little perch, and so on. In other words, " small fry " !

Anguille en Matelote à la Marinière.—Make in the same way as *Batelière* (above), but moisten with white instead of red wine, and at the last add a little cream. The garnish is the same as for the *Batelière.*

Anguille en filets à l'Orly (Fillets of Eel à l'Orly).—Take the fillets from one or more eels and cut them into strips. Season them, dip them in a light frying-batter, and fry them in very hot deep fat. Drain them, arrange them on a plate covered with a napkin, and surround them with fried parsley. Serve Tomato Sauce separately.

Pâté chaud d'Anguille à la Flamande (Flemish Eel Pie).— Prepare enough fillets of eel for the size of your pie, cut them in slices, season them, and stiffen them in oil. Line a pie mould with short crust, and cover the bottom and sides with pike forcemeat flavoured with *fines herbes* (parsley, chervil, chives and tarragon). Garnish this with the slices of eel, arranging them to alternate with layers of the forcemeat, and adding a little sorrel and young white nettle tops melted in butter. When the mould is full, pour in a few

---

* SUBSTITUTE BUTTERFISH

spoonfuls of melted butter, close it with a pastry lid well joined on, and cook for an hour and a half in a moderate oven.

Anguille à la Provençale.—Cut the eel in pieces, roll them in flour, and colour them well in half foaming butter, half oil. Add finally chopped shallot and parsley, crushed garlic and breadcrumbs; cook a little longer, and serve very hot.

Anguille à la Romanaise.—Cut the eel in pieces about two inches long, and wrap each up in a very thin slice of raw lemon without the skin, and a thin rasher of streaky bacon. Tie them up, and cook them gently in butter, in a stewpan, adding two cloves of garlic. As soon as they are cooked, take out the pieces, untie them, and arrange them on a dish. Remove the garlic, swill the stewpan with a glass of dry white wine, let it reduce, and thicken it with butter. Cover the pieces of eel with it, and sprinkle them with chopped parsley.

Anguille à la Tartare (Eel à la Tartare).—Cook the eel, whether whole and rolled in a ring or in pieces, in a white wine *court-bouillon*, keeping it rather undercooked than over-cooked. Drain it, wipe it thoroughly, egg-and-breadcrumb it, and grill it so as to finish the cooking and at the same time colour the coating of egg and breadcrumbs. Or if you like, fry it in deep fat. Arrange on a dish within a border of gherkins, and hand a Tartare Sauce separately.

Anguille au vert à la Flamande.—Cut up some small or medium-sized eels in pieces about two and a half to three inches long. Fry them lightly in butter with onion and celery cut in small pieces, moisten with enough white wine to cover the pieces, season, and add for each two pounds of eel: five ounces of finely cut sorrel, the same of watercress leaves, two ounces of white nettle-tops, a third of an ounce of parsley and the same of chervil, a little bag containing sage, herb savory and mint a sixth of an ounce of each. Boil very rapidly for twelve to fifteen minutes, and when cooked bind off the fire with four egg-yolks beaten in a little cream. Serve hot or cold.

Bouilliture d'Anguilles.—Take for preference medium-sized eels ; skin them, open them, clean them, and cut them into pieces about two inches long. Season them, and fry them quickly in *nut* oil, with onions and one or two cloves of garlic all chopped. When all are well coloured, put them into a stewpan, add a little flour, colour this lightly, and moisten with enough red wine and a little water to cover the pieces. Add a *bouquet garni*, stir until it boils, and then cook gently until the eels are cooked. (JOURDIN.)

Anguille au beurre rouge (Eel with Red Butter). See Carp with Red Butter (page 78).

GUDGEON *(GOUJON)*

The best gudgeon come from clear and rapid streams with stony bottoms. They are hardly ever prepared otherwise than fried in deep fat or in butter with *fines herbes* (parsley, chervil, chives and tarragon). They are also used as a garnish for dishes of certain other fish, e.g. *Carpe à la Chambord* (page 80), and they are then egg-and-breadcrumbed, and fried in deep fat. They are generally coated with the egg-and-breadcrumbs so that their heads and tails are left uncoated, as if they were wearing a muff; and this fashion is naturally called *en manchon*.

---

* SUBSTITUTE FLOUNDER OR BUTTERFISH

PERCH (*PERCHE*)

The perch is a beautiful and excellent fish, but it is dangerous to handle because of the pain which the little spikes of its dorsal fin may cause.

Perches à la Commère.—Allow for each person a perch of six ounces, gross. Cook the perch in salted water, slightly acidulated with lemon juice. Drain them, scrape them on each side, and put the fish back into the *court-bouillon* to make sure that they are quite clean. Drain them again, and arrange them on the serving-dish. Mask them with Butter Sauce, keeping it fairly light. Sprinkle over them a mixture of hot hard-boiled egg, white and yolk, and chopped parsley.

Perches à la Hollandaise.—Prepare and cook in advance for eight minutes a *court-bouillon* composed of water salted with a third of an ounce of salt and acidulated by a dessertspoonful of vinegar for each pint and three-quarters, and a bouquet of parsley, thyme and bayleaf. Plunge the perch, medium-sized or large one, into this, cover the pan, and poach them on the side of the stove, allowing twelve minutes for fish weighing six ounces and fifteen to twenty minutes for those weighing from eight to ten ounces. Drain and skin the perch, and put them back into the *court-bouillon*, as directed in the previous recipe. Then arrange them on your dish covered with a napkin, and surround them with quarters of boiled floury potatoes and bunches of parsley. Hand separately some slightly salted melted butter, flavoured with lemon juice and chopped parsley.

(NOTE.—The proportion of melted butter is generally an ounce for each person.)

Perches Souchet (Souchet of Perch).—Take six perch weighing six ounces each.

(1) Cut two ounces of the red part of carrot into very fine *julienne* strips, with the same amount of the white part of celery, and half an ounce of parsley root. Stew this *julienne* in butter, moisten it with half a pint and four table-spoonfuls of white wine and as much water, season with a pinch of salt, and finish cooking the vegetables in this.

(2) Clean and trim the perch, and arrange them in a shallow dish. Pour over them the boiling *court-bouillon* above, straining it through a conical sieve (but be sure to keep back the *julienne* of vegetables for later use). Put on the lid and poach the fish on the side of the stove for twelve minutes. Then drain them and arrange them on the serving-dish, keeping them hot.

(3) Reduce the *court-bouillon* by half; then bind it with an ounce and a half of flour kneaded with butter in the proportion of five parts butter to four parts flour. Let the sauce boil for a minute, then finish it off the fire with two ounces of butter. Mix with it the *julienne* which has been kept back for the purpose, add half a dessertspoonful of very small parsley leaves well blanched, and pour this sauce over the fish.

Other Preparations for Perch.—Perch can be fried (you want little perch weighing about five ounces each for this), grilled, cooked *à la meunière, à la Bercy, au gratin,* etc. Medium-sized perch can also be used in a matelote of perch, or as an ingredient in a mixed matelote.

PIKE (*BROCHET*)

The best pike are those weighing from two and a half pounds to four pounds. As the flesh of large fish is inclined to be dry, they are almost always braised.

Brochet à l'Angevine (Pike à l'Angevine).—That is to say, as cooked in Anjou. Get a pike weighing two pounds, cut it in slices across, and keep back the liver. Stiffen the slices in a sauté-pan in butter, and then moisten with Anjou wine. Season, add a little chopped shallot, grated nutmeg and English mustard, and let the fish cook and the sauce reduce at the same time. Finish with two dessertspoonfuls of double cream, and bind with the pounded liver. Add butter, correct the seasoning, and finish with lemon juice. Serve in a timbale with fried croûtons round it.

Brochet au beurre blanc (Pike with White Butter).—Cook the pike in an ordinary *court-bouillon*. Drain it, remove the skin from the two sides, arrange it on the serving-dish, and cover it plentifully with White Butter (*Beurre blanc*), for which see page 25.

Brochet au Bleu (Pike au Bleu).—The method of preparing fish *au bleu* is as follows :—The first condition is that the fish, whether large or small, must be alive. Remove the gills, and clean the fish quickly, handling it as little as possible. Cut off the fins, etc. Do not scale it, or scrape it, or even wash it, so as to leave on it the natural slime which assists in the " blueing " process. Put the fish on the drainer of a fish kettle, sprinkle it with boiling vinegar, and cover it with a *court-bouillon* prepared beforehand, warm if the fish is fairly large. Small fish weighing from five ounces to half a pound, such as trout, tench, and so on, must be plunged into boiling *court-bouillon*, after being sprinkled with the vinegar. Cook as in an ordinary *court-bouillon*, that is to say, keeping the water just trembling. Then arrange on a dish covered with a napkin, and surround with parsley. The scales should be removed at the moment of serving.

Fish cooked in this fashion can be served hot or cold. If hot, it is accompanied by slightly salted melted butter and steamed or boiled potatoes. If cold, a Ravigote Sauce (see page 40) or a Sauce Gribiche (see page 38) is handed with it.

Brochet aux Champignons de rosée.—A pike of medium size is best for this dish. Put it in the fish kettle surrounded by very small field mushrooms which have been freshly gathered. Moisten with sherry and thick brown stock, and braise it. When it is cooked, place it on a dish and surround it with the mushrooms. Reduce the cooking liquor, finish with butter, a ladleful of cream, and several drops of fine brandy, and pour this sauce (which should look like *café au lait*) over the fish.

Brochet court-bouillonné avec sauces diverses (Boiled Pike with various sauces).—When pike has been cooked in a *court-bouillon*, it can be served with any of the following sauces, and always then accompanied by boiled or steamed potatoes : Caper Sauce, *Hollandaise*, *Vénitienne*, hot *Ravigote*.

Côtelettes de Brochet à la mode de Cholet.—For fifteen cutlets, prepare a pike forcemeat in the manner described under *Pain de Brochet à la Normande* (page 94). Divide the forcemeat into portions weighing about three ounces, and shape each with floured hands into the form of a cutlet. Put these into a buttered sauté-pan, cover them with slightly salted boiling water, and poach them for about ten minutes. Then take them out, drain them, plunge them into cold water, wipe them dry and egg-and-breadcrumb them. When the time comes for serving them (so as not to keep them waiting) put them side by side in a sauté-pan containing foaming butter, and colour them golden on both sides. Drain them on a cloth, stick in the end of each a piece of uncooked macaroni to imitate the cutlet bone, and put a little frill on it. Arrange them in a circle on your dish and pour in the middle a very creamy Tomato Sauce flavoured with *fines herbes*, that is, parsley, chervil, chives and tarragon all finely chopped.

Côtelettes de Brochet purée de champignons (Pike Cutlets with Mushroom Purée).—With an ordinary pike forcemeat (see page 94) make the number of cutlets you want. Poach them and fry them as described in the recipe above. Serve them with a Mushroom Purée (see page 20) in the middle.

(NOTE.—If desired, a creamy Onion Purée can be substituted for the Mushroom Purée.)

Côtelettes de Brochet fourrées (Stuffed Pike Cutlets).—Special moulds are made for shaping various sorts of cutlets, and in this case the use of the appropriate moulds is recommended.

Prepare beforehand a salpicon of mushrooms and truffles bound with Allemande Sauce. Butter the moulds, line them at the bottom and on the sides with an even layer of pike forcemeat. Fill up the centre with the salpicon, cover with more forcemeat, and smooth with a knife. Put the moulds into a sauté-pan, add boiling salted water, and poach them as above. (On contact with the boiling water, the cutlets will come away from the moulds by themselves.) Then drain them, egg-and-breadcrumb them, fry them golden in butter, and arrange them on the serving-dish. They can be accompanied by a light purée of mushrooms, or by an Onion (*Soubise*) Sauce, or some other appropriate one.

Filets de Brochet (Fillets of Pike).—The preparation of these fillets and of the garnish and sauce can be varied according to taste and circumstance. Skin the pike, remove the fillets and cut them up as you like. Arrange them in a buttered fireproof dish, and poach them with very little liquid, basting them from time to time. The liquid will vary according to the dish you are making ; *e.g.* white wine for a White Wine Sauce. When they are cooked, glaze them at the last moment. Arrange them in a circle on a round dish, and put in the middle the sauce or garnish that you have selected.

Filets de Brochet Bonne Femme.—Butter the bottom of a shallow fireproof dish, and sprinkle it with chopped raw mushrooms, roughly chopped parsley and chopped shallot. Season with salt and pepper. On this arrange the fillets of pike, moisten with white wine and mushroom cooking liquor (see page 20), and poach them in the oven. Arrange the fillets on the serving-dish, reduce the cooking liquor, thicken it with butter, and finish it with a little Hollandaise Sauce. Cover the fillets with this, and brown lightly in the oven.

Pain de Brochet à la Normande.—(1) *The Forcemeat.* Pound a pound of pike flesh and pass it through a very fine tammy-cloth. Work in a mortar eleven ounces of ordinary choux paste without sugar, and add to it by degrees the pike flesh, nine ounces of butter, and several spoonfuls of cold Béchamel Sauce. Season with salt, pepper and nutmeg. Put this forcemeat into a basin, put it on ice, and mix into it four or five yolks of egg and four dessertspoonfuls of cream.

(2) With this forcemeat fill a well-buttered cylindrical mould, pressing it well down so that there are no air pockets inside. Poach this in the *bain-marie* for forty minutes.

(3) Meanwhile, you will have prepared a Cream Sauce (see page 32) bound with two egg-yolks, to which you will add a garnish *à la Normande*, that is, crayfish tails, poached oysters and cooked button mushrooms. Unmould the *pain*, and pour the sauce and garnish over it.

Quenelles de Brochet (Pike Quenelles).—These quenelles are made with ordinary pike forcemeat, but they are better if it is a mousseline forcemeat (see page 15). Mould them with a dessertspoon, and place them as they are moulded on a buttered shallow fireproof dish or a sauté-pan. Cover them with boiling salted water, and poach them. They are done as soon as the forcemeat feels firm to the touch. Drain them on a cloth, arrange them in a circle on the serving-dish, and pour the chosen sauce in the middle.

Quenelles de Brochet à la graisse or *Quenelles de Brochet Lyonnaise.*—(1) *The Forcemeat.* Pound a pound of pike flesh and set it aside. Now pound very finely six and a half ounces of beef kidney fat and just over three ounces of beef marrow. Then add a pound of very cold Frangipane panada (see page 17) and four egg-whites by small degrees. Put back the pike flesh with a seasoning of salt, pepper and grated nutmeg, and mix it vigorously with the pestle so as to get a perfect amalgamation. Put the forcemeat into a basin, add a little cream, and, if it is not to be used at once, keep it on ice.

(2) Mould the quenelles with a dessertspoon in the usual

way, and poach them in some good fish fumet. Drain them,
arrange them in a circle, and serve with a Sauce Bercy,
Nantua, Mornay, or some other.

Brochet à la Valvins.—Take a medium-sized fish. Skin it
on both sides, and lard it with anchovy fillets. Season it,
and wrap it in oiled or buttered paper. Then bake it in
the oven. Serve with a Ravigote Sauce, melted butter
flavoured with mustard, or Maître-d'hôtel Butter.

Brochetons (Small Pike) weighing from nine ounces to a
pound can be used in a mixed matelote, or fried in deep fat
or *à la meunière*, or grilled and served with a butter of some
kind, as with Tartare Sauce, Green Sauce, etc.

TENCH* (*TANCHE*)

The removal of the tench's scales presents some difficulty,
as they are very small, but this process will be found easier
if the fish is first scalded. It is a good fish as an ingredient
of a *Matelote à la crème* (*Matelote Marinière*, see page 86), and
it can also be served *au gratin*, *à la Bercy*, *meunière*, fried in
deep fat, and so on.

Tanche à la Poitevine.—Scale and clean carefully a tench
weighing about a pound and a half : score its sides, and
season it. Butter thickly a shallow dish, and sprinkle over
the bottom some finely minced potatoes and a large onion,
also minced. Lay the tench on this bed, sprinkle it with a
glass of brandy (*marc*), set it alight, and then moisten with
two glasses of dry white wine. Cook in the oven for twenty-
five to thirty minutes. At the last moment add a binding
of two egg-yolks and two dessertspoonfuls of well-whipped

* SUBSTITUTE DACE

fresh cream.   Stir lightly, brown very slightly, and serve.

Tanches à la mode de Touraine.—Scatter on the bottom of a buttered dish a little chopped shallot, and chopped chives and chervil.   Add also a few minced mushrooms or morels, if you can get them.   Lay on this some small tench weighing about five to eight ounces each, moisten with cream which has been boiled beforehand, and cook in the oven for twenty minutes, basting now and again.   At the moment of serving, correct the seasoning, and sprinkle the fish with chopped parsley, chives and chervil.

Tanche au beurre rouge (Tench with Red Butter).   See Carp with Red Butter (page 78).

TROUT (*TRUITES DE RIVIÈRE*)

Serve one trout, weighing four to five ounces, per head.

Truites au Bleu (Trout au Bleu).—The essential condition of this picturesque dish is that the fish should be alive. Stun them, clean them as quickly as possible, and plunge them immediately into a boiling *court-bouillon* consisting only of salted water with plenty of vinegar in it.

For quarter-pound trout, poach for ten minutes on the side of the fire.   Arrange them on a napkin with parsley round them, and serve separately melted butter and steamed or boiled potatoes.

Truites au Chablis (Trout au Chablis).—Make a *court-bouillon* with Chablis, and poach the trout gently in it. With this *court-bouillon*, make a jelly as described on page 15.   Decorate the trout with tarragon leaves, little sprigs of chervil, white or yolk of hard-boiled egg, etc., and cover them deeply with the cold jelly.

Truites Doria (Trout à la Doria).—The trout are fried *à la meunière* (page 5), and dished with a surround of little heaps of cucumber balls blanched and stewed in butter.

Truites à la Bretonne.—The trout are fried *à la meunière* (page 100), and served with a surround of shrimps' tails and mushrooms fried in butter.

Truites farcies Carême (Stuffed Trout Carême).—Soft-roed trout should be used for this dish, and should weigh from five to seven ounces each. Pass the roes through a tammy, and add to this purée chopped shallots, mushrooms, parsley and chervil, breadcrumbs, a beaten egg and a seasoning of salt and pepper. Cut the trout down the back from one end to the other, and remove the backbone. Fill them with the stuffing, and wrap each in a heavily buttered paper. Then braise them in very little liquid for fifteen to twenty minutes. Then unroll the paper, and quickly wrap each trout in a thin piece of puff-paste : arrange them on a baking-tin, and cook in a hot oven. They are usually served as they are, but they may be accompanied, if liked, by a Cream Sauce flavoured with Truffle Essence.

Truites au Fenouil (Trout with Fennel).—Butter a dish, and scatter a fine *julienne* of fennel in it. Lightly season your trout with salt and a touch of cayenne, lay them in the dish, moisten with white wine, cover, and poach the fish gently. When they are cooked, skin them, and arrange them on the serving-dish. Reduce the cooking liquor, thicken it with butter, heighten the seasoning a little, and pour this sauce over the trout. (JOURDIN.)

Truites à la Grenobloise.—These are small trout, seasoned,

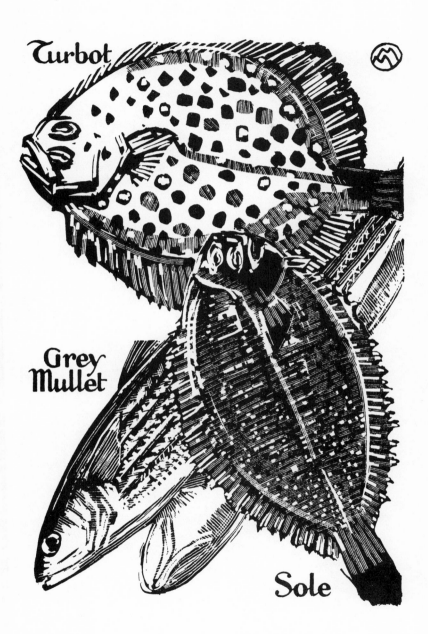

Turbot

Grey
Mullet

Sole

floured and cooked in butter, that is, *à la meunière*. Arrange them in the serving-dish and keep them hot. In the same pan in which they have cooked fry in butter some finely chopped mushrooms and a pinch of breadcrumbs, and pour this when still foaming over the fish. Finish with lemon juice and a few capers.

Truites à la Hussarde.—The trout should weigh half a pound each. Fill their stomachs with ordinary fish force-meat (page 14) mixed with Duxelles (page 13), and sew up the opening. Season them with salt and pepper.

For six trout, chop up finely a large onion, and scatter it on the bottom of a buttered dish. Lay the trout on this, moisten with half a pint of Chablis, and add two ounces of butter in little dabs, and a small *bouquet garni*. Bake in the oven for half an hour, basting frequently. Drain the fishes, remove the thread which sewed them up, and arrange them in the serving-dish. Rub the cooking liquor through a fine conical sieve with a wooden spoon, reduce it for a few seconds, bind it very lightly with Kneaded Butter, and finish with three ounces of butter and a few drops of Anchovy Essence. Cover the trout with this sauce and glaze quickly.

Truites à la mode de Héas. (Héas is a small Pyrenean summer resort near the circus of Troumouse.)

The trout should weigh about five ounces. For six trout prepare four ounces of Duxelles (see page 13) with fresh mushrooms. Season and flour the trout, and cook them in a frying-pan in clarified butter. Spread the Duxelles on the serving-dish, arrange the trout on it, and sprinkle them generously with the chopped yolk of hot hard-boiled egg mixed with chopped parsley. Sprinkle with butter cooked *à la noisette* (page 28), using about an ounce of butter for each fish. The dish should be served as quickly as possible so that the butter is still foaming when it comes to the table.

Truites à la Meunière.—Wipe the trout, season them, roll them in flour, and cook them in a frying-pan in clarified butter. Arrange them on the serving-dish, scatter chopped parsley over them, sprinkle them lightly with lemon juice, and pour over some butter cooked *à la noisette* (page 28).

(NOTE.—It should be observed that cooking fish *à la meunière*, simple as it sounds, needs some care. Too great a heat will brown the skin and the appearance and flavour of the fish will be spoiled. If the cooking is too slow, the fish get soft. Fish properly cooked in this way should be a beautiful golden brown.)

Truites à la Normande (aux ciboulettes).—Butter a dish thickly, lay the trout on it, add a dessertspoonful of water, the juice of a lemon, salt, pepper, plenty of chopped chives and some chopped parsley. Cook them in the oven for ten minutes. Meanwhile, boil as much double cream as you will want for a sauce. After the ten minutes' cooking, pour this over the fish, sprinkle with breadcrumbs, and brown in the oven.

Truites au Rubis.—Proceed as if for *Trout au Chablis* (page 97), using a good red Burgundy or Bordeaux in place of the white wine.

THREE DISHES OF RIVER-FISH

La Meurette (Bourgogne).—For this dish you will want a variety of fish such as eel, perch, little pike, tench,* trout, and so on. Scale them, clean them and trim them, and cut off their heads. Now cut them into pieces across of the

* SUBSTITUTE DACE

same size, and put them in a copper pan or earthenware basin. Sprinkle them with a good glass of brandy (*marc*), and leave them to marinate for an hour or two. Now toss in butter some minced onions and leeks, a few potatoes (which will supply the binding element), a large *bouquet garni* with celery, several crushed cloves of garlic, salt and pepper. Moisten with good Burgundy, and cook for half an hour. Pass this fumet through a fine sieve or tammy on to the pieces of fish, and let them cook in it for eight to sixteen minutes. Put some pieces of toasted bread rubbed with garlic in the bottom of a shallow dish, and put the pieces of fish on them. If the sauce is too thin, let it reduce by half, then bind it lightly with Kneaded Butter. Finish it with more butter, correct the seasoning, and pour it over the fish.

La Pouchouse (Franche-Comté).—For ten people you will want five pounds of fish : little carp, tench,* perch, eels, small barbel and pike, etc. Prepare the fish and cut them in slices across, all the same thickness but not too large. In an earthenware pan put an ounce of minced onion, four finely crushed cloves of garlic, a *bouquet garni*, the pieces of fish, salt, pepper and three or four ounces of butter. Stiffen the pieces of fish in the butter, *flambez* them with a glass of brandy (*marc*), moisten with just enough red wine to cover them, and boil for fifteen to twenty minutes. In another earthenware pan fry in butter some rather lean streaky bacon cut in dice and blanched, some button onions and button mushrooms. Take out the pieces of fish and put them into the pan with the garnish above. Reduce the cooking liquor in the other pan by half, strain it into the second pan, bind with Kneaded Butter (*beurre manié*), and simmer for a minute or two. Serve as it is, adding some small croûtons of bread fried golden in butter.

* SUBSTITUTE DACE

Waterzoï.—The following fish are suitable for making *Waterzoï* : small pike, eel, chub, little carp, tench,* perch, small barbel. If you cannot include all these fish, you should have at least three or four different kinds. You will need, for ten people, six pounds of the fish, and they should be alive.

Having cleaned them, cut them in slices across, and put them into a stewpan with salt, pepper and a bouquet of parsley stalks and a piece of celery. Moisten with water just to cover the pieces. Cook rapidly for twenty minutes so that the liquid reduces as the fish are cooking. At the last, add a little finely crushed biscuit or oven-dried bread, and boil on for another two minutes. Hand separately slices of brown bread-and-butter.

* SUBSTITUTE DACE

Chapter VII

Salt-Water Fish

WHEN we come to the fishes from the sea, Madame Prunier
has endless advice to give us. She has always been a little
puzzled why it is we cannot as a rule get such fishes as
Bass, Gurnard, Sea-bream and so on in the fishmonger's
shop, and I am inclined to think that the reason is that even
if we were to see them there we should neither recognise
them nor know what to do with them if we bought them.
This chapter should remove that reproach.

Many writers, and not least among them E. V. Lucas,
have complained that they cannot get in the hotels and
restaurants of this country any other fish than Sole (of varying quality) or Turbot. If Madame Prunier has her way,
English people will soon become much more " fish-
conscious," and by asking for the cheaper and more unfamiliar fishes will soon find that a demand is created. And
they are delicious, Bass and Grey Mullet especially, the
former being a favourite of George Moore's, who was
always complaining that it could never be found in London.

A glance through the recipes in this chapter will soon
convince the reader that here is imagination at last applied
to fish in a way which we had never dreamed it could be.
The usual boiled or fried or grilled pale before this magnifi-
cent array of dishes. Attention is particularly drawn to the
many ways of preparing Herring and Mackerel. The Skate [1]
recipes should also be noticed, and the remarkable collec-

[1] See page 150.

tion of Salt Cod dishes, remarkable to a country where this
fish is eaten only on Good Friday, and then with egg sauce
and parsnips ! Fresh Cod, too, is treated as it deserves, a
fish which Escoffier claimed to be so excellent that if it
were less common it would be held in as high esteem as
Salmon.

All of the fish treated in this chapter can be obtained in
England, some of them, like Shad and Sturgeon, being less
familiar than others.

BASS (*BAR*)

An excellent fish which might be seen more in the shops
were the demand for it greater. It resembles the salmon in
its shape, though not in the colour of its flesh, which is
very white. Its only disadvantage is that it has rather many
bones. Large bass are principally poached, and served with
melted butter, Maître-d'hôtel Butter, Hollandaise Sauce,
etc. The smaller fish can also be poached, but they are
more usually grilled, fried in deep fat or *à la meunière*, and
even filleted. Nearly all the fashions of serving salmon are
applicable to bass.

Bar au Bleu.—For this you will want a fish weighing about
three pounds. Put it in the fish kettle with half a bottle of
red wine, the same of white wine and a pint and three-
quarters of fish fumet or stock. Add fluted rounds of carrot
(which will serve afterwards as a garnish), two finely
chopped onions, two cloves, two cloves of garlic, a *bouquet
garni*, a few mushroom stalks, salt and coarsely ground
pepper. Bring to the boil, and let the fish poach on the
side of the stove for ten to fifteen minutes. Strain half of
the cooking liquor through a fine cloth, remove any grease,

bind it lightly with Kneaded Butter, and add a little Tomato
Purée and a few drops of Anchovy Essence. Arrange the
bass on a dish bordered with the carrot rings, and hand the
sauce separately.

Bar bouilli sauce Crevettes (Boiled Bass, with Shrimp Sauce).
—For six persons you will need a bass weighing about three
pounds. Cook it in a *court-bouillon* (page 13), arrange it on
a napkin in a dish, and surround it with parsley. Serve
separately a Shrimp Sauce (*Crevettes*) (page 32).

Bar braisé Cardinal (Braised Bass à la Cardinal).—For ten
people take a bass of five pounds. Braise it with very
dry white wine, basting it often. Lay it on a dish and
round it place crayfish or fine prawns with their tails
shelled. Hand a Cardinal Sauce (page 31) seasoned with
paprika pepper.

Bar braisé Polotzoff (Braised Bass à la Polotzoff).—A
medium-sized bass, of about three pounds, is wanted here.
Stuff it with mousseline forcemeat (page 15) of sole, with
chopped chives added. Braise it with a fine mirepoix
(page 16) and fresh chopped tomatoes. Reduce the cooking liquor with half-glaze (*demi-glace*) sauce, and thicken with
butter. Arrange the bass on the dish, cover it with the
sauce, and garnish it with stuffed olives, croustades of
mushrooms *à la crème*, and little tomatoes stewed in butter.

Délices de Bar Grand Vatel. (This recipe is acknowledged to J.-B. Féès.)

Fillet a bass, cut the fillets in small slices and stiffen them
in butter. Let them get cold. Now wrap each of them
in brioche paste, shape into a rectangle, and bake in the
oven. Serve separately a Bercy Sauce (page 31).

(Note.—If you like you can wrap up with the fish slices
a little " melted " sorrel mixed with chopped hard-boiled

egg-yolks. In this case, Maître-d'hôtel Butter should be handed instead of the sauce.)

Bar à la Dinardaise en Medaillons.—Cut the bass into small slices, of the same size and the shape of a medal. The fish should weigh two pounds and of course be filleted. Keep the head and tail for cooking separately. Egg-and-bread-crumb the slices and cook them in the oven on a buttered dish. Meanwhile, have prepared a *chiffonnade* of spinach and sorrel *à la crème*, put this on the serving-dish, and arrange on it the slices of bass. At each end place the cooked head and tail of the fish, and cover the whole with a light Mornay Sauce (page 34). Brown quickly in the oven just before serving.

(NOTE.—To prepare a *chiffonnade*, first carefully shred the sorrel and spinach, and remove the mid-ribs. Carefully wash the leaves, and squeeze them between the fingers of the left hand and the table top, as you cut them into fine strips with a sharp knife. Melt them in a little butter, and finish them with cream in the usual manner.)

Bar froid (Cold Bass).—This is bass poached in *court-bouillon* and left to get cold. Wipe it, arrange it on your dish, and decorate it as you wish. Mask it well with jelly, and surround it with a Salade Parisienne.

(NOTE.—Salade Parisienne is a vegetable salad with which are mixed dice of lobster or *langouste* and a binding of Mayonnaise.)

Bar rôti Jean-Bart (Roast Bass à la Jean-Bart).—For six people take a bass of three pounds or thereabouts. Incise it, on each side, season it and roast it in the oven, basting it with butter. Meanwhile cut in rings six large onions, season them, flour them and fry them in oil, keeping them crisp. Arrange the bass on a dish, surround it with the fried onions, and hand a Sauce Bercy flavoured with mustard.

Bar rôti sauce Génevoise (Roast Bass with Génevoise Sauce). —For this you will want a bass of three and a half to four pounds. Lay it in a thickly buttered baking-pan, season it, surround it with rounds of carrot, onion, celery, *bouquet garni*. Sprinkle it with butter, and roast it slowly for forty or fifty minutes. When it is cooked, put it in the serving-dish, and skin it on both sides. Moisten the cooking liquor with three-quarters of a pint of very dry white wine (for in the neighbourhood of Geneva some very good white wines are made). Reduce this by three-quarters, and strain it into a saucepan. Put it back on the fire, and add four tablespoon-fuls of cream. Reduce again, this time by half. Remove the pan from the fire, and add a binding of four dessert-spoonfuls of Hollandaise Sauce. Season as you like. Cover the bass with this sauce, and surround it with steamed potatoes cut in the shape of a hazel nut.

Bars pochés Carême (Poached Bass à la Carême).—Take some small bass weighing about half a pound each and cook them for ten minutes in a *court-bouillon* with white wine (page 13). Drain them, skin them on both sides, and keep them hot. With half of the *court-bouillon*, some cooking liquor of oysters, mussels and mushrooms well reduced, make a White Wine Sauce and bind it with two egg-yolks. Make a garnish of oysters, mussels and mush-rooms, bound with some of the sauce, and fill some little croustades with this garnish. Cover the bass with the rest of the sauce, arrange the croustades round them, and serve very hot.

Bars poêlés Gourmande.—These are little bass of a pound to a pound and a half for two or three persons. Cut them down the back from head to tail, and remove the backbone. Season them, egg-and-breadcrumb them, and cook them in clarified butter. Hand with them a Béarnaise Sauce. (Ch. ALAMAGNIE.)

Bar à l'Angevine.—Remove the backbone from a bass of three pounds. Keep the head and trimmings to make the sauce. Stuff the bass with a mixture of purée of mushrooms, one dessertspoonful of sorrel purée and half a pound of purée of spinach, all bound with a beaten egg, a little cream and some breadcrumbs, and seasoned with powdered thyme and savory. Bake the bass gently in the oven, basting it well. Arrange the fish on your dish, reduce the cooking liquor, adding two dessertspoonfuls each of vinegar and white wine and some chopped shallot, then moisten with a pint of cream, thicken with butter and then with two yolks of eggs at the last moment, and brown lightly.   (M. BOUZY.)

BRILL* (*BARBUE*)

This fish resembles the turbot, but its shape is more elongated. Whether large or small, all the recipes for small turbot and sole can be applied to it. It should be remembered, when cooking brill, that its flesh is more fragile than that of the turbot.

Barbue à l'Ambassadrice.—Take for ten people a brill of six pounds. Cut it down the back, lift up the fillets, and remove the backbone. Stuff the inside with a Chasseur garnish much reduced and strongly flavoured with tomato. Put the fillets back in place and join them with a line of mousseline forcemeat of whiting (page 15) squeezed through a forcing-bag with a grooved pipe. Then braise the fish. When it is cooked, arrange it on your dish,

* SUBSTITUTE TURBOT

surround it with little heaps of asparagus tips bound with butter and mushrooms. Reduce the cooking liquor, add cream, thicken it with butter, pour it over the fish, and brown it quickly.

Suprême de Barbue Saint-Germain.—Fillet a small brill, skinned. Trim the fillets, egg-and-breadcrumb them, and cook them in butter. Garnish, on serving, with small grilled tomatoes and croquettes of rice. Hand with them a Béarnaise Sauce.

Barbue Polignac (Brill à la Polignac).—Cook the fillets in a buttered dish, seasoned and moistened with dry white wine and a little fish fumet. Take out the fillets, arrange them on a dish, and decorate them with little strips of cooked mushrooms and truffles. Reduce the cooking liquor, add a little cream, and finish with butter. Pour over the fish and brown quickly.

COD, FRESH (*CABILLAUD*, ou *MORUE FRAÎCHE*)

Many despise cod as tasteless and watery, but no less an authority than Escoffier wrote that "if cod were less common, it would be held in as high esteem as salmon ; for, when it is really fresh and of good quality, the delicacy and delicious flavour of its flesh admit of its ranking among the finest of fish." The following recipes should help to substantiate this dictum.

Cabillaud à la Boulangère.—Take a piece (cutlet) of the size you need from the middle of the fish. Put it in a shallow fireproof dish, surround it with quartered raw potatoes and well-blanched little onions. Season with salt and pepper, brush over with melted butter and bake in the oven, basting often with butter. Sprinkle with chopped parsley on serving.

Cabillaud Crème Gratin.—With some cold cod, proceed as for *Turbot Crème Gratin* (page 187).

Cabillaud à la Flamande.—Thickly butter a sauté-pan, and lay in it the cod cutlets seasoned with salt, pepper and grated nutmeg. Add a chopped shallot, a small *bouquet garni,* lemon juice, and a little dry white wine, and poached in the oven for ten minutes. Arrange the cutlets in the serving-dish, bind the cooking liquor with a little fine breadcrumbs or finely crushed oven-dried bread. Boil up for a few minutes, and pour over the fish.

Cabillaud en Fritot.—Cut some thin slices from cod fillets, slit them so as to make a little pocket in each, and stuff them with a little fish forcemeat to which chopped mushrooms have been added. Close the slices again and lay them on a buttered dish. Poach them with very little liquid, and let them get cold. When you want to serve them, dip them in frying-batter, and fry them in very hot deep fat. Arrange them in a napkin with fried parsley, and hand a Tomato Sauce.

Cabillaud à la Mornay.—Cover the bottom of the serving-dish with creamy Mornay Sauce (page 34), arrange on this your cod cutlets poached and well drained, cover them with the same sauce, sprinkle them with grated cheese and brown them quickly.

Cabillaud à la Portugaise.—Butter a shallow fireproof dish thickly, and lay on it your cod cutlets seasoned with salt and pepper. Add a chopped onion, some crushed garlic, roughly chopped parsley, a sprig of thyme, some peeled, pressed and roughly chopped tomatoes, and moisten with white wine. Bring to the boil, and cook for ten minutes.

Arrange the cutlets on the serving-dish, reduce the cooking liquor, butter it lightly, correct the seasoning and pour it over the fish.

Cabillaud à la Provençale.—Proceed as for *Cabillaud à la Portugaise* (above), adding a *julienne* of mushrooms.

Cabillaud poché (Boiled Cod).—Cod is usually poached in salted water, but one can also use a well-seasoned and flavoured *court-bouillon*. In whichever case, and whether it has been poached whole or in cutlets, it should be accompanied by either melted butter, Caper or Hollandaise Sauce and by steamed potatoes.

COD, SALT (*MORUE*)

Salt cod should always have white flesh and the fillets should be thick. If they are thin and the colour is yellowish, these are signs of age and stringiness. Salt cod should be soaked for at least twenty-four hours to remove the saltiness, and the water should be changed every three or four hours. If it is then still too salt when you want to cook it, it should be placed for a few minutes in warm water. Six or seven ounces of salt cod should be allowed for each person.

Bouillabaisse de Morue.—Fry in six tablespoonfuls of oil, without colouration, four ounces of onion, an ounce of the white part of a leek and the same of garlic, all chopped up. Add two and a half pints of water, a good pinch of salt, a small pinch of pepper, a *bouquet garni* and a touch of saffron. Bring to the boil and boil for five minutes, then add five waxy potatoes cut in thick rounds. Boil on for another twelve minutes, add five pounds of soaked salt cod cut in little pieces about two inches square. Add also four more tablespoonfuls of oil. Continue to boil rapidly for a quarter of an hour, and a few seconds before the cooking is finished throw in a dessertspoonful of roughly chopped parsley. Pour the bouillabaisse into a timbale or a shallow dish, and serve at the same time, and on another dish, some pieces of toast which have been rubbed with a cut clove of garlic and moistened with some of the liquid of the bouillabaisse.

Brandade de Morue.—Cut three pounds of soaked salt cod in large squares, poach it in water, keeping it rather underdone, drain it and remove the skin and bones. Now add to it a third of its weight of warm mashed potatoes that have been baked in their jackets in the oven. Pound the salt cod in a mortar, mixing it and pounding it with the potatoes, and working the pestle vigorously so as to get a fine paste. With this paste, incorporate by degrees half a pint of warm olive-oil (in which one or two cloves of garlic have been put while it was warming) and the same quantity of warm cream, pounding away all the time, so as to get the Brandade white and light. Season it at the last minute, and serve it either by itself, or with little croûtons of bread fried in butter, or in little *vol-au-vent*.

(NOTE.—This Brandade is eaten largely in France during Lent, and in the South it is often eaten cold, as hors-d'œuvre.)

Crêpes de Brandade (Brandade Pancakes).—Make some very thin pancakes with unsweetened batter, garnish them with a very light Brandade, and fold them over. Serve separately a creamy White Wine Sauce. (M. COCHOIS.)

Morue Cardinal.—Make three-quarters of a pint of tomato purée, adding chopped parsley and a touch of garlic. When it is cold, mix with it two whole eggs, two yolks of eggs, and a pound of freshly cooked flaked salt cod. Pour the whole into a buttered mould, and poach it in the *bain-marie*. Turn it out at the moment of serving, and serve with a Cream Sauce (page 32).

Morue Cantabréca.—Take some well-soaked fillets of salt cod and poach them without letting them come to the boil. Fry lightly in oil two large chopped onions, add six crushed cloves of garlic, six roughly chopped tomatoes, six sweet red peppers (tinned ones would do), two finely cut leeks (the white part only), and a *bouquet garni*. Simmer for a few minutes, then moisten with a wineglassful of white wine and the same of the water the cod was cooked in. Cook for ten minutes. If you then find that the flavour of the tomatoes is not pronounced enough, add a little concentrated tomato purée. Pass through a sieve, and correct the seasoning. Flake up the salt cod, removing skin and bones. In the bottom of a fireproof dish pour some of the tomato cullis. On this lay the salt cod. Cover it with the rest of the tomato, and let it simmer for a few minutes in the oven.

Coquilles de Morue.—Make some Béchamel Sauce, adding to it some grated cheese, and mix with it some flaked cooked salt cod and minced mushrooms, or, if you prefer it, a little truffle. Garnish the buttered scallop shells with this mixture, smooth it into a dome, sprinkle it with grated cheese mixed with browned breadcrumbs, and brown quickly.

Croquettes de Morue.—Flake or cut in dice some freshly cooked salt cod, from which all skin and bones have been removed. Mix it with a very much reduced Béchamel Sauce to which grated cheese has been added. The proportion should be for a pound of the flaked cod, sixteen tablespoonfuls of the sauce and two ounces of cheese. Spread the mixture on a plate, and let it get cold. Divide it then into portions weighing about two ounces each, roll them into balls, and egg-and-breadcrumb them. Fry them in oil, and serve them on a napkin with fried parsley.

Morue à l'Espagnole.—Flake up some salt cod, and fry it in oil with finely minced onion. Then add to it some tomatoes, skinned, pressed and roughly chopped, some skinned sweet red peppers cut in *julienne* strips, a touch of saffron and a *bouquet garni.* Simmer this mixture for a quarter of an hour, and serve it either hot or cold.

Filets de Morue à l'Aixoise.—Soak the cod fillets, and stuff them with the following mixture : onion, tomatoes, garlic, parsley, capers and anchovy fillets all chopped up. Tie the fillets with cotton, put them into a baking-tin, and bake them in the oven, basting them with olive-oil. Then take them out and arrange them on the dish, mix two dessert-spoonfuls of Tomato Sauce with the cooking liquor, and pour it over the fish.

Filets de Morue frits (Fried Fillets of Salt Cod).—Cut some thin strips from fillets of soaked salt cod, wipe them in a cloth and then dip them in milk. Roll them in flour, dip them in beaten egg, and fry them in very hot oil. Serve with lemon-flavoured Tomato Sauce, or with a Sauce Rémoulade (page 40).

Croquettes à l'Américaine (Fish Balls).—Pound a half-and-half mixture of flaked cooked salt cod and fresh cod with an equal amount of the pulp from potatoes baked in the oven. Season with a touch of nutmeg. Divide the mixture into portions weighing about two ounces each, roll them into balls, egg-and-breadcrumb them, and fry them in very hot fat. Hand a Tomato Sauce with them.

Morue au gratin Carême.—Make a light Béchamel Sauce, and add to it plenty of grated cheese. Make a border of Duchesse potato (page 20) round a shallow fireproof dish, and coat the bottom with the sauce. Cover this with flaked salt cod, from which the bones and skin have been removed, mask with the same sauce, sprinkle with grated cheese, and brown in the oven.

Morue au gratin Marseillaise.—Cut the soaked cod in large cubes, poach them, drain them, and wipe them dry. Now dip them in milk, roll them in flour, and fry them golden in a very hot mixture of oil and butter. Arrange them in a dish, surround them with mussels and mushrooms, cover the whole with a light Béchamel Sauce, and brown in the oven.

Morue Grand' Mère.—Stew gently (*faire suer* : see page 17) some white parts of leeks, celery and a little onion : moisten with milk and cook with some small potatoes. Put a layer of these potatoes in a small shallow dish, alternating the layers with salt cod *à la crème* and chopped chervil. On the top put a little breadcrumbs and grated cheese mixed, and brown in the oven.

Morue grillée Saint-Germain.—Take some soaked cod fillets and cut them in two horizontally, so as to make two fillets of each. Dip them in yolk of egg beaten with cream, salt and pepper. Roll them then in breadcrumbs, and flatten them well. Just colour them under the grill, and finish cooking them in a buttered dish in the oven. Serve with them a Béarnaise Sauce (page 30).

Morue à l'Italienne.—Cut the salt cod in square pieces, roll them in flour, and colour them in oil. Add a few skinned, pressed and roughly chopped tomatoes, a touch of garlic, *fines herbes* (parsley, chervil, chives and tarragon), and finish cooking them. Arrange in a crown, decorate each piece with criss-crossed anchovy fillets, and garnish the middle with black olives. Hand a Pilaff rice (page 21) separately.

Langues de Morue à la façon des Pêcheurs (Salt Cods' Tongues à la façon des Pêcheurs).—Roll the tongues in flour, and fry them in oil with finely minced onions and crushed garlic. Moisten with a little fish fumet or water, season with pepper and cook for a quarter of an hour. Add some little potatoes or large ones cut in quarters, and finish cooking.

Morue à la Limousine.—Cut the salt cod in quarters and blanch it. Then plunge it into cold water and drain it. Line a sauté-pan with large dice (*brunoise*) of onion and white of leek, adding some chopped garlic and a *bouquet garni*. Add the salt cod, moisten with very little water, and cook it. Make separately a white *roux*, which you will moisten with equal parts of oil and the blanching liquor of the cod, and cook it for twenty minutes. Also cook in boiling water several small potatoes, keeping them rather firm. Now put in another sauté-pan the pieces of cod, add the potatoes, some chopped chervil, cream, and the sauce strained through a conical sieve (*chinois*). Bring to the boil for a minute, then keep on the side of the stove until the moment for serving up.

Morue à la Lyonnaise.—Fry some sliced onions golden in butter, and add nearly the same amount of *sauté* potatoes which have been kept soft. In another pan, fry the flaked, boned and skinned salt cod, add the onions and potatoes, fry the three together briskly, shaking the pan to ensure their mixture, and finish with a few drops of lemon or vinegar. Put into a timbale and sprinkle with chopped parsley.

Morue à la Marinière.—Garnish the bottom of a stewpan with butter, finely chopped onion, crushed garlic, capers, anchovies, parsley, pepper and a little Tomato Sauce. Put the pieces of salt cod on this bed, add a little more butter in small pieces, cover tightly and cook for an hour.

Morue à la Milanaise.—Cut up the salt cod in slices, season them with pepper, dip them in beaten egg, then roll them first in grated cheese and then in breadcrumbs. Fry them in a frying-pan in oil and butter, arrange them on the dish, and sprinkle them with lemon juice. Hand a Tomato Sauce.

Morue à la Moscovite (hors-d'œuvre).—Poach the salt cod, but keep it a little underdone. Remove skin and bones, and finish cooking it in cream with a little chopped fennel. When it is cold, add lemon juice, *fines herbes* (parsley, chervil, chives and tarragon) and a touch of cayenne. Serve separately a Cucumber Salad.

Morue à la Napolitaine.—Cooked and flaked salt cod, bound with Cream Sauce (page 32), between two layers of spaghetti cooked in the usual manner. Sprinkle with browned breadcrumbs and grated cheese, dot over with butter, and brown lightly.

Morue à l'Oseille.—Put a layer of thinly cut sorrel in a fireproof dish, on it put a layer of thin slices of salt cod fillets, and on them another layer of sorrel. Add some small bits of butter, and cook in a slow oven. Towards the end of the cooking, sprinkle with a little browned breadcrumbs and brown in the oven.

(NOTE.—If you find the flavour of sorrel a little too acid by itself, you can use here a mixture of one-third spinach to two-thirds of sorrel.)

Morue à la Paysanne.—Cook some small floury potatoes in salted water, then skin them and cut them into rounds.

Put a layer of them in a shallow dish, add a layer of flaked salt cod, and season with pepper, *fines herbes* (parsley, chervil, chives and tarragon), and add a few bits of butter. Fill the dish with alternate layers in this way, heat up well, and serve.

(NOTE.—If preferred, half butter and half cream may be used.)

Morue pochée (Boiled Salt Cod).—Cut the salt cod into square pieces weighing about six ounces, and poach them for ten minutes. Serve with steamed or boiled potatoes and some kind of sauce, such as White Butter, Caper, Hollandaise, Cream, etc.

Morue à la Provençale.—Proceed as for *Morue à la Lyonnaise* (page 116), but substitute oil for butter, and add garlic, capers and black olives.

CONGER (*CONGRE*, ou *ANGUILLE DE MER*)

Except in bouillabaisse, high cookery does not use this very firm-fleshed fish. In household cooking it can be used for making fish stock : its flesh can be cut in thin strips, marinated for some time, and then cooked *à l'Orly*, that is to say, egg-and-breadcrumbed or dipped in batter and fried in deep fat, being served with a Tomato Sauce. It is also sometimes cut in slices, cooked in salted water, and served with a white sauce. Here is one very pleasant way with it.

Congre sauté aux Câpres.—Take the part of the fish from the stomach to the head, and cut it across in pieces about eight inches wide. Bone these as you would a saddle of lamb, then remove the skin on each side. Brush them over with milk, roll them in flour, and cook them gently, after seasoning them with salt and pepper, in foaming butter.

When they are served, add a few capers and pour over the butter, which should be nut-brown (*noisette*) and not black.

EEL-POUT (*LOTTE*)

This fish, which is also called Blenny or Gunnel, is not very often found for sale in England. It is a firm-fleshed fish, the principal value of which lies in its liver. Filleted, it can be prepared in slices, with a garnish and sauce, according to taste.

Lotte à la Bourguignonne (Eel-pout à la Bourguignonne).— Poach the eel-pout in a cooking liquor of red wine, herbs and spices prepared beforehand, drain it, and arrange it on the serving-dish, surrounding it with mushrooms and button onions stewed in butter. Stain the cooking liquor and reduce it, bind it with Kneaded Butter, butter it, and pour it over the fish and its garnish. On serving, put some heart-shaped croûtons of fried bread round the dish.

Lotte au four (Baked Eel-pout).—Lard the piece you are going to roast, season it, and wrap it in a well-buttered piece of paper. Put in the bottom of your baking-dish some carrot, onion and a *bouquet garni*, put the eel-pout on this, and add a little white wine and the cooking liquor of mushrooms (page 20). Cook in a good moderate oven for fifteen minutes per pound. When the cooking is two-thirds done, remove the paper, and finish cooking the fish without it, basting nearly all the time. Strain the cooking liquor, reduce it by half, thicken it with butter, and hand it separately.

Foie de Lotte (Eel-pout's Liver).—This is cooked like Carp's Soft Roe (see page 81) in salted and acidulated water. You can also cook it with butter : but it must be remembered that it will take rather longer than the carp's roe. It can also be used to garnish little china cases, or served in scallop shells, au gratin, and so on.

Quenelles de Lotte.—With the flesh of the eel-pout, make a forcemeat in the same way and in the same proportions as described for Pike Forcemeat (page 94). The force-meat may be truffled, if liked. To make and poach the quenelles, follow the recipe for Quenelles of Pike (page 94).

GURNARD* (*GRONDIN*)

A fish with an enormous bony head, which must not be confused with the red mullet. There are two varieties commonly found, the pink gurnard and the grey. Several of the recipes for red mullet can be applied to the gurnard, but it must be remembered that its flesh is very much firmer than that of the former fish. The gurnard's best use is the bouillabaisse, but the following recipe will be found pleasing.

Grondins Beurre Blanc.—Poach some gurnard fillets in a well-seasoned *court-bouillon.* Reduce a quart of the cooking liquor, with the addition of chopped shallot, to half a wine-glassful. Put butter in this, and bring quickly to the boil. As soon as it boils strain it through a fine conical sieve, and salt and pepper it. Serve the fish with steamed potatoes, and hand the butter separately.

HADDOCK, SMOKED (*EGLEFIN FUMÉ*)

Whether whole or in fillets, this fish is poached in plain water to which a little milk is added. The time of cooking, after the liquid comes to the boil, is five to ten minutes for

* SUBSTITUTE MULLET

a whole haddock weighing about a pound, or twice as long
for the same weight in fillets.   It is served with fresh melted
butter and steamed potatoes.

HALIBUT (*FLÉTAN*)

This fish, which is very little known in France, is very
much appreciated in England and Holland for the sake of
its delicate and palatable flesh.   It is a little like the brill in
appearance, but longer, its shape being more like that of a
very large lemon sole.   As in the case of brill, the various
fashions of preparing small turbots and the different preparations of sole and fillets of sole can be applied to the halibut.

HERRING (*HARENG*)

For some reason or other there has always been a definite
prejudice in the politer kitchens in England against this
really delicious fish.   It may be because English people know
so few different ways of presenting it at table.   The numerous
recipes that follow should help to disabuse them of the
belief that the herring makes a poor and uninteresting dish.

Harengs à la Bretonne.—Take some soft-roed herrings, egg-
and-breadcrumb them, and fry them in clarified butter.
Remove the roes, and rub half of them through a sieve.
Mix a little Dijon mustard with the purée, and thicken it
with melted butter.   Egg-and-breadcrumb and fry the rest
of the roes.   Put the cullis of roes in the bottom of the
serving-dish, arrange the herrings upon it, and surround
them with the fried roes.

Harengs à la Calaisienne.—Cut the herrings down the back,
and remove the backbones.   Stuff them with their roes,

hard or soft, mixed with soaked breadcrumbs, chopped shallots and parsley, salt, pepper, a little cream and a little softened butter.   Put the two fillets together again, wrap each herring in buttered paper, and cook them in the oven. Serve a Maître-d'hôtel Butter with this dish.

Harengs à la Diable (Devilled Herrings).—Score the herrings on each side and spread them with mustard seasoned with a little cayenne pepper.   Sprinkle them with breadcrumbs, and grill them, basting them with melted butter.

Harengs farcis (Stuffed Herrings).—Proceed as for *Harengs à la Calaisienne*, but substitute an ordinary forcemeat, to which chopped hard-boiled eggs have been added, for the Calaisienne forcemeat.   Wrap in paper, and cook in the oven.   Serve with them, but separately, some melted butter or a Maître-d'hôtel Butter.

Laitances de Harengs (Herrings' Roes). See Carp's Roe (page 81).

Harengs marinés (Soused Herrings).   See under Hors-d'œuvre (page 46).

Harengs à la Paramé.—Stiffen the herrings in butter, and then put them into buttered paper bags with a very dry Duxelles (page 13), several drops of lemon juice, and a little butter.   Fold over the ends of the paper bags, and finish cooking the herrings in the oven.

Harengs à la Portière.—Cook the herrings in butter in a frying-pan, spread them with mustard, and add a little chopped parsley.   Finally pour over them some nut-brown butter (*beurre noisette*), swill the hot frying-pan with a few drops of vinegar, and pour this over as well.

Harengs Mesnil-Val.   (See page 47.)

Filets de Harengs Maconnaise.—Make some cooking liquor

with vegetables (onion, carrot, celery) cut in large dice (*brunoise*), seasoning, and red wine (Macon), and cook for half an hour. Poach your filleted herrings in this, and serve them garnished with mushrooms, glazed button onions and croûtons of fried bread. Cover with Sauce Maconnaise.

Filets de Harengs Trophy.—In 1936 Madame Prunier inaugurated a Trophy for the best herring catch of the season, and this dish was composed to celebrate the event by her chef, Mons. Cochois.

Fry fillets of herrings in clarified butter, and serve them in this way. Two fillets on each plate, roughly chopped tomatoes tossed in butter on top, then another fillet to make a sandwich. Cover with a light Sauce Thermidor, and brown lightly.

JOHN DORY (*SAINT-PIERRE*)

This hideous fish has a rather firm but delicious flesh. It is hardly ever cooked except in fillets, and it can be treated in any of the ways described for fillets of sole. The flesh of the John Dory is excellent for making fish forcemeat. Its name must not be confused with the *daurade*, which is the sea-bream.

LAMPREY (*LAMPROIE*)

Although this fish is caught in England, notably in the River Severn, it is very seldom to be seen in the fish-shops. It is a sort of eel, but finer and fatter than the common eel. It must be scalded before the skin can be removed, and it can be prepared in any of the ways prescribed for the eel. English people will be most familiar with it in its potted form.

LEMON SOLE (*LIMANDE*)

This fish is usually looked on as an economical substitute for the sole, and indeed it is susceptible to a number of sole recipes. The small ones are inclined to be thin, and for that reason are often dipped in batter before they are fried.

MACKEREL (*MAQUEREAU*)

Mackerel are best in the spring, and they should never be used unless they are perfectly fresh.

Filets de maquereau à la Batelière.—Season the fillets, brush them with oil or with melted butter, and grill them. Hand with them a Green Sauce (*Sauce Verte*) (page 40), or a hot Ravigote Sauce (page 40).

Maquereaux Antiboise.—Fillets fried in butter, and served garnished with roughly chopped tomato and thin strips of the white part of leeks and of celery both stewed in butter. Pour some nut-brown butter (*beurre noisette*) over the fish on serving, and finish with a few drops of lemon juice.

Maquereau bouilli sauce au persil (Boiled Mackerel with Parsley Sauce).—Cut off the end of the head, cut the mackerel down the back, and bisect the backbone, but do not separate the two fillets. Put it in a shallow dish with enough cold water to cover it, add salt, a little vinegar and a few sprigs of parsley. Bring to the boil quickly, and let it boil for a few seconds. Then finish cooking it by poaching on the side of the stove for twelve to fifteen minutes, according to its size. Drain it on a cloth, scrape off the skin, and serve it in a long dish garnished with parsley. Serve separately a Parsley Sauce (*persil*) (page 35).

Maquereau bouilli sauce Fenouil (Boiled Mackerel with

Fennel Sauce).—Cook the mackerel as above, adding a pinch of fennel. Skin it, arrange it on a dish, and cover it with Fennel Sauce (*fenouil*) (page 32).

Maquereau Bonnefoy (Filleted Mackerel Bonnefoy).—Cook the fillets *à la meunière* (see page 5). Lay them on a hot dish, surround them with steamed or boiled potatoes, and cover them with a Sauce Bordelaise made with white wine and finished with chopped tarragon.

Maquereau à la Boulonnaise.—Use soft-roed fish if possible. Cut them in slices across and poach them in a *court-bouillon* with vinegar. Drain the slices, skin them, arrange them in a dish, and surround them with poached mussels. Strain through a cloth the quantity of the *court-bouillon* sufficient for the sauce, and bind it with enough white *roux* to make it the right consistence. Finish it with butter, and cover the slices and their garnish with it. Surround the dish with slices of the soft roes, egg-and-breadcrumbed and fried.

Maquereau à la Calaisienne. See *Harengs à la Calaisienne* (page 121).

La Cotriade de Maquereaux.—Fillet some mackerel weighing about half a pound each, and make a fish fumet with the heads and bones. Meanwhile, chop up finely some raw potatoes, slice some onions in rings, roughly chop some tomatoes. Butter a shallow fireproof dish thickly, and put the seasoned vegetables on it in layers, adding parsley, thyme and bayleaf. Lay the mackerel fillets on top, moisten with the fumet you have made, sprinkle with butter, put on the lid, and cook in the oven. Sprinkle with roughly chopped parsley on serving.

(NOTE.—It is usual, in the locality where this dish is eaten, to drink cider with it.)

Maquereau à la Dieppoise.—Fillet the fish, and poach the

fillets with white wine and mushroom cooking liquor (page 20). Drain them, dish them, surround them with shrimps, mussels and mushrooms, cover with White Wine Sauce, and brown quickly.

(NOTE.—When mackerel are poached in *court-bouillon*, whether whole or in fillets, the skin should always be removed before serving.)

Maquereau farci à la Béarnaise.—Open the mackerel by the stomach and remove the backbone. Stuff it with Pike or Whiting Forcemeat (page 14) made with *fines herbes* (parsley, chervil, chives and tarragon), and reshape the fish to its original form. Put it in a thickly buttered dish, season with salt and pepper, sprinkle with white wine, and cook it in the oven for half an hour. Lay on a dish, and cover with Béarnaise Sauce (page 30).

Maquereau Francillon.—Fillet the mackerel, grill the fillets, and serve them on croûtons of fried bread which have been spread with a mixture of Maître-d'hôtel Butter and a purée of anchovies. Surround with straw potatoes (*pommes paille*), and hand a Tomato Sauce.

Maquereau à l'Indienne.—Cook a mackerel in *court-bouillon*, drain it, skin it, lay it on a bed of Rice à *l'Indienne* (page 21), and cover it with Curry Sauce.

Laitance de Maquereau (Mackerels' Roes). See Carp's Roe (page 81).

Maquereau à la Meunière.—Fillets fried à *la meunière* (page 5).

Filets de Maquereaux Nantaise (Fillets of Mackerel Nantaise).—In an earthenware dish sprinkle some chopped raw mushrooms, onion, parsley, chives and shallots, all chopped up. Arrange on this bed some fillets of mackerel seasoned with salt and pepper, moisten with white wine

(Muscadet), sprinkle with a few breadcrumbs, and cook in the oven. Serve in the same dish.

Maquereau à la Normande.—Cut the mackerel down the back and withdraw the backbone. Flatten the fish lightly, and poach it in a fish fumet (page 15). Dish, surround by a Normande garnish (page 23), and cover with Sauce Normande (page 35).

Filets de Maquereau en Papillotes (Maquereau in Paper Bags).—Grill the fillets, put them in an oiled piece of paper between two layers of dry Duxelles (page 13) to which have been added some *fines herbes* (parsley, chervil, chives and tarragon) and some light fish glaze (page 16). Sprinkle with melted butter and lemon juice, fold the paper, and bake in a hot oven until the bag blows out.

MULLET, GREY (*MULET*, ou *MUGE*)

This fish is distinguished from the bass by its large scales : it is sometimes used instead of it, but it is not of the same quality. Beside those that follow, all the recipes already given for bass may be used for grey mullet.

Mulet aux Courgettes.—Score the mullet, season it, and put it into a thickly buttered fireproof dish. Surround it with tiny vegetable marrows (*courgettes*) cut in rounds, add some *fines herbes* (parsley, chervil, chives and tarragon), sprinkle plentifully with melted butter, and cook it in a slow oven. Serve as it is, in the same dish.

Mulet Madrilène.—Brush a baking-tin over with oil, and put in the bottom some thin rings of onion, skinned halves of tomatoes, quarters of sweet red peppers, and a half-root of fennel which has first been blanched. Season the mullet, lay it on the dish and moisten it with good Muscat. Bake in a slow oven, fifteen minutes to the pound, basting frequently. Serve as it is, in the same dish.

Mulets en Matelote (Matelote of Grey Mullet).—Use small mullet for this, about ten to twelve ounces each ; and cook in the same way as Matelote of Eel (page 85).

Mulet pochée au beurre blanc. See *Brochet au beurre blanc* (page 91).

Mulet rôti à l'Oseille.—For six people you will want a mullet of three to four pounds. Score it down the sides, and cut it down the back from head to tail. Season it, brush it over with oil, and cook it for ten minutes in the oven. Meanwhile have prepared a thickly buttered fireproof dish, put in it a little chopped shallot, some roughly chopped chervil and half a pound of sorrel cut in thin strips. Let the sorrel " melt " over the fire. Turn the mullet over on to this bed of sorrel, sprinkle it with melted butter, and cook it in a hot oven for twenty-five to thirty minutes.

Mulet à la Niçoise.—Fillet some small mullet, and cook them *à la meunière* (page 5), seeing that they are nicely browned. In the dish in which the fillets will be served, put some butter and oil, a touch of chopped shallot, roughly chopped tomatoes, parsley and a little thyme chopped up, half a glass of brandy and a little breadcrumbs. Sprinkle with butter, lay the fillets on this bed, and put into a hot oven for ten to fifteen minutes. Serve as it is.

MULLET, RED (*ROUGET*)

There are two sorts of mullet generally known in cookery : the red mullet and the surmullet. The latter can be recognised by its redder colour and the golden streaks on its back. The red mullet is the one which has been called the " woodcock of the sea," and is the commoner of the two. It is an excellent fish, which many prefer to eat with its insides, or at any rate its liver, still intact. The best ways of cooking it are either by grilling or frying in butter, and the recipes that follow are, in the main, derived from these two processes.

Rougets Danicheff.—Poach the fish with chopped shallot, a fine *julienne* of truffles, and very little white wine and mushroom cooking liquor (page 20). Dish them ; reduce the cooking liquor, add a little cream, and cover the red mullet with it. Hand separately boiled or steamed potatoes.

Rougets Francillon.—Grill the red mullet, and serve them on toasts cut to the shape of the fish and spread with a mixture of Anchovy and Maître-d'hôtel Butters. Surround with straw potatoes (*pommes paille*). Serve separately a thin buttered Tomato Sauce.

Rougets au gratin. See *Daurade au gratin* (page 146), and proceed in the same way, having regard to the smaller size of the mullet.

Rougets grillés (Grilled Red Mullet).—Score their sides and season them. Smear them with good olive-oil, and put them on a very hot grill. They can be accompanied by plain melted butter or by Anchovy or Maître-d'hôtel Butters, and steamed potatoes should be served with them.

Rougets grillés Mirabeau (Grilled Red Mullet à la Mirabeau).—Score a fine red mullet, and grill it. Serve it garnished with a Mirabeau garnish and Anchovy Butter, the last handed separately.

(NOTE.—The Mirabeau garnish consists of criss-crossed anchovy fillets and stoned olives.)

Rougets à l'Italienne.—Cook the mullet *à la meunière* (page 5). Dish them, and surround them with fairly coarsely minced mushrooms tossed in butter, and cover with Duxelles Sauce (page 13). If you like, you can also garnish this dish with very small tomatoes skinned and stewed in butter.

Rougets à la Juive.—Small mullet should be used for this dish, and they should be floured and fried in oil. Serve separately a Tartare Sauce (page 40).

Rougets à la Livournaise.—Score and season the mullet ; arrange them in a shallow fireproof dish, and cover them with chopped tomatoes which have been lightly stewed (*fondues*) in oil with chopped shallot, a tiny bit of crushed garlic, salt and pepper. Add a little good white wine, sprinkle with browned breadcrumbs and melted butter or oil, and cook in the oven for fifteen to twenty minutes, according to the size of the fish. When serving, sprinkle over a few drops of lemon juice and scatter over a few capers.

Rougets à la Nantaise.—Grill the mullet, and arrange them on a dish bordered with scalloped slices of lemon, and cover them with a sauce made in this way. Put some white wine with very finely chopped onion in a saucepan, and reduce almost completely : add a little meat glaze, the insides and liver (and the roe if there is one) of the fish, these last well crushed. Pass through a tammy, thicken with butter, and finish with a little chopped parsley and chervil.

Rougets à la Niçoise.—Grill the mullet or fry them in oil. Dish them, and cover them with roughly chopped tomatoes lightly stewed in oil, this *fondue* being reduced and seasoned with a touch of garlic. Garnish the tops of the fish with anchovy fillets and stuffed olives. Serve Anchovy Butter separately.

Rougets à l'Orientale.—In proportion to the number of

mullet, lightly brown in oil some chopped onion ; add roughly chopped tomatoes, a *bouquet garni*, white wine, a touch of garlic, chopped sweet red peppers, a little of an infusion of saffron and coriander seeds, and salt and pepper. Cook this for a quarter of an hour, and reduce it. Fry the mullet in very hot oil, arrange them in your dish, cover them with the stewed tomato mixture, and decorate round with slices of unpeeled lemon.

(NOTE.—This dish can also be served cold, and as such often forms part of the hors-d'œuvre.)

Rougets en papillotes.—Grill the mullet, or fry them in butter. Take a sheet of oiled paper for each mullet, and spread on it a spoonful of very dry Duxelles Sauce (page 13) ; lay a mullet on this, cover it with the same sauce, and roll up the paper and fold it. Put the paper bags in the oven, and let them get a light brown, when they will be done.

Rougets au Plat. See *Merlans au Plat* (page 194).

Rougets à la Polonaise.—Cook them *à la meunière* (page 5), and dish them. Cover them lightly with reduced fish fumet (page 15) bound with yolk of egg and cream. Scatter over them some hot hard-boiled eggs and parsley, both chopped, mixed with very fine breadcrumbs, and pour over all some nut-brown butter (*beurre noisette*).

Rougets à la Vénitienne.—Fry the mullet in oil. Dish them, and surround them with button mushrooms, and olives stuffed with anchovy puree. Cover with Sauce Vénitienne (page 36).

Rougets Montesquieu.—Have the mullet filleted, season them and dip them first in melted butter, and then in chopped onion and parsley. Fry them in butter, and sprinkle with a few drops of lemon juice on serving.

ROCKFISH

This is more or less a comprehensive name for a number of fish which are seldom displayed in the fishmonger's in a whole state.   It has been known for some years as Rock Salmon, but the use of this name, owing to its confusion with Salmon, is to be discouraged.   The fish treated here under this heading are : Saithe, Monk, and Flake.   These are variously known also as Coalfish or Green Cod (Pollack in Scotland), Angler or Frog-fish, and different sorts of Dogfish.   The corresponding fish in the French edition of this book are *Colin* (Saithe) and *Lotte-de-mer*, or *Baudroie* (Monk or Angler-fish).

All the preparations given for Cod can be used for these fishes, and when cold they are admirable for making coquilles, Mayonnaises and salads.   The *Lotte-de-mer* (which should not be confused with the Eel-pout—*Lotte*) is especially used for bouillabaisse, and it is also one of the ingredients of the *Bourride* (page 197).   In France it is prepared in smoked fillets, which are grilled or cooked in butter and served accompanied by a highly seasoned sauce. It is also used in the following attractive dish.

Lotte au gratin.—A fillet is boned and skinned and cooked as follows : lay it in a buttered fireproof dish in which you have first put a seasoned layer of very finely chopped shallot and onion and chopped parsley and mushrooms.   Moisten with a glass of dry white wine, and cook in the oven.   When done, arrange the fish on your serving-dish ; reduce the cooking liquor, thicken it with butter, and then add a little White Wine Sauce. Cover the fish, sprinkle with bread-crumbs only, and brown quickly.

SALMON (*SAUMON*)

The salmon, king of the migrant fishes, admits of every sort of preparation, whether by boiling, grilling or braising ; an infinite variety even when we exclude the dishes made from salmon already cooked. We give here a few, leaving it to the reader to exercise his skill and ingenuity in improvising others.

The salmon, which is at its best from January to September, can be cooked in the following ways : poached or braised whole ; as a piece (*tronçon*) of varying size taken from the middle of the fish ; as a cutlet (*darne*), that is, a slice about an inch and a half thick ; or in slices (*tranches*) about half an inch thick and weighing about half a pound.

Saumon court-bouillonné (Boiled Salmon).—For the method and time of cooking, see note on page 8.

When the salmon is cooked, it is laid upon a napkin on the serving-dish, and surrounded by sprigs of curly parsley. At the same time there are handed steamed or boiled potatoes and one or two of the following sauces : Hollandaise, Caper, Mousseline, Anchovy, Shrimp, Oyster, *Nantua*, *Vénitienne*, hot *Ravigote*, or *Génevoise* ; for which see the chapter on Sauces.

(NOTE.—With the whole fish or large pieces two sauces are usually served.)

Saumon braisé (Braised Salmon).—Put the fish, or the piece, in the grill in the fish kettle lined in the usual way for braising (page 7), and let it stew gently (*suer*) in the oven for eight to ten minutes. Then moisten it up to half-way with white or red wine, according to the recipe you are following. The cooking is done with the lid on, slowly, with frequent basting, for ten minutes to each pound of fish.

Cadgery de Saumon. See page 137.

Côtelettes de Saumon (Salmon Cutlets).—Salmon cutlets can be made in two ways :

(1) Make the necessary amount of salmon forcemeat, following the recipe for Pike Forcemeat (page 94), substituting salmon for pike, and follow the exact recipe for *Côtelettes de Brochet* (page 92).

(2) The cutlets can be made with the same preparation as that for Salmon Croquettes (page 135). They are, after all, only croquettes shaped like cutlets, which are accompanied by some cullis or sauce according to choice.

Coquilles de Saumon.

These are made with various sauces in the following manner : cover the bottom of the scallop shells with a spoonful of the sauce chosen, garnish them with flakes of cooked salmon completely freed from all skin and bones, cover this with more of the sauce, and brown quickly in the oven. The coquilles should be silver ones, or instead of these, ordinary scallop shells.

Au vin blanc.—Garnish the shells with salmon, cover with White Wine Sauce, and brown quickly.

A la Mornay.—Garnish the shells, cover with Mornay Sauce (page 34), sprinkle with grated cheese and melted butter, and brown quickly.

Sauce Crevettes.—Add to the salmon some shrimps, and cover with Shrimp Sauce.

Au Gratin.—Garnish the shells, cover with Duxelles Sauce (page 13), sprinkle with very fine browned bread-crumbs and melted butter, and brown quickly. Take the shells from the oven, and on serving squeeze over them a few drops of lemon juice and add a little chopped parsley.

Froides.—Garnish the bottom of the shells with a little seasoned macédoine of vegetables or a fine *julienne* of lettuce leaves. Add the salmon, cover with Mayonnaise Sauce, or Green Mayonnaise Sauce, and surround the shells with a little border of chopped hard-boiled egg (yolk and white) mixed with chopped parsley.

Coulibiac de Saumon. See *Pâté chaud de Saumon* (page 139).

Croquettes de Saumon (Salmon Cutlets).—(1) Make a salpicon with the following ingredients : a pound of salmon, half a pound of cooked mushrooms, four ounces of shelled shrimps, two ounces of truffles. The binding sauce should be a very much reduced Béchamel, with six egg-yolks added for every pint and three-quarters. The proportion of sauce to salpicon is just over half a pint to each pound of the salpicon. Mix the salpicon with the sauce, pour it out on a dish and spread it. Brush over the surface with butter, and let it get cold.

(2) Divide the mixture into portions weighing about two ounces or a little over, and shape them into rectangles, ovals, or cutlets, according to the description on the menu. Egg-and-breadcrumb them, using very fine crumbs. Keep them in a cool place, if they have long to wait. When ready to serve them, plunge them into very hot fat, drain them on a

cloth, and serve them in a circle with fried parsley in the middle. Hand the appropriate sauce with them.

Darne de Saumon pochée.—Make a *court-bouillon* (without vinegar) in sufficient quantity for your needs. Plunge the salmon cutlets in it, bring quickly to the boil, draw the pan to the side of the stove, and let the fish poach for six to ten minutes according to the thickness of the cutlets.

(NOTE.—The *court-bouillon* usually employed for poaching fish is one containing White Wine Vinegar. We advise this for large pieces of fish which have to be cooked slowly, but we think the vinegar should be left out in the case of the smaller cutlets, because the acidity tends to spoil the colour of the salmon.)

These poached cutlets are always accompanied by steamed or boiled potatoes, and by some such sauce as Hollandaise, Béarnaise or Anchovy. Or they can be served with Maître-d'hôtel Butter, plain melted butter, and so on.

Darne de Saumon Bourguignonne.—Poach the cutlet with red wine. Dish it, and surround it with a Bourguignonne garnish, and finish the sauce as on page 31.

Darne de Saumon à la Chambord.—Proceed exactly as for *Carpe à la Chambord* (page 80).

Darne de Saumon à la Daumont.—Poach the cutlet in *court-bouillon* without vinegar. Dish it, and surround it by large cooked mushrooms, little pastry bouchées filled with cray-fish tails bound with Nantua Sauce, and quenelles moulded in a small spoon of creamy, truffled fish forcemeat. Hand Nantua Sauce with it.

Darne de Saumon à la Riga (Cold).—Poach the cutlet in *court-bouillon* without vinegar, and let it get cold. Remove the skin, and cover the cutlet thickly with white fish jelly.

Dish it, and surround it by little hollowed sections of cucumber, blanched, marinated and garnished with a macédoine of vegetables bound with Mayonnaise Sauce, tartlets garnished with the same macédoine, and hard-boiled egg-halves filled with caviar. Finally put a border of pieces of jelly round the dish.

Escalopes de Saumon.—Cut some fillets of salmon, skin them, and cut them in slices weighing about three to four ounces each. Trim them, and poach them on a buttered dish with very little red or white wine, mushroom cooking liquor and fish fumet. Serve them with a garnish and sauce as desired.

Kadgiori ou Cadgery de Saumon (Salmon Kedgeree).—This dish can be made for using up cold cooked salmon, turbot, brill, rockfish, cod, and so on. First make six ounces to half a pound of Pilaff rice (page 21), as well as three-quarters of a pint of White Wine Sauce flavoured, if you like, with curry powder. Flake up a pound of cooked salmon, removing all skin and bone ; warm it up in salted water, drain it thoroughly and mix it with the sauce, adding five hard-boiled eggs, cut in large dice while hot. Arrange in a timbale or shallow dish alternating layers of fish and rice. Finish with a layer of rice, and pour over some nut-brown butter (*beurre noisette*) on serving.

Médaillons de Saumon.—Cut some slices, half an inch thick, from a salmon fillet, trim them into little oval shapes, and poach them gently. Let them get cold. Then cover them either with a Mayonnaise, Rémoulade or Green Sauce bound with jelly, or with a white or pink Chaudfroid Sauce, and varnish them with jelly. Arrange in a circle on a round dish.

(NOTE.—The trimmings of the *médaillons* can be poached

separately and used for a Salmon Salad, or some other purpose.)

Mousse de Saumon (Hot).—Pound finely a pound of salmon flesh with a third of an ounce of salt, a good pinch of pepper, and two whites of eggs added by degrees. Pass through a tammy, and put the forcemeat into a basin. Work it for a few minutes with a spoon, and put it on ice for an hour. Then working it with the spatula, mix in about three-quarters of a pint of cream, thick and fresh, and lastly two small well-whisked egg-whites. With this preparation fill your well-buttered mould, and poach it for forty to forty-five minutes. The mousse is cooked when it feels rather firm and elastic to the touch. It is inadvisable to turn the mousse out immediately on its removal from the *bain-marie* : it is better to leave it for seven or eight minutes so that it shrinks a little inside the mould. This hot mousse can be served with any of the sauces appropriate to salmon.

Mousse de Saumon (Cold).—Pound in a mortar a pound of cold cooked salmon, braised for preference. Pass it through a tammy, put it into a basin and incorporate with it in this order: six tablespoonfuls of very good cold melted jelly, eight tablespoonfuls of Fish Velouté and eight tablespoonfuls of cream which must be whipped before being added. Correct the seasoning if necessary. This mousse can be moulded in two ways—in a mould already well lined with very clear jelly and decorated, or in a silver or glass dish. Under the influence of Escoffier, modern kitchen methods have been considerably simplified, and the moulding with the jelly lining, which is a long and painstaking business, has been practically abandoned. This is how you mould it in the silver or glass dish. Take a dish which will just hold the mousse, pour the mousse into it, smooth the top into a slight dome, and decorate it with truffle. Then varnish the top as many times as is necessary to give the mousse a thick coating of jelly. Keep the mousse in the refrigerator or ice-chest until needed to serve.

Mousselines de Saumon.—Mousselines are really nothing more than large quenelles made of the same composition as Hot Mousse of Salmon (page 138), moulded with dessert-spoons and poached in the same way as all other large quenelles. They can also be made with a forcing-bag to the size of an ordinary meringue. Mousselines can also be made in little timbale moulds, and poached in the *bain-marie*. They are accompanied, if desired, by a light garnish and by some sauce or other as occasion demands. What sauce and garnish must be decided by the chef when planning his menu.

Mayonnaise de Saumon (Salmon Mayonnaise).—Garnish the bottom of a salad-bowl with *julienne* strips of lettuce seasoned with salt and a few drops of vinegar. Arrange on this cold flaked salmon, with every vestige of skin and bones removed, in the proportion of between three and four ounces for each person. Cover the whole with a highly seasoned Mayonnaise Sauce ; decorate with anchovy fillets, stoned olives and capers, and set in the middle a small lettuce heart. Surround the dish with hard-boiled eggs and quartered lettuce hearts alternately. On serving, a further border can be arranged of thin rings of radish and gherkin, tarragon leaves, and so on.

Pâté Chaud de Saumon or *Coulibiac.*—This Hot Salmon Pie, which hails from Russia, is a dish which must be eaten once, and then many times after. But you must have a company of ten or twelve people to eat it. For this number you will require : two and a half pounds of paste for

Coulibiac (page 18) ; a pound and a half of salmon fillet, cut in small slices, stiffened in butter and allowed to get cold ; half a pound of large semolina or rice cooked in white consommé ; three hard-boiled eggs, white and yolk chopped together ; four ounces of mushrooms and a large onion, chopped, tossed together in butter, and let grow cold, with a tablespoonful of chopped parsley ; three ounces of dried Vésiga (the dried marrow of the sturgeon), soaked in cold water for five hours to ensure its full swelling, then cooked for four hours in slightly salted water, and then very coarsely chopped. (It has been found that Vésiga swells to five times its original size during soaking and cooking. In this case, its final weight will be fifteen ounces.)

METHOD.—With two-thirds of the paste, roll out a rectangle sixteen inches long by ten inches wide. Garnish the middle of it with successive layers of semolina or rice, slices of salmon, Vésiga, and mushrooms, onions and egg. Finish with a layer of semolina or rice. Roll out the rest of the paste, and lay this on top of the garnish. Draw up the edges of the lower rectangle of paste, moistening them lightly, and join them well to the edges of the top layer, so that the garnish is completely enclosed. Now keep the Coulibiac in a fairly warm place for a good half-hour, so that the paste rises slightly. Then brush it over with melted butter, sprinkle it with very fine browned breadcrumbs, and make a slit in the top for the steam to escape. Put it in a good moderate oven, in a place where the heat will come especially from the bottom. Bake for fifty minutes, and when removing it from the oven, pour inside it five or six dessertspoonfuls of melted butter.

Saumon au Beurre de Montpellier (Salmon with Montpellier Butter).—The fish used for this dish can be either whole or

in large or small slices.   In any case, it must first be poached,
and then let get cold.   Skin it and cover it with Montpellier
Butter (page 27).   Decorate it with truffles in whatever
way you like, but the more usual decoration is in the form
of scales with crescents in truffle.   Mask with cold melted
white fish jelly.   Arrange the piece on a dish, and surround
it with halves of hard-boiled egg on end, and the yolks
outside.   Decorate the dish outside further with pieces of
jelly and the Montpellier Butter.

OBSERVATION ON COLD DRESSED FISH.—Where a whole
fish is concerned, only one or both sides of the fish are
skinned, according to its position on the dish.   If it is laid
on one side, then the side on top only should be skinned ;
but if the fish is set on its stomach, then the skin must be
removed from both sides.   Opinions are divided on this
question of dressing the fish, some chefs refusing to allow
the position on the stomach, while others, followers of
Dubois, admit this position.

Saumon froide à la Parisienne (Cold Salmon à la Parisienne).
—For this dish it is usual to have a small or medium-sized
fish, or piece of a fish, that has been poached in *court-bouillon*
and allowed to get cold.   Remove the skin from the middle
in such a way as to leave a rectangle of bare flesh.   Cover
this skinned part only with Mayonnaise Sauce mixed with
jelly, and when this has set, decorate it with white and yolk
of hard-boiled eggs, tiny sprigs of chervil, tarragon leaves,
and so on.   Mask heavily with white jelly and decorate with
Montpellier Butter (page 27), through a forcing-bag.   Surround with small artichoke bottoms garnished with Salade
Russe bound with thick Mayonnaise Sauce.

Quiche de Saumon fumé (Smoked Salmon Tart).—Line a
flan case with short-crust pastry.   Beat up lightly, as if for

an omelette, four whole eggs and two yolks, mix with them three-quarters of a pint of fresh cream, season with salt, pepper and grated nutmeg, and pour this mixture into the flan case. Sprinkle over the top some small dabs of butter, and add enough thin slices of smoked salmon to cover the cream. Bake in a very hot oven for thirty-five minutes. Serve immediately, or the salmon will get tough. The slices should remain on top of the flan and be lightly covered with cream.

(NOTE.—This mixture can equally well be cooked in little moulds as a hot hors-d'œuvre.)

Saumon braisé à la Régence.—Stuff the fish, or the piece of the fish, with forcemeat (see page 14). Braise it on a bed of vegetables and herbs (page 7) with a fine white Bordeaux. Do not moisten too deeply. When the fish is cooked, dish it, and surround it with a garnish consisting of little quenelles of truffled fish forcemeat moulded with a teaspoon, large decorated quenelles, slices of poached soft roes cooked in butter, large trussed crayfish that have been cooked in *court-bouillon*. Serve separately a Normande Sauce (page 35) to which has been added the reduced cooking liquor of the fish.

Tourte de Saumon à la mode de Valençay (Salmon Tart à la mode de Valençay).—Skin and trim a salmon cutlet, about an inch and a quarter thick and weighing about a pound and a half. Season it and let it marinate in Champagne for two hours. Chop up some shrimps or prawns, crayfish tails and oysters, and bind them either with a purée of truffles or of mushrooms, according to your views regarding which flavour should predominate in the final dish. With the carcasses and trimmings of the crayfish, make a Red Butter in the usual manner (see page 26:

Beurre d'Écrevisses).   Now line a rather deep flan case with short-crust, lay the cutlet in the middle, and surround it with medium-sized whole truffles.   Spread the chopped mixture over the cutlet, cover it with a pastry lid, and join the edges well.   Gild with egg, make a slit in the top, and cook in a moderate oven for an hour and a quarter.   On taking the tart from the oven, pour into it the Crayfish Butter which you have just warmed.   Serve at once.

Tranches de Saumon (Slices of Salmon).—It is often found convenient, especially in restaurants (and, I may say, in small families), to cook and serve salmon in slices.   These should not be less than seven ounces in weight, and they may be grilled, poached, or fried *à la meunière* (page 5).

Grillées.—The slices should be seasoned with salt and pepper, brushed over with oil, and grilled by a fierce heat on both sides to make sure of the outside bring " sealed." They are then finished by more moderate heat.   They can be served on Anchovy Butter, Maître-d'hôtel, Bercy, and so on.

Pochées.—Plunge the slices into boiling *court-bouillon* without vinegar, and then keep the liquid just moving. Ten minutes will be enough.   Lay them on a dish covered with a napkin, surround them with steamed or boiled potatoes and parsley, and hand a suitable sauce.

A la meunière.—Season the slices with salt and pepper, roll them in flour, and cook them in clarified butter.   Continue as for all fish cooked *à la meunière* (page 5).

(NOTE.—In whatever way the slices are cooked, the bone in the centre must always be removed after they are cooked and before serving.)

SALMON TROUT (*TRUITE SAUMONÉE*)

The salmon trout is much in demand for choice dinners, and as it is a smaller fish than the salmon it is never cut up, but always served whole, except in certain cold preparations in which it is served in fillets on a mousse of some kind. Recipes for these fashions will be found in the *Guide Culinaire* by Escoffier, Ph. Gilbert and Fétu. As all the preparations of salmon, whether hot or cold, can be used for salmon trout, they will not be repeated here. But the following two recipes may be found acceptable :

Truite Saumonée braisé, sauce Génevoise (Braised Salmon Trout, Génevoise Sauce).—Put a salmon trout weighing about two pounds in a baking-dish with vegetables cut in rounds (see directions for Roasted Bass, page 107). Sprinkle with butter, and put the dish in the oven when the vegetables have acquired a light colour. Moisten with half a bottle of good red wine, and cook for thirty to forty minutes. Drain the fish, and dish it. Strain the cooking liquor into a saucepan. Reduce it to half, and then add a light Kneaded Butter, whisking vigorously. Take it off the fire, butter it generously, correct the seasoning, and hand this sauce separately. Serve also steamed or boiled potatoes, if you will.

Truite Saumonée fourrée, aux Crevettes roses (Salmon Trout stuffed with Prawns).—This is a dish for ten people, and you will want a fish weighing about four pounds. Open it at the stomach, and remove the backbone ; season with salt and cayenne. Stuff it with a forcemeat made with pike or salmon (page 14), thickened with cream well seasoned and with Prawn Butter added to it. Wrap the fish up in a thickly buttered piece of paper, and tie it up, not too tightly, however. Put the fish on the drainer of the fish kettle, moisten with three-quarters of a pint of fish fumet, half a bottle of Chablis, and add two ounces of butter in small bits. Now braise the salmon trout in the oven, allowing about fifty minutes, and basting it frequently. Then drain it and unwrap it, skin it carefully, and dish it on its stomach. Now arrange all the way down its back some cooked button mushrooms, and on each mushroom stick a fine prawn, with its tail shelled and legs cut off. Cover with White Wine Sauce, which has been made with the reduced cooking liquor, enriched with cream, thickened with butter and bound with Hollandaise Sauce. Season the sauce rather highly. Surround the fish with pastry barquettes, each garnished with a large quenelle of pike forcemeat decorated with truffle, and slices of lobster tails masked with Sauce Américaine.

SEA-BREAM (*DAURADE*)

The appearance of this fish is very like that of the fresh-water bream, but it is fleshier. Besides the recipes that follow, small and medium-sized sea-bream may be grilled, or cooked *à la meunière*. They can also be treated in many of the ways given for fillets of sole. The very large sea-bream are always cooked in *court-bouillon*, and served with a well-seasoned sauce.

Daurade Bercy (Sea-Bream à la Bercy).—Score the sea-bream, season it and lay it in a buttered shallow fireproof dish, in which you have first sprinkled chopped shallot and roughly chopped parsley. Moisten with white wine, sprinkle with melted butter, and cook in the oven with frequent basting. Arrange the fish on the serving-dish, reduce the cooking liquor, thicken it with butter, mask the fish with it, and brown quickly in the oven or with a salamander.

Daurade à la Bretonne.—For six people, take a sea-bream of about two and a half pounds. Make a forcemeat as follows : fry lightly in butter, as if for a Duxelles, half a pound of chopped mushrooms and a good dessertspoonful of chopped shallot ; season with salt and pepper, add parsley, a touch of rosemary and eight tablespoonfuls of white wine. Let it reduce, then take it off the fire, and finish with three or four ounces of breadcrumbs and a lightly beaten egg. Stuff the fish with this forcemeat, lay it on a thickly buttered dish, surround it with finely minced potatoes, and add a *bouquet garni*. Moisten with a wineglass of water, and cook in the oven for thirty-five to forty minutes. Serve in the same dish, as it is.

Daurade farcie (Stuffed Sea-Bream).—Cut the fish down the back from head to tail, and take out the backbone without misshaping the bream. Season it inside with salt and pepper, and stuff it with a creamy fish forcemeat (page 14), to which you have added some chopped *fines herbes* (parsley, chervil, chives and tarragon). Put the two fillets together, and cook them in the same way as *Daurade à la Bercy* (page 145).

Daurade au four (Baked Sea-Bream).—Score the sea-bream, and season it with salt and pepper. Put it in a generously buttered shallow fireproof dish, and moisten it with fish fumet and white wine. Cook in the oven, basting frequently. When the fish is cooked, it should be found to be browned, and the liquid reduced to the proper consistence of the sauce.

Daurade au gratin (Sea-Bream au gratin).—Spread a few dessertspoonfuls of Gratin Sauce (page 33) in the bottom of a dish, and add a little chopped shallot and roughly chopped parsley. Put the fish on this bed, surround it with raw mushrooms cut in rather thick slices, cover it with Gratin Sauce, sprinkle with browned breadcrumbs and melted butter, and bake in the oven until browned. This will take about thirty to forty minutes, according to the size of the fish. On removing it from the oven, squeeze over it a little lemon juice, and scatter over it some roughly chopped parsley.

Daurade à la Menagère.—Proceed as for *Daurade à la Bercy* (page 145), but add some minced mushrooms. A few minutes before the cooking is finished sprinkle with browned breadcrumbs, and add a few little dabs of butter to make a thin brown crust.

Daurade rôtie (Roasted Sea-Bream).—Lard a sea-bream finely with alternate strips of bacon fat and anchovy fillets. Wrap it in oiled paper, and bake it in the oven. After cooking, swill the baking-dish with a little white wine, reduce it, and thicken it with butter.

SHAD (*ALOSE*)

This is a very popular fish both on the Continent and in America, but it is little known in England.

Alose à l'Angévine (Shad as in Anjou).—Make a force-meat, according to the directions on page 14, with six ounces of raw soft roes, breadcrumbs soaked in milk and squeezed dry, and finely chopped parsley chives, herb savory and a little basil. Clean, scrape and trim the shad, wash it, wipe it thoroughly, stuff it with the forcemeat, and sew it up. Cut in fine *julienne* strips half a pound of young cabbage, blanch them, and plunge them at once in cold water.   Spread this cabbage in a long fireproof dish, adding the minced white part of three leeks and a small handful of finely cut sorrel.   Put the shad on top, season it with salt and pepper, add three-quarters of a pint of cream that has been boiled beforehand, and braise the fish in the oven, basting it frequently.   Serve it as it is.

Alose à l'Avignonnaise (Shad as at Avignon).—(This recipe was contributed by M. Auternand.)   Chop up finely a pound and a half of sorrel, add a large chopped onion, three or four pressed and chopped tomatoes, and a crushed clove of garlic.   Fry these lightly in olive-oil, season with salt and pepper, and add at the last some chopped parsley and a small handful of fresh breadcrumbs to bind the mixture. Meanwhile fry the shad in olive-oil in an earthenware dish that has a lid.   Spread out on the dish a bed of sorrel, lay the shad on it, cover this in turn with the rest of the sorrel, sprinkle over two dessertspoonfuls of oil, and braise the fish in the oven (preferably a baker's oven) for eight to ten hours.   After this lengthy cooking, the sorrel will have lost its slightly bitter flavour, the bones will have all melted, and the result will be a delicious dish which was formerly celebrated by the poet, Auguste Marin.

Alose au Beurre blanc (Shad with White Butter).—Poach the shad in a *court-bouillon* rather strongly flavoured with white wine, and when it is dished mask it with a few spoonfuls of White Butter (see *Beurre blanc*, page 25), and serve the rest of the butter separately.

Alose farcie et rotie (Stuffed Baked Shad).—Stuff the shad with a forcemeat made with raw soft roes, as described in *Alose à l'Angévine* (page 147).   In the bottom of a fireproof dish, or of a baking-tin, scatter a dessertspoonful of chopped shallot and the same of chopped parsley.   Lay the stuffed shad on this, having scored it and seasoned it with salt and pepper. Add a few spoonfuls of white wine, cover with a thickly buttered greaseproof paper, and cook in a fairly hot oven for three-quarters of an hour. During cooking, brush the fish over pretty often with melted butter. On serving, sprinkle with a little chopped parsley.

Alose au Gratin (Shad au Gratin). See *Sole au Gratin* (page 167). The shad may be cooked whole, in fillets or in cutlets, as preferred.

Alose grillée à l'Oseille (Grilled Shad with Sorrel).—Cut the shad down lengthways, and remove the backbone. Season with salt and pepper, brush over with plenty of oil, lay it on a very hot grill, and grill it over a hot but not flaming fire. Dish the shad, sprinkle it with melted butter, and hand separately a purée of braised sorrel. If the acidity of the sorrel is not liked, the purée may be made of a third spinach and two-thirds sorrel.

(NOTE.—The directions given above are, of course, for a kind of grill which is unobtainable in private houses. With a gas or electric grill, the cook's judgment must be used to approximate the heat of the grill to that described above.)

Alose grillée avec Beurres et Sauces divers (Grilled Shad with various Butters and Sauces).—Whether the shad is cooked whole with its backbone removed, as described in the last recipe, or simply scored on each side, or cut in slices about an inch thick, it is advisable first to marinate it with finely chopped onion, parsley stalks, thyme, bayleaf, lemon juice and olive-oil. Soak a whole shad for one hour, but if cut in pieces then twenty to twenty-five minutes will be enough.

Serve with the following Butters : Maître-d'hôtel, Bercy, Anchovy, Shallot, Ravigote, etc. (pages 25-29). Or with these Sauces : Béarnaise, Mustard or *Sauce Matelote* with either red or white wine.

Œufs d'Alose au Bacon (Shad's Roe with Bacon).—Divide the hard roe of a shad in portions, and wrap each in oiled paper. Grill them gently. At the same time grill some thin rashers of bacon. Unwrap the pieces of roe, arrange them on a dish, lay a rasher of bacon on each, and hand a Maître-d'hôtel Butter separately.

Œufs d'Alose à l'Orange (Shad's Roe with Orange).— Season the hard roe of a shad, and cook it in butter. Dish it, squeeze over it a few drops of lemon juice and scatter over it a little chopped parsley. Surround with orange sections, and sprinkle with foamy nut-brown butter (*beurre noisette*).

(NOTE.—Shad's Roe can also be prepared *à la meunière*, in paper bags (*en papillote*) or *sur le plat*.)

Tranches d'Alose à la meunière (Shad Cutlets à la meunière). See under Salmon (page 143), and proceed in the same manner.

SKATE (*RAIE*)

The best of the various sorts of skate is that known as the Thornback (*bouclée*), for its flesh is more delicate and it is not subject to the alkaline odour of some other kinds. Generally skate is sold in our fishmongers' shops ready prepared for cooking, but in case the whole fish is bought, here are the directions for dealing with it. As far as the cooking is concerned, these directions apply, of course, to the skate ready prepared for cooking.

The Cooking of Skate.—The skate must first of all be scrubbed and washed in plenty of water so as to remove stickiness; the "wings" are then detached (they are the only eatable parts) and cut into pieces weighing from five ounces to half a pound. They are then cooked in water which has been fairly strongly salted and acidulated with lemon juice or vinegar. The pieces are then drained and skinned (the latter operation being accomplished by scraping each side), and the extremity is cut off as it consists only of bone. The pieces are then put back into the cooking liquor, where they are kept warm for their final preparation.

Raie au Beurre Noir (Skate with Black Butter).—It is in this manner that skate is most often served. Have the cooked pieces very hot, drain them, wipe them dry, and arrange them on the dish. Season them with salt and pepper, and sprinkle them with capers and chopped parsley. Pour over plenty of Black Butter (*Beurre Noir*) and a dash of vinegar which has been swilled in the hot pan. Steamed potatoes should be handed separately.

Raie en Fritot (Fried Skate).—Cut the skate into small pieces, season them with salt and pepper, and let them lie for an hour with minced onion, parsley stalks, thyme, bay-leaf, lemon juice and olive oil. When they are wanted, take off the bits of the marinade, wipe them dry, dip them in frying batter, and fry them in very hot deep oil. Garnish them with fried parsley, and hand a Tomato Sauce.

Raie au Gratin (Skate au Gratin).—This dish can be prepared in two ways: with ordinary cooked skate, or with the "wings" of small raw skates.

In the first place the procedure for Rapid Gratin must be used, as the skate is already cooked, and all that is needed is the quick browning. But in the second case it is a Complete Gratin that is needed, as the browning and cooking must be done at the same time.

For cooking *Au Gratin*, see pages 10 and 11.

Raie avec Sauces diverses (Skate with various Sauces).—The skate having been prepared and cooked as already described, it can be served with a Cream Sauce, a Caper Sauce, or a Béchamel Sauce made with leeks in the Breton fashion. Served cold, it can very happily be accompanied by a *Sauce Gribiche* (see page 38).

Croûtes au Foie de Raie (Skate's Liver on Toast).—This is a much appreciated and delicate dish generally served as a hot hors d'œuvre. In England it makes an admirable savoury.

Poach the liver in the *court-bouillon* used for cooking the skate, adding a few vegetables and herbs (*aromates*). Cut out some rounds of breadcrumb about two inches in diameter, fry them in clarified butter, and scoop out a little of the inside. Garnish them with the liver cut in dice or very small slices, sprinkle with Nut-brown Butter (*Beurre Noisette*), a little chopped parsley and lemon juice, and serve very hot.

SMELTS (*EPERLANS*)

The small smelts are always fried, either *en brochette*, that is, several impaled on a skewer through their eyes, or *en buisson* like Gudgeon (page 88). Larger ones may be prepared in certain ways like whiting, that is, *à l'Anglaise*, *Bercy*, *au gratin*, *au vin blanc*, *aux fines herbes*, etc. (see pages 191-195). But it must be remembered in adapting these recipes for smelts, the length of cooking time must be shortened in proportion to the size of the fish.

SOLES AND FILLETS OF SOLE
(*SOLES ET FILETS DE SOLES*)

Among the prime fish the sole is certainly one of the best, and is always in great favour with gourmets. Its very fine and light flesh lends itself to every sort of treatment. Of all soles, the Dover sole is particularly appreciated.

In cookery, soles are prepared either whole or in fillets— whole when the party is a small one, and in fillets when there is a large number of guests and in restaurants. But, with the exception of a few special dishes, the same preparation applies to the whole as to the filleted sole. The following instructions are given as a matter of interest, because in England this preparation is done by the fishmonger, in the case of small establishments.

To prepare a Whole Sole for Cooking.—Cut off the head diagonally at the end of the fillets. Trim the end of the tail, turn back lightly the black skin (the skin of the back) either at this end or the other, take hold of it with a corner of a cloth, and pull it off with a sharp tug. The white skin does not need to be removed, but it should be carefully scraped. Then clean the sole inside, trim the fins round it, and lightly raise the fillets on the skinned side by the back-bone, so as to facilitate cooking.

To fillet a Sole for Poaching.—When filleting a sole it is unnecessary to cut off the head. Skin it on both sides, in the manner described above, but pull off the skin from the tail end. Then with a thin-bladed knife raise the fillets from the backbone on both sides, cutting close to the bone. Keep the bones for Fish Fumet (page 15). Now with a lightly moistened cutlet-bat flatten the fillets gently, so as to break the fibres in the flesh. Fillets can be prepared either flat, or folded in half lengthways as they are, or with a stuffing of some sort between. They can also be prepared in paupiettes, as follows : spread the fillets with fish force-meat, roll them round so that the stuffing is inside, and tie them round with a few turns of thread or cotton so that they will keep their shape, which is that of a large cork.

To poach Soles and Fillets of Sole.—In poaching soles the ingredients used are red or white wine, Mushroom Cooking Liquor (page 20), or Fish Fumet (page 15). That is to say, one of these only, or two, either wine and mushroom liquor, or wine and fish fumet. The poaching must be done without the liquid boiling. It must be kept just moving, especially in the case of fillets poached flat, for boiling will make them curl up.

Grilled Soles.—When whole soles or fillets are grilled, the cooking should be done by a very moderate heat.

In the following pages there are given, in one series, recipes for whole soles and for fillets. Each recipe is headed according to the way the sole should be prepared, *e.g.* whole, filleted, in paupiettes, or in some cases in more than one of these ways.

(NOTE ON SAUCES.—In almost every case the poaching liquid of the sole should be reduced, and added to the sauce accompanying it.)

Soles Aiglon (filleted).—Poach the fillets flat in white wine. Arrange them on a purée of mushrooms mixed with a third of its volume of onion purée (*Soubise*). Make with White Wine Sauce, and surround with little pastry fleurons cooked without being first gilded.

Sole Alexandra (whole).—Prepare the fish as for *Sole Colbert* (page 162). Arrange it on a bed of roughly chopped tomatoes stewed in butter, and substitute Béarnaise Sauce for the Maître-d'hôtel Butter.

Sole Alphonse XIII (fillets).—Cook the fillets flat in butter. Place each on half a fried aubergine, which has been garnished with dice of sweet red peppers and tomatoes stewed to a mash (*fondue*) in butter.

Sole Alsacienne (fillets).—Poach the fillets flat with white wine. Lay them in a bed of braised sauerkraut, cover them with Mornay Sauce, sprinkle with grated cheese, and brown quickly.

Sole à l'Ambassadrice (fillets).—Roll each fillet round the base of a stuffed crayfish head, and poach with white wine. Dish them in a crown, with the crayfish heads outwards. Hand *Sauce Normande*.

Sole à l'Américaine (whole or filleted).—Poach the sole in an Américaine cooking liquor. Dish surrounded by slices of lobster tail cooked *à l'Américaine* and by button mushrooms. Hand *Sauce Américaine*.

Sole à l'Amiral (whole).—This should be a large sole poached with white wine and fish fumet. Arrange on the serving-dish, and garnish with crayfish tails and mushrooms round it. Cover with White Wine Sauce, with the sole's cooking liquor added and finished with Crayfish Butter. Surround with a few mussels and oysters cooked *à la Villeroy* (page 229). Decorate with slices of truffle.

Sole à l'Andalouse (paupiettes).—Roll the fillets in paupiettes, and poach them with mushroom cooking liquor and butter. Arrange each paupiette on a small tomato-half garnished with Rice *à l'Indienne* mixed with dice of sweet red peppers. Surround with fried slices of aubergine, and sprinkle with foaming butter. Border the dish with thin slices of lemon.

Sole à l'Anglaise (whole or filleted).—The sole when whole is prepared like *Merlans Colbert* (page 193). The fillets are egg-and-breadcrumbed. In either case they are cooked in clarified butter, and served with a Maître-d'hôtel Butter.

Sole Archiduc (paupiettes).—These are fillets stuffed with whiting forcemeat flavoured with *fines herbes* (parsley, chervil, chives and tarragon) and paprika pepper, and rolled up in paupiettes. Poach them, arrange them in a crown with a salpicon of lobster, mushrooms and truffles bound with White Wine Sauce, in the middle. Cover with a creamy Nantua Sauce, put a slice of truffle on each paupiette, and surround them with little quenelles and fried oysters.

Sole Argenteuil (fillets).—Fillets poached flat, arranged on a bed of green asparagus tips bound with butter, and covered with a White Wine Sauce.

Sole Arlésienne (whole).—Poach in the same way as *Turbotin Dugléré* (page 189), adding a touch of garlic. Dish ; reduce the cooking liquor, add to it some tiny vegetable-marrows (*courgettes*) cut in the shape of olives that have been stewed in butter and finished with cream. Pour these and the liquor over the sole, and surround with fried onion rings.

Sole à l'Armoricaine (whole or in fillets).—Prepare in the same way as *à l'Américaine* (page 155), but bind the sauce with yolk of egg and cream. The garnish here is slices of lobster and soft roes egg-and-breadcrumbed and fried.

Sole Bagration (fillets).—Fillets poached flat, covered with Mornay Sauce, sprinkled with grated cheese and browned. On serving, arrange at each end of the dish a heap of small lozenge-shaped bread croûtons fried in butter.

Sole Bannaro (fillets).—Brush the fillets with melted butter, roll them in fresh breadcrumbs, and cook them flat in the oven with clarified butter. Dish them, surround them with banana rings fried in butter, and sprinkle them with nut-brown butter (*beurre noisette*) to which have been added some blanched and splintered fresh almonds and lemon juice.

Sole Batelière (fillets).—Stuff the fillets, fold them in half, and poach them. Place each on a pastry barquette garnished with mussels and mushrooms bound with Cream Sauce. Cover with White Wine Sauce flavoured with *fines herbes* (parsley, chervil, chives and tarragon), and on each fillet lay a small fried gudgeon.

Sole Beaufort (whole).—The sole is grilled. Dish it, cover it with Maître-d'hôtel Butter, and surround it with a garnish consisting of lozenge-shaped bread croûtons fried in butter, spread with spinach mixed with mushroom purée, masked with Mornay Sauce and browned in the oven.

Sole Bénédictine (fillets).—Folded poached fillets, arranged on a bed of Brandade of Salt Cod (page 112) and masked with Cream Sauce.

Sole Bercy (whole or filleted).—Poach the fillets flat with white wine, mushroom cooking liquor, chopped shallot and butter. Reduce the cooking liquor, thicken it with butter, pour it over the fillets, and brown quickly.

Sole Bergère (whole or filleted).—Poach the sole with a little white wine, fish fumet, chopped shallot and raw mushrooms finely minced. Cut some crumb of bread into fine *julienne* strips, and fry them in butter. Dish the sole ; reduce the cooking liquor, butter it lightly, bind it with a little Hollandaise Sauce, and add a pinch of chopped parsley. Pour this over the fish, sprinkle the *julienne* of breadcrumb over it, and brown quickly.

Sole Bolivar (whole).—Remove the backbone from the sole without spoiling the fish, which you must then stuff with fish forcemeat flavoured with onion and tomato. Moisten with white wine and fish fumet, and poach gently. Dish, mask with White Wine Sauce, and brown quickly.

Sole Bonne Femme (whole or filleted).—Proceed as for *Sole Bercy* (page 157), but add finely chopped mushrooms. Dish, reduce the cooking liquor, bind it with a little fish Velouté, thicken with butter, pour it over the fish, and brown it quickly.

Sole Bordelaise (whole or filleted).—Poach the sole or the fillets flat with red wine and chopped shallots and seasoning. Dish it ; reduce the cooking liquor, add a little half-glaze sauce (*demi-glace*) and an appropriate amount of melted meat glaze; thicken with butter. Pour this over the sole, and surround with little pastry bouchées garnished with a salpicon of mushrooms bound with the same sauce.

Sole Bourguignonne (whole or filleted).—Poach the sole or the fillets flat with red wine and butter. Dish with a Bourguignonne Sauce, and garnish.

Sole à la Bretonne (whole or filleted).—Poach the soles or the fillets flat with white wine and fish fumet. Dish ; reduce the cooking liquor, and add fresh cream. Surround the sole with cooked button mushrooms, pour the sauce over, and brown quickly. Finally, scatter some capers over the sauce, and put pastry fleurons round the dish.

Sole Bréval (whole or filleted).—Proceed as for *Sole Bonne Femme* (above), with the addition of roughly chopped tomato.

Sole Byron (whole).—Poach the sole with red wine. Dish it, and garnish it with button mushrooms. Cover with *Sauce Gênoise* with truffles, to which the cooking liquor of the sole has been added. Surround with heart-shaped croûtons of fried bread.

Sole Cancalaise (whole or filleted).—Poach the sole or the fillets flat with mushroom cooking liquor and oyster water. Dish ; garnish with poached and bearded oysters, prawns or shrimps and button mushrooms. Cover with White Wine Sauce, and brown quickly.

Sole Cardinal (fillets).—Cover the fillets with fish force-meat, fold them over and poach them. Dish them with a surround of slices of lobster tail, cover with Cardinal Sauce, and put a few slices of truffle on top.

Sole Carême (whole).—Poach the sole with white wine and fish fumet. Dish, and garnish with poached and bearded oysters and poached slices of soft roe. Cover with a White Wine Sauce flavoured with celery, and surround with little puff-paste fleurons.

Sole Carmen (whole).—Grill the sole. Dish it, and lay on it strips of sweet red pepper and tarragon leaves. Serve separately a Maître-d'hôtel Butter, slightly flavoured with tomato and mixed with small dice of sweet red pepper.

Sole Castiglione (fillets).—Prepare as for *Dugléré* (see *Turbotin Dugléré*, page 189), adding mussels and truffles.

Sole à la Catalane (paupiettes).—Roll the fillets in paupiettes and poach them with white wine and mushroom cooking liquor. Put each paupiette in a small scooped-out tomato which has been poached in the oven, and garnish with a mash (*fondue*) of onions. Cover with Bercy Sauce, and brown quickly.

Sole Carvalho (fillets).—Poach the fillets flat with white wine. Dish them, cover them with Béarnaise Sauce to which you have added the reduced cooking liquor of the sole, and decorate with blanched tarragon leaves. Put at each end of the serving-dish a heap of roughly chopped tomatoes stewed in butter.

Sole Caylus (whole).—Poach the sole. Dish it, and surround it with tomato halves that have been stewed in butter and are garnished with a fine *julienne* of carrot, celery and the white part of leeks. Cover with Mornay Sauce, and brown quickly.

Sole Cécilia (whole or filleted).—Cook the fish *à la meunière* (page 5). Surround it with asparagus tips bound with butter. Sprinkle with a mixture of breadcrumbs and grated cheese, then with melted butter, and brown in the oven.

Sole au Chambertin (whole).—Poach the sole with Chambertin. Dish it; bind the cooking liquor with Kneaded Butter, cover the sole with it, and surround it with small fried gudgeon.

Sole à la Chambord (whole). See *Carpe à la Chambord* (page 80), and proceed in the same way, being careful to keep to the same proportions.

Sole au Champagne (whole or filleted).—Poach the sole or the fillets flat with Champagne. Dish them, cover them with White Wine Sauce to which has been added the reduced cooking liquor from the sole, and surround them with small fried gudgeon.

Sole aux Champignons (whole or filleted).—Poach the sole or the fillets flat with white wine and mushroom cooking liquor. Dish them; surround them with cooked button mushrooms, and cover them with White Wine Sauce to which has been added the reduced cooking liquor of the sole.

Sole Chauchat (whole or filleted).—Poach the sole or the fillets flat with white wine and fish fumet. Dish it; and surround it with slices of freshly boiled potatoes. Cover with White Wine Sauce to which the reduced cooking liquor of the sole has been added, and brown quickly.

Sole Cherbourg (fillets).—This consists of stuffed and folded fillets poached with white wine and mussel cooking liquor. Dress them in a turban shape, and garnish the middle with a salpicon of prawns or shrimps, oysters and mussels bound with White Wine Sauce. Cover the fillets with Shrimp Sauce.

Sole Chérubin (fillets).—Fold the fillets and poach them with white wine. Place each on a barquette garnished with mushrooms *à la crème,* cover with White Wine Sauce, and on each fillet make a criss-cross decoration with thin strips of smoked salmon.

Sole Choisy (whole or filleted).—Poach the sole or the fillets flat with white wine. Dish them, and surround them with a *chiffonade* of lettuce melted in butter and thin *julienne* strips of truffle. Mask with White Wine Sauce, and surround with fleurons.

Sole Cingalaise (fillets).—Fold and poach the fillets with white wine. Lay them on a bed of Pilaff rice (page 21), to which you have added sweet red peppers cut in dice. Cover with a Curry Sauce.

Sole Clara Ward (whole or filleted).—Fry the sole or the fillets *à la meunière* (page 5). Dish it; surround it with diced or olive-shaped pieces of celeriac stewed in butter, and diced artichoke bottoms tossed in butter. Pour over some foaming butter at the last.

Sole Clarence (paupiettes).—Spread on the fillets some whiting forcemeat flavoured with anchovy purée, roll them in paupiettes and poach them with fish fumet. Arrange them in a crown, garnish the centre with poached soft roes and shelled prawns or shrimps, cover with White Wine Sauce, and decorate with anchovy fillets.

Sole Claudine (fillets).—Stuff the fillets with forcemeat, fold them and poach them with white wine, a mirepoix bordelaise (page 17), roughly chopped tomato and lobster cullis. Dish in little oval cases garnished with a salpicon of lobster bound with Sauce Américaine. Strain the cooking liquor, reduce it, thicken it with butter, and cover the fillets with it. Scatter over them at the last a little chopped parsley.

Sole Colbert (whole).—Raise the fillets on the skinned side of a sole so as to expose the backbone, and break this in two or three places in order to facilitate its removal when the fish is cooked. Egg-and-breadcrumb the fish, press the fillets down again, and fry it in deep fat. Then when it is cooked remove the pieces of backbone, and stuff the inside with Maître-d'hôtel Butter.

Sole Coquelin (fillets).—Cover the fillets with fish forcemeat flavoured with reduced tomato, add an oyster for each fillet, and fold them over. Poach them with white wine, and dish each on a tomato stewed in butter. Cover with White Wine Sauce, decorate each fillet with a slice of truffle, and brown quickly.

Coquilles de Soles Saint-Jacques.—Cut the filleted soles in slices or thin strips, and poach them with white wine and fish fumet. Drain them and put them in scallop shells with slices of lobster tails stiffened in butter and cooked minced mushrooms. Reduce the cooking liquor, finish it as in *Sole Bonne Femme* (page 158), pour it over the contents of the shells, and brown quickly.

Sole aux Courgettes (whole).—Cook in butter some minced little vegetable-marrows and roughly chopped parsley, adding chopped rosemary and basil. Lay the sole on a buttered shallow fireproof dish, cover it with this mixture, sprinkle it with browned breadcrumbs and melted butter, and cook in the oven. On serving, add lemon juice and chopped parsley.

Sole Montorgeuil (fillets).—(This recipe is acknowledged to M. Cochois.) Poach the fillets flat with white wine and mushroom cooking liquor. Dish them; cover them with Mornay Sauce, sprinkle them with grated cheese, and brown quickly. Surround them with a ribbon of Tomato Sauce, and at each end of the dish arrange a small heap of little vegetable-marrows (*courgettes*) *à la crème*.

Sole aux Crevettes (whole).—Poach the sole with white wine. Dish it, and surround it with shelled prawns. Cover with Prawn or Shrimp Sauce. Down the middle of the sole stick a row of prawns with their tails shelled.

Sole Crillon (fillets).—Poach the fillets with white wine, and arrange them on the serving-dish alternately with thin slices of lobster tails. Add to the cooking liquor equal parts of Sauce Américaine and thick fresh cream. Reduce it, thicken it with butter, and finish with a liqueurglassful of brandy and a touch of cayenne. Cover the fillets with this sauce, put several slices of truffle on each, and surround them with fleurons. (A. ARGENTIÉ.)

Croustade de Sole Marquise.—Fold the fillets and poach them in butter. Garnish a very low *vol-au-vent* crust with Nantua quenelles, that is quenelles flavoured with crayfish, crayfish tails, and mushrooms bound with Sauce Normande. Cover with Nantua Sauce, and arrange the fillets with a fine slice of truffle on each.

Sole Cubat (whole or filleted).—Poach the fish with fish fumet. Arrange them on a fairly thick mushroom purée, with slices of truffle on them. Cover with Mornay Sauce, sprinkle with grated cheese, and brown quickly.

Sole à la Daumont (whole).—Raise the fillets of the sole on the skinned side, so as to be able to withdraw the backbone without damaging the shape of the fish. Stuff the inside with fish forcemeat made with the addition of a crayfish cullis, press back the fillets so as to shut in the forcemeat, turn the fish over on to a buttered dish (that is, stuffed side downwards), and poach it with white wine and mushroom cooking liquor. Arrange the sole on the serving-dish, cover it with Shrimp Sauce, and surround it with the following garnish : large mushrooms stewed in butter and garnished with a salpicon of crayfish tails, truffled quenelles, and slices of soft roes egg-and-breadcrumbed and fried.

Sole Dauphine (fillets).—Fold the fillets in half, poach them in butter, wipe them, and cover them with Villeroy Sauce (page 37). When they are cold and the sauce is set, egg-and-breadcrumb them and fry them in clarified butter. Dish them in a crown, and put in the middle a salpicon of lobster, quenelles, mushrooms and truffles bound with White Wine Sauce. Hand a Nantua Sauce separately.

Sole Deauvillaise (whole).—Poach the sole with four ounces of onion stewed in butter without colouration, and with thin cream. Dish it ; pass the cooking liquor through a sieve, and finish it with butter and fresh cream. Cover the sole with this sauce, and surround it with fleurons of puff-paste.

Délice de Sole Marquise de Polignac.—For this you will want a sole weighing about a pound and three-quarters. Skin it on both sides, and fillet it. Keep the backbone, leaving the head on it. Cut the fillets diagonally in half, beat them a little so as to soften the fibres, and spread them with a fine forcemeat of whiting seasoned with paprika pepper, and to which you have added the raw eggs or coral of a lobster passed through a fine tammy. Put the backbone of the sole on a thickly buttered dish, arrange the fillets on it, season them, moisten them with Pommery, and poach them gently. Now drain the fillets, take the backbone from the dish, and put it on the serving-dish, and on it the eight fillets in two rows with eight peeled and cooked mushrooms in the middle. Reduce the cooking liquor by three-quarters, add four dessertspoonfuls of fresh cream, take the pan from the fire, and finish with four dessertspoonfuls of Hollandaise Sauce. Pass the sauce through muslin. Cover the fillets (which have been kept hot) with this sauce, and garnish them with eight fine trussed crayfish, which have been cooked in a highly seasoned *nage* (page 17).

(NOTE.—The fillets should be coated with the sauce only at the very last minute.)

Sole Dieppoise (whole or filleted).—Poach the sole or the fillets flat with white wine. Dish them ; surround them with prawns or shrimps, mushrooms and mussels. Cover with White Wine Sauce, and brown quickly.

Sole Dorée (whole).—Fry the sole *à la meunière* (page 171) in clarified butter, seeing that it is nice and golden on each side. Serve as it is, drained, with slices of peeled lemon.

Sole Doria (whole or filleted).—Fry the sole or the fillets *à la meunière* (page 171). Garnish with little heaps of cucumber cut olive-shaped, stewed in butter and bound with cream.

Sole Dugléré (whole).—For this dish you use a large sole, either cut in slices across or cooked whole. Follow the recipe for *Turbotin Dugléré* (page 189).

Sole à la Duse (fillets).—Stuff the fillets, fold them and poach them with fish fumet. Arrange them in a turban shape on a bed of Pilaff rice (page 21), and garnish the centre with shelled prawns or shrimps bound with Nantua

Sauce. Cover generously with a thin Mornay Sauce, and brown quickly.

Sole Édouard (fillets).—Poach the fillets flat with white wine and fish fumet. Arrange them on a very fine salpicon of lobster and truffles bound with an equal amount of mushroom purée. Cover with Bercy Sauce made red with lobster shells, and brown quickly.

Épigrammes de Filets de Sole.—Stuff, fold, and poach the fillets. Let them get cold, then egg-and-breadcrumb them, and grill them gently. Dress in a turban with a sauce or garnish of some kind in the middle, the name of the garnish being stated in the name of the dish : e.g. *Épigrammes de Filets de Sole à la Dieppoise.*

Sole à la Fécampoise (whole or filleted).—Sole or fillets poached flat with white wine and the cooking liquor of mussels. Dish them, garnish them with mussels and shrimps, and cover with Joinville Sauce. Surround with soft roes egg-and-breadcrumbed and fried.

Sole à la Florentine (whole or filleted).—Poach the sole or the fillets flat with fish fumet. Dish on a bed of leaf spinach stewed in butter. Cover with Mornay Sauce to which you have added the reduced cooking liquor from the sole, sprinkle with grated cheese, and brown quickly.

Sole à la Française (whole).—Poach the sole with white wine and fish fumet. Dish it, and cover it lengthways, one half with White Wine Sauce and the other half with Sauce Vénitienne. Surround with little croustades made of Duchesse potato garnished with mussels *à la poulette*, and with trussed crayfish cooked in *court-bouillon.*

Sole François-Ier (fillets).—Stuff the fillets with a mousse-line of lobster, fold them, and poach them in fish fumet. Serve them on half-aubergines garnished with

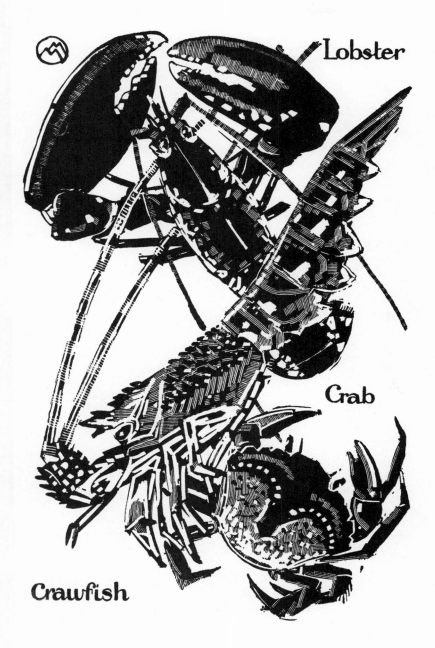

Lobster

Crab

Crawfish

a *Chasseur* garnish, and cover them with tomato-flavoured Béarnaise Sauce. Pour round the reduced cooking liquor to which you have added some fresh cream.

Sole Gallia (whole or filleted).—Poach the sole or the fillets flat with mushroom cooking liquor. Dish them ; garnish them with *julienne* strips of mushrooms and truffles ; cover them with a creamy White Wine Sauce, and surround the dish with little round scalloped croûtons fried in butter.

Sole Galliéra (whole or filleted).—Proceed as for *Sole Choisy* (page 161), replacing the *julienne* of truffles by a *julienne* of mushrooms.

Sole Grand Duc (fillets).—Stuff the fillets, fold them, and poach them with mushroom cooking liquor. Arrange them in turban shape, cover them with Mornay Sauce, and brown them quickly. Garnish the centre with asparagus tips bound with butter, and surround them with stuffed and poached crayfish heads.

Sole Grand Prix (fillets).—These should be fine fillets poached flat in a fine white wine and butter. Dish, and cover with *Sauce Vénitienne*. Arrange on the sole some mushrooms coated with Prawn Sauce, and surmounted by a piece of truffle cut to represent a jockey's cap. (E. KIENTZ.)

Sole Granville (whole or filleted).—The sole or the fillets flat are poached in fish fumet. They are dished and garnished with prawns or shrimps, mushrooms and truffles, and covered with White Wine Sauce. The dish should be bordered with little *canapés* spread with Soft Roe Butter (page 27).

Sole au Gratin (whole or filleted).—Cover the bottom of a shallow fireproof dish with rather thick Duxelles Sauce (page 13). Lay the sole or the fillets on it, surround them with raw mushrooms cut in rather thick slices and overlapping each other, put on the sole itself a few cooked mushrooms, cover with Duxelles Sauce, sprinkle with browned breadcrumbs, dot with butter, and brown in the oven. (See notes on *Complete Gratin*, page 11.) On taking from the oven, add lemon juice and chopped parsley.

Sole Grimaldi (paupiettes).—Garnish the bottom of a timbale crust with spaghetti bound with butter and cream, and add the flesh from a lobster tail cut in dice. Add six cooked paupiettes of sole, and cover them with Prawn or Shrimp Sauce. Cover with more spaghetti, add another six paupiettes, and finish with a layer of the sauce. Put the lid on the timbale, and serve it on a napkin.

Sole Henriette (fillets).—Bake some large waxy potatoes in their jackets. Cut a slice from the skin, and withdraw the pulp from the inside without breaking the skin. Now fill the skins two-thirds full with a salpicon of poached fillets of sole bound with White Wine Sauce seasoned with paprika pepper. Cover with Mornay Sauce, sprinkle with chopped nuts, and brown quickly. Serve on a napkin.

Sole aux Huîtres (whole or filleted).—Poach the sole or the fillets flat. Dish them; surround with poached and bearded oysters, and mask with White Wine Sauce to which the reduced cooking liquor of the oysters has been added.

Sole Île de France (whole).—Poach the sole, dish it, and surround it with *julienne* strips of mushroom and truffle. Cover with Bercy Sauce, brown quickly, and at each end of the dish lay a heap of asparagus tips bound with butter and a heap of roughly chopped tomatoes stewed in butter.

Sole à l'Indienne (fillets).—Fold the fillets, poach them, and lay them on a bed of Rice *à l'Indienne* to which you have added peeled and splintered fresh almonds. Cover with Curry Sauce.

Sole Jean-Bart (fillets).—Arrange in a dome shape on a dish a salpicon of prawns or shrimps, mushrooms and little mussels bound with thick Béchamel Sauce. Arrange on this raw and well-flattened fillets of sole, sprinkle with melted butter, and poach them at the mouth of the oven. Now cover with White Wine Sauce, sprinkle with chopped truffle, and surround with large mussels put back in their shells, covered with Mornay Sauce, and browned.

Sole Joinville (fillets).—Mask the fillets with a mousseline of fish (page 15). Fold them, and poach them with mushroom cooking liquor. Arrange them in a turban shape on a salpicon of prawns or shrimps, mushrooms and truffles bound with Joinville Sauce. Cover with the same sauce, put a slice of truffle on each fillet, and stick a small crayfish on top of it.

Sole Judic (fillets).—Fold the fillets and poach them. Arrange them in a crown, putting each on a small braised lettuce-half. Garnish the centre with little fish quenelles, cover with Mornay Sauce, and brown quickly.

Sole en Julienne (fillets).—Cut the fillets in thin *julienne* strips. Dip them in milk and then in flour, and fry them in very hot deep fat. Arrange them in a heap on the serving-dish on a napkin with fried parsley.

(NOTE.—Instead of being fried in deep fat, the fish can be fried in clarified butter.)

Soles Jules Janin (whole).—Remove the backbone of a large raw sole. Garnish the inside with a mousseline of whiting to which plenty of Duxelles and *fines herbes* (parsley, chervil, chives and tarragon) have been added. Press the fillets back, and arrange down the join a line of slices of mushrooms and truffles alternately. Braise the sole with Rhine wine, and when it is dished reduce the cooking liquor, thicken with butter, enrich with cream, and pour it over the fish, browning it quickly.

Sole Ledoyen (whole).—Butter a shallow fireproof dish, and strew in it two chopped shallots, a dessertspoonful of roughly chopped parsley and two minced mushrooms. Add two dessertspoonfuls of white wine and as much fish fumet, and the juice of a quarter of a lemon. Season the sole, lay it on this bed, skinned side downwards, sprinkle it with very finely sieved white breadcrumbs, pour over some melted butter, and put it in the oven. At the end of ten minutes surround the sole with shelled cooked Dublin Bay prawns' tails (*langoustines*), a few dice of truffle, two dessert-spoonfuls of thick cream and a thin ribbon of melted meat glaze. Put in the oven for another five minutes, so that the whole is a nice golden-brown. If you like, you can add, on serving, a surround of heart-shaped croûtons of bread fried in butter.

Sole Louisiane (whole).—Cook the sole *à la meunière* (page 171). On serving, arrange on it rounds of bananas and sweet peppers fried in butter, surround it with a ribbon of Tomato Sauce, and pour over some foaming butter. Finally, sprinkle it with chopped chervil and tarragon.

Sole Maconnaise (whole or filleted).—Proceed as for *Sole Bourguignonne* (page 158), using a good Macon instead of Burgundy.

Sole Marchand de Vins (whole).—Proceed as for *Sole Bercy* (page 157), using red wine instead of white.

Sole Maréchal (whole).—Poach the sole with fish fumet. Dish it, and surround it with little heaps of mushroom salpicon and of roughly chopped tomatoes stewed in butter. Reduce the cooking liquor, thicken it with butter and a little fish glaze, cover the fish with it, and brown quickly.

Sole Marguery (fillets).—Poach the fillets flat with white wine and fish fumet. Dish them, and surround them with mussels and shrimps. Cover with a very creamy White Wine Sauce, and brown quickly.

Sole Marinière (whole or filleted).—Poach the sole or the fillets flat with white wine and the cooking liquor of mussels. Dish, and surround with mussels, and cover with Bercy Sauce to which the reduced cooking liquor of the sole has been added.

Sole à la Marseillaise (whole or filleted).—Proceed as for *Sole au Vin Blanc* (page 181), with the sauce flavoured with saffron.

Sole à la Meunière (whole or filleted).—Flour the sole or fillets, and fry them in clarified butter. Arrange on a dish bordered with channelled slices of lemon, sprinkle lightly with lemon juice, scatter over some roughly chopped parsley, and cover with nut-brown butter (*beurre noisette*).

(NOTE.—Whole soles and filleted soles *à la meunière* may be garnished as desired. In that case the name of the garnish will follow the word *meunière*, e.g. *Sole meunière à l'orange, aux champignons*, etc.)

Sole Mexicaine (paupiettes).—Roll the fillets in paupiettes, poach them with white wine and fish fumet, arrange them on large grilled mushrooms garnished with roughly chopped tomato which has been stewed in butter with okra and sweet peppers cut in dice. Cover with White Wine Sauce, and surround with a ribbon of Tomato Sauce.

Sole Mirabeau (fillets).—Poach the fillets flat. Arrange them side by side, and cover each alternate one with White Wine Sauce, the others with Sauce Bourguignonne. Make a little thread of white sauce on the red, and of red sauce on the white, and decorate with anchovy fillets and blanched tarragon leaves arranged in a cross.

Sole Miroton (fillets).—Poach the fillets flat with white wine and fish fumet. Dish them on a rather creamy mushroom purée, and scatter on the fillets some roughly chopped *fines herbes* (parsley, chervil, chives and tarragon). Cover with highly seasoned Bercy Sauce, and brown quickly. (ALAMAGNIE.)

Sole Mogador (fillets).—Spread the fillets with a fine fish forcemeat and with a slice of truffle at the end, fold them, and poach them with white wine and fish fumet. Arrange them in turban shape on a border of mousseline forcemeat, and put in the middle a Nantua garnish bound with Nantua Sauce. Cover with the same sauce, and surround with trussed crayfish cooked in *court-bouillon*.

Sole Moïna (fillets).—Fold the fillets, flour them, cook them in butter in a sauté-dish, and dish them in turban shape. Swill the pan with Port wine mixed with a little meat glaze, thicken this with butter, and pour it over the fillets. Garnish the centre with small quarters of artichokes, and morels (*morilles*) *à la crème*.

(NOTE.—Morels, which are a sponge-like fungus, can be occasionally found in England in the spring ; but they can be bought dried, and only need soaking to be cooked in the same way as the fresh ones, though the dried ones are not, of course, so delicious.)

Sole Monseigneur (whole).—Poach the sole with Chambertin. Dish it, reduce the cooking liquor, thicken it with butter, and cover the sole with it. Surround by quenelles made of mousseline forcemeat, truffles and very small poached eggs.

Sole Montreuil (whole or filleted).—Poach the sole or the

fillets flat with white wine and mushroom cooking liquor. Dish, and surround with little potato balls steamed or boiled. Cover with White Wine Sauce.

Sole Montrouge (fillets).—Fold the fillets and poach them. Arrange them on barquettes which have been garnished with a salpicon of prawns and mushrooms bound with Prawn or Shrimp Sauce. Cover the fillets, half with White Wine Sauce and half with Shrimp Sauce, and place a nice white cooked channelled mushroom on each fillet.

Sole Mornay (whole or fillets).—Poach the sole or fillets flat with fish fumet. When dished, cover it with Mornay Sauce, sprinkle with grated cheese, and brown quickly.

Sole aux Moules (whole or filleted).—Poach the sole or fillets flat with white wine and the cooking liquor of mussels. Dish surrounded by mussels, cover with White Wine Sauce, and brown quickly.

Sole Murat (fillets).—Cut the fillets in strips the size of a gudgeon, and fry them in butter. Mix with them the same quantity of potatoes and artichoke bottoms also fried in butter. Serve in a timbale, sprinkled with roughly chopped parsley and with nut-brown butter (*beurre noisette*) poured over at the last.

Sole Narbonnaise (whole).—Fry the sole *à la meunière* (page 171). Dish it, and surround it with minced mushrooms fried in butter, and little potatoes cooked *à la Parisienne*. Sprinkle with nut-brown butter (*beurre noisette*), and scatter over some chopped *fines herbes* (parsley, chervil, chives and tarragon).

(NOTE.—*Pommes Parisienne* are potatoes cut in pieces a little smaller than a hazel-nut. These are seasoned and cooked in butter until golden. When they are cooked, they are rolled in melted meat glaze, and sprinkled with chopped parsley.)

Sole à la Nantua (whole or filleted).—Poach the sole or fillets flat. Dish them, and surround them with a Nantua garnish (page 23). Cover with Nantua Sauce.

Sole Nelson (whole or filleted).—Poach the sole or fillets flat with fish fumet. Dish them, and cover them with White Wine Sauce, and brown quickly. Put a heap of *Pommes Noisette* at each end of the dish, and surround the fish with soft roes egg-and-breadcrumbed and fried.

(NOTE.—*Pommes Noisette* are potatoes cut to the size and shape of a hazel-nut and cooked golden in butter.)

Sole Newburg (whole or filleted).—Poach the sole or the fillets flat. Dish them and surround them with slices of lobster prepared *à la Newburg* (page 217), cover with Newburg Sauce, and put some slices of truffle over the sauce.

Sole Niçoise (whole).—Poach the sole, dish it, and cover it with White Wine Sauce finished with Anchovy Essence. Surround it with heaps of roughly chopped stewed tomatoes, and on the sole lay some olives stuffed with Anchovy Butter.

Sole Normande (whole or filleted).—Poach the sole or the fillets flat with white wine and the cooking liquor of mussels. Arrange on the serving-dish with a Normande garnish (page 23), and cover with Normande Sauce.

Sole Opéra (paupiettes).—Roll the fillets in paupiettes, and poach them with white wine and mushroom cooking liquor. Lay each paupiette in a tartlet garnished with asparagus tips bound with butter, and put a slice of truffle on top of it. Surround the paupiettes with a thread of buttered meat glaze.

Sole Orly (fillets).—Season the fillets and egg-and-breadcrumb them, or dip them, if you·wish, in frying-batter : there is no strict rule about this. Fry them in deep fat, serve them on a napkin with fried parsley, and hand a Tomato Sauce with them.

Sole Ostendaise (fillets).—Fold the fillets, and poach them with white wine and the liquor from the oysters which you will use in the garnish. Arrange them in turban shape, garnish the middle with poached oysters, cover with Normande Sauce, and surround with little quoit-shaped croquettes made with a salpicon of fillets of sole, truffles and mushrooms bound with a thick Béchamel Sauce.

Sole Otéro (fillets).—Bake some large waxy potatoes in their jackets, cut a slice off their sides, and remove the pulp. Fill the scooped-out shells three-parts full with a salpicon lobster, place in each a folded and poached fillet of sole, cover with Mornay Sauce, and brown quickly in the oven. Put a slice of truffle on each fillet, and serve.

Sole Parisienne (fillets).—Poach the fillets flat with white wine. Dish them surrounded by minced mushrooms and slices of truffle, cover with White Wine Sauce, and border with little potatoes *à la Parisienne* (page 173) and trussed cooked crayfish.

Sole Portugaise (whole or filleted).—Poach the sole or the fillets flat with white wine and fish fumet. Dish them, surround them with a stew (*fondue*) of tomatoes with cooked minced mushrooms added, cover with White Wine Sauce, and brown quickly. Sprinkle some chopped *fines herbes* (parsley, chervil, chives and tarragon) on top.

Sole sur Planche (whole).—Planked sole. Cook the sole *à la meunière*. Put it in a paper bag (*papilotte*) with a thread of Béarnaise Sauce down the middle and slices of truffles. Close the paper bag, set it on an ebony " plank " which has been heated beforehand, and let the bag brown in the oven.

Sole Prat (fillets).—Poach the fillets flat. Dish them and surround them with small cooked mushrooms. Treat as for *Sole au Vin Blanc* (page 181), but use Noilly-Prat Vermouth instead of the white wine.

Sole Prince Albert (fillets).—Fold the fillets in boat-shape, and poach them with white wine. Dish, cover with Prawn or Shrimp Sauce, and put a small peeled mushroom on each fillet.

Sole Prunier (fillets).—Poach the fillets with white wine and mushroom cooking liquor. Dish them, and surround them with poached and bearded oysters. Place over them peeled mushrooms and slices of truffle, and cover with a White Wine Sauce. (A. LENOBLE.)

Sole Rachel (fillets). Spread some fillets with fish force-meat with slices of truffle stuck in it, and poach them flat, taking great care in doing so. Cover the serving-dish with Shrimp Sauce, arrange the fillets on the sauce, and surround them with heaps of asparagus tips bound with butter. Stick a prawn with its tail shelled on each fillet.

Sole Régence (whole or filleted).—Poach the sole or the fillets flat with a good white wine. Dish, surround with a Régence garnish, and cover with a thin White Wine Sauce.

Sole Rémoi (whole or filleted).—Cook the fish *à la meunière* (page 171). Dish it on a fine truffled purée of mushrooms, and sprinkle with nut-brown butter (*beurre noisette*). Add a few slices of truffle before serving.

Sole Richelieu (whole).—Prepare this in the same manner as *Sole Colbert* (page 162), and cook in clarified butter. Garnish the inside of the fish with Maître-d'hôtel Butter, and put a line of truffle slices on the fish.

Sole Rivièra (fillets).—Cut the fillets in strips the size of a gudgeon, and fry them in butter. Mix with artichoke bottoms and mushrooms (both cut in a thick *julienne*) which have also been fried in butter, and toss the three ingredients together for a minute or two to make sure of their mixing well. Dish them, and add a small heap of roughly chopped fresh tomatoes stewed in butter. At the last pour over some foaming butter and finish with a squeeze of lemon juice.

Sole Rochelaise (whole or filleted).—Poach the sole or the fillets flat with red wine and chopped onion cooked in butter. Dish, and surround with poached mussels, oysters and soft roes. Cover with the reduced cooking liquor lightly bound with Kneaded Butter and thickened with butter. Put round a border of small croûtons fried in butter.

Sole Rossini (paupiettes).—Spread the fillets with fish forcemeat to which has been added a quarter of its volume of *foie gras* purée. Roll them in paupiettes, and poach them in some very good white wine. Dish them, cover them with White Wine Sauce, and scatter chopped truffle on it. Surround by very small tartlets stuffed with the same forcemeat as was used for the fillets, this having been cooked on each tartlet at the mouth of the oven. On top of each tartlet put an olive-shaped truffle.

Sole Rouennaise (whole or filleted).—Proceed exactly as for *Sole Rochelaise* (above). When the fish is covered with the sauce, surround it with small smelts egg-and-breadcrumbed and fried, trussed crayfish and small heart-shaped croûtons fried in butter.

Sole Royale Montceau (fillets).—Fold the fillets, and poach them with white wine and fish fumet. Garnish the bottom of a low croustade with quenelles of pike and slices of lobster tail on each quenelle. Cover with Sauce Armoricaine, add the fillets of sole, and put slices of truffle on them.

Sole à la Russe (whole).—Poach the sole with white wine with the addition of vegetables designated *à la Russe*, that is to say, grooved and very thin rounds of carrot and fine slices of a small onion.   Dish the sole, cover it with White Wine Sauce to which you have added tiny sprigs of chervil, and brown quickly.

Sole Saint-Germain (whole or filleted).—Brush the fish or fillets with melted butter, roll in fine white breadcrumbs, and grill them gently.   Serve surrounded by *Pommes Noisette* (page 174), and on the fish lay some blanched tarragon leaves.   Hand a Béarnaise Sauce separately.

Soufflé de Filets de Sole Royal.—Cut the fillets in strips the size of a gudgeon, poach them with Barsac, and drain them.   Add some fumet of sole to the cooking liquor, reduce it to a glaze, and roll the fillets in it.   Prepare a cheese soufflé mixture, using half Cheshire and half Parmesan cheese, and put this and the fillets of sole in alternate layers in a buttered timbale.   Finish with a layer of the mixture, and cook like an ordinary soufflé.   Serve separately a White Wine Sauce made with Barsac.

Soles Soufflées.—For six people you will want six small soles, each weighing about six or seven ounces.   Fillet them, trim the backbones, and put these in a buttered dish with a little fish fumet, put them in the oven for a few minutes, and keep them by.   Pound six of the fillets of the soles, adding a little pike or turbot flesh, with seasoning and a small white of egg.   Pass through a tammy, put the forcemeat in a bowl and work it on ice, adding three dessertspoonfuls of fresh thick cream and then six egg-whites stiffly beaten.   Correct the seasoning, and add a touch of cayenne.   Now arrange the backbones on a dish, spread on each a layer of the forcemeat about a quarter of an inch thick, and on this bed lay the fillets, three on each backbone. Cover these with more forcemeat, smooth it over, sprinkle with clarified butter, and put into a very hot oven. Fifteen minutes, with frequent basting, will be enough. On serving, surround the dish with little croustades garnished with a salpicon of lobster, truffles and mushrooms bound with Sauce Américaine. Hand separately a high seasoned Normande Sauce. (P. ESCALLE.)

Sole Suchet (fillets).—Poach the fillets with white wine and fish fumet, adding a *julienne* of truffles and of celery and the red part of carrot stewed beforehand in butter. Dish the fillets, and cover them with White Wine Sauce to which has been added the *julienne* of vegetables and truffles, well drained.

Sole Suédoise (fillets).—Poach some macaroni, and bind it with grated cheese and butter. Poach the fillets with half white wine, half fish fumet. Arrange alternately on a buttered shallow fireproof dish sole and macaroni alternately. Cover with White Wine Sauce, and brown quickly.

Sole Sylvette (fillets).—Poach the fillets flat with Madeira. Dish them surrounded by artichoke bottoms and minced mushrooms. Reduce the cooking liquor, thicken it with cream and butter, and pour it over the fillets.

Sole Sylvia (paupiettes).—Roll the fillets in paupiettes, poach them, and dish each on an artichoke bottom. Cover with Mornay Sauce, brown quickly, and sprinkle with chopped truffle.

Sole Talleyrand (fillets).—Spread a layer of spaghetti *à la crème* on the bottom of a buttered shallow fireproof dish ; arrange on it the raw fillets of sole, cover with a light White Wine Sauce, and cook in the oven until the fillets are done. On removing from the oven, add some slices of truffle, and serve in the dish as it is.

Sole Thérèse (paupiettes).—Roll the fillets in paupiettes after stuffing them with truffled whiting forcemeat. Poach them and dish them. Put a slice of truffle on each paupiette, surround them with little hazel-nut-shaped potatoes boiled or steamed, and cover with White Wine Sauce flavoured with essence of truffles.

Sole Thermidor (whole).—Poach the sole with white wine. Dish it, surround it with slices of cooked mushrooms, and cover it with a Bercy Sauce flavoured with mustard.

Timbale de Sole à la Bottin.—Cut the fillets in strips the size of a gudgeon, and cook them as for *Sole Bercy* (page 157), adding a little meat glaze. Add slices of lobster, shelled prawns or shrimps, and mussels, and put into the timbale. Reduce the cooking liquor, thicken it with butter, and pour it into the timbale. Serve very hot.

Sole Tosca (fillets).—Mask the fillets with a mousseline forcemeat of sole to which has been added a fine salpicon of lobster, truffles and mushrooms. Fold them, egg-and-breadcrumb them, fry them in oil, and arrange them in a crown. Garnish the centre with a stew (*fondue*) of tomatoes very much reduced, and surround the dish with onion rings dipped in batter and fried.

Sole Trouvillaise (whole).—Poach the sole. Dish it, and surround it with a Dieppoise garnish (page 22), cover it with White Wine Sauce, and brown it quickly. Put a border of fleurons round the dish, and down the middle a row of poached oysters.

Sole Urville (fillets).—Fold the fillets, and poach them : put each in a barquette, and cover with *Sauce Américaine.*

Sole Valois (whole).—Poach the sole, and dish it. Cover

it with White Wine Sauce made with a reduction of
Béarnaise Sauce, and put a ribbon of meat glaze round
the dish.

Sole Varsovienne (whole).—Prepare this like *Sole à la
Russe* (page 178), adding (1) some little triangles (*paysanne*)
of celery in the cooking mixture, and (2) a light **Caviar**
Butter in the sauce.

Sole Vendôme (fillets).—Poach the fillets flat. Dish them,
and cover them with White Wine Sauce flavoured with
tomato. Surround the fish with little mousselines of lobster.

Sole Vénitienne (whole).—Poach the sole with white wine.
Dish it, and serve covered with *Sauce Vénitienne*.

Sole Victoria (whole).—Poach the sole with fish fumet.
Dish it, and surround it with small slices of lobster tail,
cover it with *Sauce Victoria*, and brown quickly. Add
some slices of truffle after browning.

Sole Vierville (whole).—Poach the sole with white wine
and fish fumet. Arrange it on a bed of fresh tomatoes
which have been peeled, roughly chopped, and cooked with
fish fumet. Season well. Reduce the cooking liquor, add a
little White Wine Sauce and as much Hollandaise Sauce,
cover the sole with it, and brown quickly. (CHAUMEIX.)

Sole au Vin Blanc (whole or filleted).—Poach the sole or
the fillets flat with white wine. Dish them, cover them
with White Wine sauce, and brown quickly.

Sole Viveur (whole).—Prepare a *ju ienne* of celery and
sweet peppers stewed in butter and finished by cooking
in fish fumet. Poach the sole with white wine and fish
fumet ; dish it, surround it with the *julienne* of celery and
sweet peppers, and a *julienne* of mushrooms and truffles.
Cover with fairly highly seasoned *Sauce Américaine*, and
put slices of lobster on the sauce. Serve very hot.

Sole Walewska (fillets).—Garnish the fillets with slices of lobster and of truffles, fold them, and poach them with fish fumet. Arrange them in the dish, cover them with Mornay Sauce, and brown them quickly.

Sole Wilhelmine (fillets).—Bake some large waxy potatoes in their jackets, remove a slice of the skin, and take out the pulp without breaking the skins. Fold, and poach the fillets in fish fumet. Garnish the scooped-out potatoes with a purée of little marrows (*courgettes*) *à la crème*, and poached oysters. Then put a fillet in each, cover with Mornay Sauce, and brown quickly.

COLD FILLETS OF SOLE (*Filets de Sole froids*)

Aspic de Filets de Sole.—(1) Poach the fillets, let them get cold, and decorate them according to your taste. Line a mould with fine white fish jelly, and arrange the fillets in it, placing them upright along the sides. Garnish the empty space inside with a salpicon of fillets of sole, mushrooms and crayfish tails. Finish by filling up the mould with the jelly, and let it set. Turn it out when wanted on a dish bordered with pieces of jelly.

Aspic de Filets de Sole.—(2) Spread the fillets with truffled fish forcemeat, roll them in paupiettes, poach them and let them get cold. Line a mould with jelly, and arrange the paupiettes in it, alternately with quenelles truffled and decorated. Finish as above.

Filets de Sole Moscovite.—(1) Make some little paupiettes stuffed with creamy fish forcemeat, poach them, let them get cold, and coat them with jelly. Make some little cases out of thick slices of blanched cucumbers by hollowing them out and channelling them outside. Fill these with the paupiettes, and surround them when dished with a thin border of fresh caviar. Hand separately a Mayonnaise Sauce to which have been added some lobster flesh cut in dice and some caviar.

Filets de Sole Moscovite.—(2) Make a border of cold lobster mousse. On it arrange, alternately, little fillets of sole stuffed with the same mousse, folded and poached; *médaillons* of lobster flesh coated with jellied Mayonnaise and decorated as you like. On each fillet place a mushroom stuck with a prawn. Cover the whole thing thickly with jelly. Garnish the middle with tomatoes, peeled, scooped out and garnished with prawns or shrimps bound with Mayonnaise. Hand separately a Green Sauce (*Sauce Verte*).

STURGEON (*ESTURGEON*)

The sturgeon is a migratory fish like the salmon, and is found especially in the great rivers of Russia. It is in season from March to July. Its principal importance lies in the fact that its roe supplies the world-famous caviar. Its flesh, which is firm and dry, needs a good deal of culinary skill to make it palatable.

Esturgeon Basquaise.—Thin slices of raw sturgeon, seasoned and egg-and-breadcrumbed like an *escalope* of veal, are cooked gently in clarified butter, and served garnished with braised fennel. Béarnaise Sauce is handed with this dish.

(NOTE.—The fennel is, of course, the Florence Fennel or *Finocchio*.)

Esturgeon à la Bordelaise (Cold).—Braise a piece of sturgeon with white wine, let it get cold, and cut it in thin slices. Arrange these slices on a dish, surround them with stoned olives, peeled mushrooms cooked, and button onions stewed in butter. Cover the whole with a white jelly made with the braising liquor. At the time of serving, surround the dish with little tartlets filled with caviar.

(NOTE.—A salad of celery, beetroot and horseradish may be served at the same time.)

Darne d'Esturgeon à la Bourgeoise.—Take a cutlet from the sturgeon, not too thick. Season it with salt and pepper, and put it in a baking-dish which you have already garnished with minced carrot, onion and celery and with a few parsley stalks. Moisten moderately with white wine and fish fumet, and braise gently. When cooked, remove the cutlet and dish it. Strain the cooking liquor, reduce it by half, bind it with Kneaded Butter, and add to it several dessertspoonfuls of fresh cream. Skin the piece of sturgeon, cover it with this sauce, and surround it with little potatoes cut in the shape of olives and boiled in salted water.

Fricandeau d'Esturgeon.—Cut the sturgeon in slices about an inch and a half thick, and lard them like a *fricandeau* of veal. Braise them in just the same way as the meat is braised. This *fricandeau* is accompanied by the braising liquor, and any garnish you think suitable—for example, little glazed onions, stuffed olives, and so on.

(NOTE.—During Lent, the *fricandeau* of sturgeon can be served with a vegetable such as spinach, sorrel, celery, little marrows, potatoes *gratinées*, *cèpes*, morels (*morilles*), and so on.)

STERLET

This fish, which also comes from the rivers of Russia, is much appreciated by the gourmets of that country, but it is rarely seen in Paris or London. It belongs to the same family as the sturgeon, and the same recipes can also apply to it.   The eggs of the sterlet furnish a very fine caviar, and its marrow, like that of the sturgeon, supplies the Vésiga which is so essential an ingredient of the Coulibiac (see page 139).

TUNNY FISH (*THON*)

This fish is regularly caught on the West and Mediterranean coasts of France, and by amateurs off the coasts of this country.   Where it is fished commercially, its most important use is for preserving in oil, and this preserve makes a much appreciated hors-d'œuvre in various fashions. In household kitchens it is served hot in the following ways, and always in cutlets (*darnes*) about two inches thick.   (It may be noted here that in French cookery the term *rouelle* is applied to the tunny cutlet instead of the more usual *darne*.)

Thon à la Bonne Femme.—Blanch the cutlet for seven or eight minutes, drain it, wipe it, colour it in oil on both sides, and take it out.   In the same oil lightly fry an onion, add a tablespoonful of flour, cook it for a few minutes, then moisten with half water and half wine (three-quarters of a pint), and half a wineglassful of vinegar.   Add salt and pepper, two chopped tomatoes and a *bouquet garni*.   When this liquid is boiling, put back the tunny cutlet, and cook slowly for an hour.   On the moment of serving, mix with the sauce a few gherkins cut in thin rounds, as well as some chopped parsley.

Thon braisé.—Put the tunny in a stewpan which has been lined with large rounds of carrot and onion and a *bouquet garni*, and let it stew gently in the oven for a quarter of an hour.   Add a wineglassful of white wine, reduce it almost completely, then moisten with stock to the height of the cutlet. Cook gently for an hour and a quarter. With this Braised Tunny you can serve a purée of sorrel or spinach, or a highly seasoned sauce. At the same time serve the braising liquor, strained and reduced.

Thon grillé.—For grilling, the cutlet ought to be thinner, about an inch thick only. Season it with salt and pepper, and marinate for an hour beforehand with a minced onion, some parsley stalks, thyme and bayleaf, oil, white wine and lemon juice. Then wipe it dry, brush it over with oil, and grill it gently. When it is almost done, sprinkle both sides with fine browned breadcrumbs. Instead of grilling the cutlet, you can cook it in the oven if you prefer. Whichever way it is cooked, serve at the same time a Rémoulade or Tartare Sauce.

TURBOT (*TURBOT*)

The flesh of the turbot is firm, white and extremely palatable. It should be chosen large, with thick fillets and a very white underside. Large turbot are usually served as *relevés* for a large party, but in restaurants (and increasingly in the home as well) turbot is served in slices and in fillets. The recipes for cooking these fillets are the same as those for Chicken Turbot (*Turbotins*), and a large number of recipes for cooking fillets of sole can also be applied to them. But for the proper treatment of a whole turbot, a turbot kettle of the right size with its drainer is essential.

Turbot bouilli ou poché (Boiled Turbot).—Having prepared the turbot for cooking, make a fairly deep incision down the backbone on the back, which is the brown side. Put the fish in the kettle, on the drainer. Cover it with cold water, to which you have added milk (in proportion of one-

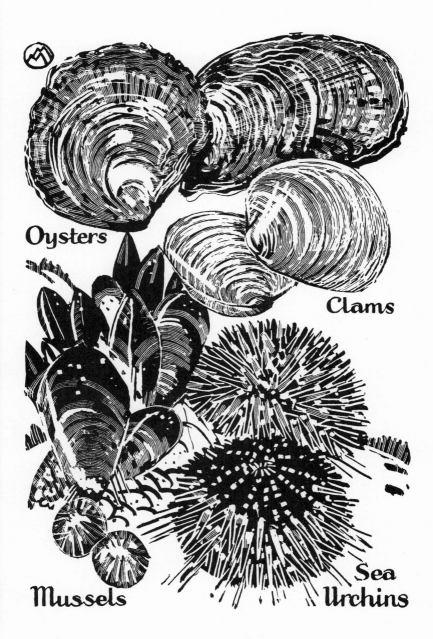

Oysters

Clams

Mussels

Sea
Urchins

eighth of the water) and a few slices of peeled lemon with the pips removed. Bring to the boil slowly, draw aside to a corner of the stove, where the liquid will continue just moving. Rapid boiling will do no good, as it will only result in breaking the fish. Poach for seven to ten minutes per pound according to the thickness of the fish. To serve the turbot, slide it gently from the drainer on to a napkin in the serving-dish, and surround it with parsley. It is advisable to smear the surface of the fish with a piece of butter to give it brilliance. With it should be served steamed or boiled potatoes, and one or two of the following sauces : Hollandaise, Mousseline, Caper, Shrimp, Lobster, *Vénitienne,* Béarnaise, White Wine, *Américaine,* or melted butter, Maître-d'hôtel Butter, etc., etc.

Turbot Prince Albert.—Braise the turbot on a bed of vegetables and herbs (*aromates*) with a good white wine. After cooking, arrange the turbot on the serving-dish and surround it by large peeled mushrooms, tartlets garnished with crayfish tails bound with Nantua Sauce, large truffled quenelles, and oysters and mussels egg-and-breadcrumbed and fried. Cover the fish with White Wine Sauce, flavoured with oysters and with Crayfish Butter added. Also arrange two rows of truffles on the fish. Serve some of the same sauce separately.

Cadgery de Turbot.—With cold turbot, proceed as for *Cadgery de Saumon* (page 137).

Turbot Crème Gratin.—Butter a shallow fireproof dish, border it with Duchesse potatoes, making a wall about an inch and a half high, and gilding the top with egg. Put in the middle several spoonfuls of Mornay Sauce, add the flaked turbot, which has been warmed up beforehand, in sufficient quantity to come two-thirds of the way up the border of potato. Fill up with Mornay Sauce, sprinkle with grated cheese, and brown in the oven in such a way that the top of the border does not get too brown.

Coquilles de Turbot.—These are made in the same way as all other coquilles with sauces such as Mornay, or White Wine, *au gratin* with Duxelles Sauce, and so on.

CHICKEN TURBOT (*TURBOTINS*)

The following recipes are for small turbot, commonly known in England as Chicken Turbot, and for fillets of large turbot as spoken of on page 186.

Turbotin à l'Américaine.—Braise the chicken turbot, and dish it. Surround it with large channelled mushrooms and slices of lobster flesh, and cover it with Sauce Américaine to which has been added the reduced braising liquor.

Turbotin farci à l'Amiral.—For six people you will want a chicken turbot weighing from three to four pounds. Make an incision to the backbone on the brown side, from head to tail. Lift the fillets near the backbone so as to form a pocket, and stuff this pocket with lobster forcemeat to which have been added the raw " coral " and some very much reduced tomato purée. Draw the fillets together, so as to enclose the stuffing well. Turn the fish over, and lay it in a suitably sized dish which has been thickly buttered. Moisten with a glass of Champagne, and nearly as much fish fumet. Cook very gently in the oven, basting frequently, for about forty minutes. Arrange the fish on the serving-dish. Reduce the cooking liquor by half, and add to it as much *Sauce Américaine*, rather highly seasoned and finished with chopped tarragon. Cover the fish with some of the sauce, and hand the rest.

Turbotin Bonne Femme.—Proceed exactly as for *Sole Bonne Femme* (page 158).

Turbotin à la Daumont.—Braise it in the manner described under *Turbotin à l'Amiral* (page 188), but do not stuff it. Dish it, surround it with croquettes of crayfish tails, mushrooms, large truffled quenelles, and soft roes egg-and-breadcrumbed and fried. Cover with Nantua Sauce with chopped truffles added to it. Border the dish with puff-paste fleurons. Serve the rest of the sauce separately.

Turbotin Dugléré.—Braise the chicken turbot with chopped shallot, roughly chopped tomatoes, sprigs of thyme, *fines herbes* (parsley, chervil, chives and tarragon) and white wine, salt and pepper. When cooked, dish it, reduce the cooking liquor, thicken it with butter, add to it a little White Wine Sauce, cover the fish, and brown quickly. With breadcrumbs fried in butter write the word " Dugléré " on top.

Turbotin au Grand Vin.—Braise the chicken turbot with a *grand vin*, whether Champagne, Sauterne, Chablis, Port, Sherry, etc. Dish it, reduce the braising liquor, thicken with butter, enrich with cream, and pour this sauce over the fish. Surround with puff-paste fleurons.

Filets de Turbotin.—These fillets can be treated in every respect in the same way as fillets of sole. (See the chapter on Sole, pages 153-183.)

Fricassée de Turbotin Grand'mère.—For six people you will want a chicken turbot weighing two pounds and a sole weighing one pound, each cut in pieces weighing two ounces each. Stew in butter some button onions and mushrooms cut in quarters, add three-quarters of a pint of cream, and cook for ten minutes. Put in the pieces of fish, season, and cook gently for a quarter of an hour. Then take out the pieces of fish, and arrange them in the serving-dish. Reduce the cooking liquor by half, bind it with two yolks of eggs, add lemon juice, and pour the sauce and the garnish over the pieces of fish. Surround with croûtons of bread fried in butter. Hand separately some mussels which have been egg-and-breadcrumbed, fried in oil and kept very dry.

Turbotin au Gratin.—Proceed as for *Sole au Gratin* (page 167), having regard, as to times, to the size of the fish.

Turbotin à la Mirabeau.—Braise the chicken turbot with red wine. With the braising liquor make a Génevoise Sauce. Cover the fish with this sauce, but make outside a border of White Wine Sauce on which you will lay some anchovy fillets. Make a decoration in the middle of the fish with blanched tarragon leaves.

Turbotin à la Parisienne.—Braise the chicken turbot with white wine. Meanwhile, cook a lobster *à la nage* (page 213). Arrange the fish in the serving-dish. Remove the flesh from the lobster tail without damaging the shell, and cut it in slices. Put the lobster on the turbot, brushing over the shell with melted butter to make it shine. Surround the base of the lobster shell with a mousse of whiting, on which you will arrange alternately the lobster slices and slices of poached soft roes. Serve separately some steamed potatoes and a sauceboat of Nantua Sauce.

Turbotin Régence.—Braise the fish with white wine. Dish it, and surround it with quenelles of fish forcemeat flavoured with crayfish cullis, mushrooms, slices of poached soft roes, poached oysters and slices of truffles. Cover with White Wine Sauce flavoured with truffle essence.

Turbotin Soufflé.—Loosen the fillets as described in *Turbotin à l'Amiral* (page 188). Stuff the opening with a mousse of turbot or other fish, to which have been added chopped truffles and stiffly whisked whites of eggs. Wrap the fish

in a buttered paper, and turn it over on to a buttered shallow
fireproof dish.   Sprinkle it with melted butter, and bake it
in the oven.   Lay it in the serving-dish, surround it with fine
whole truffles and small croquettes of truffled fish mousse.
Hand separately a Hollandaise Sauce flavoured with essence
of truffles.

WEEVER (*VIVE*)

A fish with firm flesh most suitable for inclusion in a
bouillabaisse.   It is not easily come by in this country,
though the Editor has lively childhood recollections of it,
as a denizen (no doubt when very young and small) in sea-
shore pools.   There are a number of recipes which can be
applied to it from those given for whiting, but the comparative firmness of its flesh must be taken into account in
calculating the time of cooking.   Care must be taken, in
handling it, owing to its poisonous and prickly fins.

Filets de Vives Briéval.—Butter a dish, and put in it some
minced mushrooms, chopped shallots, a few chopped onions
and fresh tomatoes roughly chopped and with their pips
removed ; season with salt and pepper.   Lay on this the
skinned fillets of the weevers, add a little dry white wine,
cover with buttered paper, and cook in the oven.   Reduce
the cooking liquor, thicken it slightly with butter, add a
little White Wine Sauce and chopped parsley, pour it over
the fillets, and brown quickly.

WHITING* (*MERLAN*)

The whiting has a delicate but fragile flesh, and the best
way to prepare it is whole.   But there are a number of
recipes for fillets of whiting well worth considering.   Below

* SUBSTITUTE FROST FISH

are given a number of recipes for this fish, whole and filleted.

Merlans à la mode Anglaise.—Open the fish down the back, remove the backbone, egg-and-breadcrumb them, using fresh breadcrumbs, and cook them in clarified butter. Serve Maître-d'hôtel Butter separately.

Merlans Bercy.—Butter a dish, sprinkle it with chopped shallot and parsley, and lay the fish on this. Season them with salt and pepper, moisten with white wine, and cook in the oven with frequent bastings. Dish the whiting, reduce the cooking liquor by half, thicken it with butter, pour it over the fish, and brown quickly.

Merlans Boitelle.—Prepare the whiting as for *Merlans Bonne Femme* (below). Arrange them in a dish bordered with Duchesse potato lightly coloured in the oven, and arrange round them slices of freshly boiled potatoes.

Merlans Bonne Femme.—Cook the whiting as indicated for *Merlans Bercy* (above), but add minced mushrooms. Finish the sauce with a little Hollandaise Sauce, or with a yolk of egg beaten in a little water.

Merlans à la Bretonne.—Fry the whiting *à la meunière* (page 5) : add capers, shelled shrimps, and edge the dish with slices of lemon.

Merlans à la Cancalaise (fillets).—Poach the fillets with white wine. Arrange them in the serving-dish, surround them with shelled shrimps or prawns and poached oysters, cover them with White Wine Sauce or Normande Sauce, and brown quickly.

Merlans Cécilia (fillets).—Fry the fillets *à la meunière* (page 5). Dish them surrounded by asparagus tips bound with butter, sprinkle with grated cheese, and brown in the oven. Add a few slices of truffle.

Merlans Colbert.—Open the whiting down the back, and remove the backbone, breaking it at the beginning of the head and near the tail. Season it, egg-and-breadcrumb it, and fry it in deep fat. Dish, and serve covered with Maître-d'hôtel Butter.

Merlans Crawford.—This dish is cooked in the same way as *Merlans Richelieu* (page 195), the difference being that it is cooked without its head, served with a Béarnaise Sauce, and sprinkled with chopped truffles.

Merlans à la Dieppoise (fillets).—Poach the fillets with fish fumet. Dish them with a surround of shrimps, mussels and button mushrooms. Cover with White Wine Sauce, and brown quickly.

Merlans à la Diplomate.—Remove the backbone as for *Merlans Colbert* (above). Stuff the fish with a mixture of coarsely chopped mushrooms which have been tossed in butter with chopped shallot, parsley, tarragon and roughly chopped tomatoes, all bound with a little Mornay Sauce. Close the whiting, and poach them with a little fish fumet. Drain them, dish them, cover them with Mornay Sauce, sprinkle them with grated cheese, and brown quickly.

Merlans Doria (fillets).—Fry the fillets *à la meunière* (page 5). Dish them, and surround them with little balls of cucumber, stewed in butter and bound with cream.

Merlans au Gratin.—Score the whiting on the back, and proceed as for *Daurade au Gratin* (page 146).

Merlans à l'Hôtelière.—Egg-and-breadcrumb, and fry the whiting as for *Merlans Colbert* (above). Dish them on Maître-d'hôtel Butter to which you have added some Duxelles (page 13) and a few drops of meat glaze.

Merlans Jackson (fillets).—Poach the fillets with fish fumet and white wine. Cover the bottom of the serving-dish with onion purée (*soubise*), to which you have added chopped parsley and tarragon. Drain the fillets well, and lay them on this purée. Reduce the cooking liquor, thicken it with butter, cover the fillets with it, and brown quickly.

Merlans en Lorgnette.—Loosen the fillets by the backbone, and break the bone just by the head. This will leave the whiting whole, but without a stiff backbone. Egg-and-breadcrumb them, roll them into paupiette shape, and secure them by means of a small skewer. Fry them in deep fat just before you want them, remove the skewer afterwards, and serve them on a napkin with fried parsley. Hand a light Tomato Sauce. (Also called *Merlans en colère.*)

Merlans à la meunière. See page 5.

Merlans au Plat.—Score the whiting on the back, and lay them in a buttered fireproof dish in which they will be served. Moisten with fish fumet and white wine, add a few dabs of butter, and cook in the oven, basting them frequently until they are done. The fish should be then partly browned, and the cooking liquor reduced to a syrupy consistence.

Quenelles de Merlan.—These quenelles are made with a creamy whiting forcemeat (see page 14), and are moulded with two dessertspoons dipped in hot water. Fill one of the spoons with the forcemeat, shaping it smoothly into a dome so that the quenelle approaches the shape of an egg. Detach it by slipping the other spoon under it, and put each quenelle as soon as made on a buttered baking-dish. When all are done, cover them with slightly salted boiling water, and poach them for twelve minutes without letting the water boil, but keeping it just moving. Drain the quenelles on a cloth, arrange them in a crown on a round dish, and cover them with the sauce chosen. This

may be Cream, Onion, White Wine, Normande, etc. They
can also be covered with Mornay Sauce, sprinkled with
cheese, and quickly browned.

(NOTE.—For this kind of quenelle, there are special
moulds which much simplify the process.)

Mousse de Merlan (Hot).—Pound a pound of whiting
flesh with a fifth of its amount of white breadcrumbs soaked
in milk and pressed, salt and pepper, and two whites of
eggs added very gradually. Pass through a tammy. Put
the purée into a basin, and work it on ice with a spatula,
mixing in about twelve tablespoonfuls of thick fresh cream
little by little. Poach this forcemeat in a mould in the
bain-marie, and serve with it whatever sauce you choose.
In certain cases the forcemeat may be enriched by chopped
truffle.

Mousse de Merlan (Cold). See Cold Mousse of Salmon
(page 138), and proceed in the same way.

Merlans Richelieu.—Prepare exactly as *Merlans Colbert*
(page 191), but serve with a few slices of truffle on each.

Merlans Verdurette (fillets).—Egg-and-breadcrumb the
fillets, and fry them in clarified butter. Dish them on the
serving-dish. Meanwhile fry some minced fresh *chantarelles*
(*girolles*) or *cèpes* in oil, until they are cooked and lightly
browned. Drain away the oil, substitute a piece of butter,
add chopped shallot and a teaspoonful each of chopped
parsley, chervil and chives, and four leaves of tarragon
also chopped. Fry together for a few seconds, and pour
the whole, still foaming, over the fillets. The juice of
half a lemon can also be added now, if liked. (P. NEVEU.)

(NOTE.—It is unlikely that the ordinary housewife will
be able to buy fresh *cèpes* or *chantarelles* ; but both these
fungi grow in our woods, and those who are lucky enough

to live near spots where they can be found may like to try this simple recipe for themselves.)

Grillade au Fenouil (Grilled Fish with Fennel).—This extremely delicious dish from the south of France is simple to do, but requires a double grid with legs on each side, which will fit over the dish. This recipe can be applied to various fish, but it is particularly good when made with John Dory (*Saint-Pierre*). The fish is grilled in the usual manner, and then laid in the double grid. On a large dish a heap of dried fennel is laid, the fish on the grid is put over this, and the fennel is lighted. As it burns, the fish is turned over, so that each side receives some of the fragrant flavouring of the burning herbs.

MIXED TIMBALES

Timbale Argentié.—(This timbale is dedicated by M. Bouzy to an old colleague.) Garnish the timbale with little paupiettes of sole stuffed with salmon forcemeat, poached and boned frogs' legs, sliced mushrooms, shelled prawns, all bound with a creamy and highly seasoned Sauce Américaine. Stick round the outside some prawns with their tails shelled. Serve separately Rice *à la Créole*.

Timbale de Maître Escoffier.—For the garnish, cook some large macaroni, keeping it rather firm. With the help of a paper cornet, fill the macaroni with a fine whiting force-meat, cut them in short lengths, and poach these for a few minutes in salted water. Mix together in a Cream Sauce the macaroni, the white part of some scallops stewed in old brandy (*vieille fine*), and cream, mushrooms, slices of *langouste* and quenelles made with whiting forcemeat.

Timbale Marivaux.—Garnish the timbale with slices of

lobster and crayfish tails cooked with Sherry, truffled quenelles of salmon, little stewed morels (*morilles*), or, if they cannot be obtained, small stewed mushrooms. Mix these with a thick cullis made from the shells and heads of the lobster and crayfish, thickened with cream and flavoured with a few spoonfuls of Hollandaise Sauce and a touch of paprika pepper.

Timbale Prunier.—Garnish paupiettes of sole stuffed with fine whiting forcemeat, large mushrooms cut in slices, poached and bearded oysters, and truffles ; bind with White Wine Sauce. (A. LENOBLE.)

Tourte Carème.—Blanch some *nouilles* (noodles), bind them with cream, and mix them with the fillets of fish, *e.g.* John Dory, rockfish, turbot or fillets of sole cut in small slices. Bind the whole with a sauce made with the cooking liquor of mussels and of mushrooms, and finished with yolks of egg and cream. Garnish the tart with this mixture ; sprinkle with grated Gruyère cheese, and brown quickly just before serving.

Vol-au-vent du Vendredi-Saint.—Garnish the vol-au-vent with large quenelles made with whatever fish forcemeat you like, shelled prawns or shrimps, mussels and button mushrooms. Make a sauce with the cooking liquor of the mussels and mushrooms, and finish it with yolks of eggs and cream. Garnish the vol-au-vent just before you want to serve it.

MIXED FISH DISHES

La Bourride.—This is a regional dish from Provence, and this is how you make it for six persons. With six cloves of garlic, a pinch of salt, two yolks of eggs and three-quarters of a pint of olive-oil, make an *Aïoli* (see page 37).

Put a dozen slices of bread a quarter of an inch thick in a dish. Now cut in slices across (*tronçons*) three pounds of fish, such as whiting, bass, sea-bream, conger, and so on ; in other words, what you can get, but there should not be less than three sorts. Line a sauté-pan with a large onion cut in rings, a sprig of fennel, and thyme, a bayleaf, and a little piece of dried orange-peel. Add the fish, moisten with two and a half pints of hot water, season with salt and pepper, bring to the boil quickly, and boil for twelve minutes. Sprinkle the slices of bread with a few spoonfuls of the fish liquor, just enough to soak them. Now mix in a saucepan eight yolks of eggs and six tablespoonfuls of the *Aïoli*. Dilute this little by little with the rest of the fish liquor strained through a fine conical sieve. Stir it on a low fire until the mixture is thick enough to coat the spoon (like an English custard), but do not let it boil or it will curdle. The result should be a smooth and very light cream. Pour it over the soaked slices of bread so that they are well covered, and serve at once, with the pieces of fish in a separate dish, and the rest of the *Aïoli* in a sauceboat.

La Chaudrée Charentaise.—Make a very rich fish fumet with the bones of turbot and soles, the white part of leeks, parsley, chervil, celery, thyme, bayleaf, pepper and salt, bound with a light purée. In this fumet cook pieces weighing four ounces each of turbot, John Dory, conger, rockfish (rock salmon), skinned and boned, for a quarter of an hour, as well as gurnards,* mackerel and small soles for eight minutes. The resulting dish should have the appearance of an Irish stew of which the liquor has been strained. Hand separately some slices of toast, and sprinkle the dish with parsley and chervil before serving.

* SUBSTITUTE MULLET

Chapter *VIII*

Shellfish

In culinary matters the French are far more punctilious than we are, and where we speak glibly of shellfish, they divide that wide term into shellfish (*coquillages*) and molluscs, and crustaceans (*crustacés*) such as crabs, lobsters, crayfish, *langouste*, and so on.

Here again is a great diversity of recipes which will come as a pleasant surprise to us who mostly eat our oysters raw and our lobsters cold. And while I am on the subject of oysters, let me say, without in any way belittling our own natives (which I personally believe are second to none in the world), that it is the duty of everyone interested in food to try those oysters that come from France, and while being cheaper are so nearly as good. In particular the *Marennes*, a greenish oyster, and the plump little *Belons*. The bright-green *Portugaise* is affected by some, and the amateur will find pleasure in instructing his friends in the different sorts of this delicious mollusc.

Mussels are another shellfish which ought to be enjoyed more in this country, and those who have tasted and appreciated *Moules Marinière*, for example, at a restaurant, will be glad to find out how to prepare them themselves.

Of the larger crustaceans, I should like to sing the praises of the *langouste*, or crawfish, which makes many admirable dishes, and is less expensive than the lobster. This creature must not be confused with the fresh-water crayfish (*écrevisse*),

about which I should like to add a few words. This little
creature used to be easily obtainable many years ago in the
Thames, and all over the country ; and while it has disappeared, at any rate from the lower reaches of the Thames,
it is still to be found in streams and small rivers up and
down the country. Many people with a stream running
through their estates still hold crayfish parties, and the
house-party goes down to the stream by night to catch
these little creatures. But I suspect that crayfish-catching
has gone out of fashion because we have forgotten what to
do with them when once they are caught, and here again
is Madame Prunier offering instruction and, I hope, setting
a pleasant and profitable fashion once more.

CLAMS

See directions for cooking under Hors-d'œuvre, Soups,
etc.

CRABS (*CRABES*)

Crabs should be boiled in a special *court-bouillon* or *nage*
for shellfish, for which a recipe is given on page 17. The
time allowed should be a quarter of an hour for each pound.
After cooking, remove the flesh and the creamy parts from
the inside of the shell, as well as the flesh from the claws.
Great care should be taken in shelling, for nothing would
be more unpleasant than to find little bits of shell in the
flesh. The body shells should be kept intact.

Crabe en barquettes à l'Armoricaine (Barquettes of Crab à
l'Armoricaine).—Mix the crab flesh with *Sauce Armoricaine* (page 30), and use the mixture for garnishing the
barquettes.

Crabe à la Bretonne.—Put some white wine into a pan with

a *bouquet garni* chopped, and shallots and mushrooms, and reduce it. Add a little Béchamel Sauce, butter it, mix in the crab flesh, and simmer for seven or eight minutes. Fill some shells (*coquilles*), cover with Cream Sauce (page 32), sprinkle with grated cheese, and brown quickly.

Crabe en Croustade à la Nantua (Croustades of Crab à la Nantua).—Mix the crab flesh with *Sauce Nantua* (page 34) flavoured with truffle essence, and garnish the croustades with it.

Crabe diablé (Devilled Crab).—Lightly fry in butter some chopped onion and shallot. Remove, and swill the pan with a few drops of brandy, adding then a little Dijon mustard, a little Béchamel Sauce, and the flesh of the crab. Season according to taste, and garnish the crab shells with this mixture.

Crabe à l'Indienne (Curried Crab).—Lightly fry some shallots, mushrooms and tomatoes all chopped up. Add a little Béchamel Sauce, four ounces of rice cooked with curry, and the same quantity of crab flesh. Simmer for twenty minutes, and fill the crab shells, or some scallop shells, with the mixture.

Crabe au Paprika.—Toss lightly in foaming butter half a pound of crab flesh. Add some cream, a little Béchamel Sauce, a pinch of paprika pepper, enough breadcrumbs to bind it, and two yolks of eggs. Make some round toasts, put a spoonful of the mixture on each, and make them very hot in the oven just before serving.

Pilaff de chair de Crabe (Pilaff of Crab).—Butter a mould or pudding-basin, and line the bottom and sides with a fairly thick layer of Pilaff Rice (see page 21). Fill up the middle with crab flesh bound with the sauce asked for : White Wine, Curry, Shrimp, *Américaine*, *Newburg*, etc. Unmould the Pilaff, and surround it with a few spoonfuls of the sauce used.

Rissoles de Crabe Lorientaise (Crab Rissoles Lorientaise).— Bind the crab flesh with Mornay Sauce with plenty of cheese in it. Roll out some puff-paste five inches wide and as long as you like, and place on it, about an inch and a half apart, little heaps of the crab flesh about the size of a pigeon's egg. Moisten the edges of the paste, fold it in half, pinch the edges together, and cut out the little rissoles with a plain or fluted pastry-cutter. Gild them with egg, and cook them in a very hot oven for twelve minutes before serving them.

(NOTE.—By all accepted rules, rissoles should be fried in deep fat and not baked. But the way it is done in Lorient is given here.)

CRAWFISH (SEA-WATER) (*LANGOUSTE*)

In view of the confusion which exists between the names of crawfish (*langouste*) and crayfish (*écrevisse*), it has been thought better to refer in these pages to the former as the *langouste*. In appearance it is like a large lobster without the big claws, and although it is fished a good deal off these shores, the bulk of the catches go abroad where it is more appreciated than here. Its flesh is a good deal firmer than that of the lobster, but it is no less savoury in flavour. Nearly all the hot lobster dishes can be made with *langouste*, for which see pages 209-223 under Lobster. It lends itself more readily than the lobster to the preparation of cold dishes, particularly for banquets. Dressed *à la Parisienne*, it always gains the admiration of the diners, especially when two *langoustes* are dressed in this way face to face.

Langouste à la Parisienne.—Stretch the langouste on a board so as to keep its tail out flat, attach it firmly, and cook it in a *court-bouillon*. Let it get cold. Remove the membrane under the tail, and take out the tail flesh, being careful not to damage the shell, which is needed for dressing it. Remove also from the head the parts which are edible, flesh and creamy parts. Cut up the tail flesh in slices of the same thickness, and make on each a decoration in truffle well set in jelly. Now place the shell on a block of crumb of bread shaped like a wedge, and fix it firmly on. (The empty shell may be refilled with a *julienne* of lettuce leaves.) Arrange the slices of the tail on the top of the shell, slightly overlapping each other. Surround the langouste with artichoke bottoms each garnished with a little heap of vegetable salad, in which have been mixed the flesh from the head cut in dice and bound with jellified Mayonnaise, and with hard-boiled egg-halves stuffed with their own yolks mixed with chopped truffle and bound with jelly. Hand a Mayonnaise Sauce separately. Set round the outside of the dish some slices of jelly.

(NOTE.—The correctness and beauty of this fashion depends above all on the taste and skill of the cook who is responsible for it.)

Langouste à la Russe.—Cook the langouste, and cut the slices from the tail, as has been described above in *Langouste à la Parisienne*. Cover the slices with Mayonnaise Sauce to which have been added the creamy parts from the langouste's head, the whole sieved and bound with jelly. Decorate each slice with a fluted slice of truffle and two tiny sprigs of chervil. Mask them with jelly. Arrange the shell and the slices in the same way as for the *Langouste à la Parisienne*, but surround it alternately with artichoke bottoms and

small scooped-out tomatoes, both filled with Salade Russe
bound with jellified Mayonnaise, the salad sprinkled with
chopped truffle.   Border the dish with slices of jelly, and
hand a Sauce Russe.

(NOTE.—In certain cases, and according to taste, you
can add as a garnish little barrel-shapes of hard-boiled egg,
in which some caviar takes the place of the yolk.)

Langouste Wladimir.—For two people you will want a live
langouste weighing about a pound and a quarter or a little
more.   Cut it in half lengthwise, remove the flesh, and make
with it a mousseline forcemeat as directed under *Mousse
d'Écrevisses* (page 206). With this forcemeat, to which
a few dice of the langouste flesh should be added, garnish
the shell without filling it too full, then put the two halves
together so as to give the langouste its original shape.
Wrap it up now in buttered paper bands, and tie these round
with thread.   Then poach the langouste in a *bain-marie* for
twenty-five minutes.   When ready to serve, take off the
paper, and arrange the two half-shells on a napkin.   Hand
a *Sauce Américaine* (page 30) with them.

CRAYFISH (*ECREVISSES*)

These little river shellfish are not very well known in
England at the present time, although many of our streams
abound with them.   Many years ago they were popular
enough, and of late efforts have been made to interest the
public in them here.   The principal difficulty about them
is the fact that when people have once caught them, they
do not know what to do with them : a problem which the
following pages should help to solve.

In the kitchen there are three kinds of crayfish, or rather, three different sizes. The small ones, which average just over an ounce to an ounce and a half, are used for soups ; the medium-sized ones, averaging two ounces, are used for garnishes ; while the large ones, weighing about three ounces, are used in the recipes that follow.

It must be noted that before any other preparations the crayfish must be washed well in plenty of cold water, and gutted. This latter operation consists in removing the intestinal tube with the point of a small knife. It will be found in the opening under the middle phalanx of the tail, and care should be exercised in pulling it out so as not to break it. Its presence in the crayfish when cooked would cause an unpleasant bitterness.

Aspic de queues d'Écrevisses (Crayfish Aspic).—Coat a border mould with white jelly, and decorate it as you will. Set the decoration with a little more jelly, and on this arrange, slightly overlapping each other, the shelled tails of crayfish cooked *à la Bordelaise* (see page 206). Cover with a layer of jelly, and make another layer of crayfish tails, this time arranging them the other way round. Fill up the mould in this way with alternate rows of jelly and crayfish, and when it is full, finish with a layer of jelly. Keep it on ice, and unmould it at the last moment before serving.

Écrevisses à la Bombay.—Fry the crayfish in oil with a *Mirepoix bordelaise* (see page 17). Moisten with white wine and good fish fumet, add a *bouquet garni*, some roughly chopped tomatoes and a pinch of curry powder. Cover and cook for ten minutes. Arrange the crayfish in a timbale, strain and reduce the cooking liquor, finish it with cream flavoured with milk of almonds, correct the seasoning, and pour it over the crayfish. Hand separately some Rice *à l'Indienne* (see page 21).

Écrevisses en buisson.—Cook the crayfish for ten minutes in a *nage* (see page 17) rather heavily flavoured with white wine. Let them get cold in it. Arrange them in the utensil specially made for this dish, mixing them with freshly picked curled parsley.

Écrevisses à la Bordelaise.—Fry the crayfish in butter with a *Mirepoix Bordelaise* (see page 17). When the shells get very red, pour over a glass of brandy and set it alight. When the flames have died down moisten with white wine, add peeled, pressed and roughly chopped tomatoes, a *bouquet garni*, a little meat glaze, salt and a touch of cayenne. Cover, and cook for ten minutes. Arrange the crayfish in a timbale, reduce the cooking liquor, thicken it with butter, pour it over the crayfish, and finish by sprinkling them with a little roughly chopped parsley.

Écrevisses à la Magenta.—Fry the crayfish as for *à la Bordelaise*, and finish cooking them in the same way, using as moistening the cooking liquor of lobster *à l'Américaine*, and seasoning with a little basil.

Écrevisses à la Marinière.—Fry the crayfish in butter, add onion and celery both finely minced, moisten with white wine, season, and cook them. Arrange them in a timbale, reduce the cooking liquor by half, thicken it with butter, and pour it over the crayfish. Sprinkle at the last with a little roughly chopped parsley.

Mousses et Mousselines d'Écrevisses (Cold).—Shell some crayfish (tails and claws) cooked *à la Bordelaise*. Pound the flesh finely, add the necessary amount of Fish Velouté, and pass through a tammy. To each pound of the purée allow six tablespoonfuls of very strong jelly and half a pint of cream well whisked. Mix the jelly into the purée, and put it on ice. When it begins to set, add the cream.

(NOTE.—*Mousses* are made in large moulds ; *mousselines* in little ones, one for each person. Whether the moulds are large or small, they ought to be first lined with jelly before the mixture is put into them.)

Écrevisses à la Nage.—Get ready a *nage* (see page 17) well flavoured with white wine, and when this boils, throw the crayfish into it. Cook for seven minutes, and serve them in the *nage* itself, hot or cold. If they are served cold, let them get cold in the liquid itself.

Gratin de Queues d'Écrevisses à la Nantua (Crayfish au Gratin as in Nantua).—Have at least half a dozen crayfish for each person, two small mushrooms, one fresh truffle for every five, a pint of cream and a quarter of a pound of butter. Peel and wash the mushrooms, and cook them with water, salt and lemon juice. Melt a little butter, throw in the crayfish, season them, moisten with a glass of dry white wine and the mushroom cooking liquor. Cook for six minutes, then take out the crayfish and drain them. Shell their tails and claws, reduce the sauce, and add the cream and a dessertspoonful of Béchamel Sauce. Crush up the crayfish shells with the four ounces of butter, add them to the sauce, and pass all through a sieve twice. Now put into a dish the uncooked truffles cut in strips, the crayfish tails and claws, and the mushrooms dipped into the sauce and sprinkled with grated cheese, and browned. Keep the bottom of the dish in a *bain-marie* so as to prevent the sauce from curdling.

Écrevisses à la Newburg. See *Homard à la Newburg* (page 217), and proceed in the same way.

Écrevisses Sans-Gêne.—Bake in their jackets some large waxy potatoes. Remove a slice from each, remove the pulp, and coat the inside of the skin with a *Sauce Améri-*

caine (page 30). Fill them two-thirds full with crayfish tails cooked in a *nage*, and little truffled quenelles of fish. Finish with a Mornay Sauce, sprinkle with grated cheese, and brown in the oven. As you take them from the oven, put a slice of truffle in the middle of each, a crayfish head at each end, and the claws stuck round the edges.

Soufflé d'Écrevisses.—Allow three dozen crayfish for six persons. Get ready a cheese soufflé mixture, that is to say, a very much reduced Béchamel Sauce flavoured with grated Parmesan, salt, and a little nutmeg. Add three yolks of raw eggs and the well-whisked whites in the proportions usually advised in making soufflés. Pour the mixture into a buttered soufflé-dish with alternate layers of crayfish tails, and truffles in slices or dice. Cook like an ordinary soufflé.

Timbale de queues d'Écrevisses.—In a mould about three inches high (that is, of the shape of a timbale) bake a pastry case " blind," with a lid of pastry. When the rice or dried peas have been removed from the case, gild the inside with egg, and let it dry at the mouth of the oven. Cook some medium-sized crayfish *à la Bordelaise* (page 206), and shell them. Mix them with whatever sauce you have chosen, adding little quenelles of truffled fish forcemeat, button mushrooms and slices of truffles. At least half of the contents should be crayfish tails. Pour this mixture into the pastry timbale, crown the top with empty crayfish heads, put on the pastry lid, and serve on a napkin.

Suprêmes d'Écrevisses au Grand Vin.—First prepare the crayfish in the *Bordelaise* fashion (page 206), substituting a fine vintage wine for the usual white wine. Shell the crayfish tails, and keep them aside. With the shells and the heads, etc., make a *Mousse*. Arrange the mousse in a shallow timbale or a glass dish, and put it on ice. When

it has set, make a decoration with the crayfish tails and slices
of truffles and set it with jelly.

Écrevisses à la Viennoise.—Cook the crayfish in a good
court-bouillon with white wine, and arrange them in a dish.
Reduce the cooking liquor, thicken it with butter and
season it with paprika pepper. Pour it over the crayfish
and sprinkle them with a little roughly chopped parsley.

DUBLIN BAY PRAWNS (*LANGOUSTINES*)

These are quite well known in England, and are very
often seen in the shops. They can be prepared in the same
way as Crayfish, and the very large ones in the various
fashions given for Lobster (pages 209-223). They can be
a very good imitation of the *Scampi* of Venice.

Pilaff de Langoustines. See *Pilaff de Crevettes* (page 233),
and proceed in the same way, using Dublin Bay Prawns
instead of Prawns.

ESCALLOP (*COQUILLE SAINT-JACQUES*)
See SCALLOP (pages 234-238)

LOBSTER (*HOMARD*)[1]

Homard à l'Américaine (Lobster à l'Américaine).—For six
people you will want three live lobsters weighing about a
pound and a quarter each. First, fry lightly in oil a *Mirepoix*

---

[1] For the killing of lobsters a humane method advocated by the R.S.P.C.A.
is described in their pamphlet, *The Killing of Crabs and Lobsters for Table,* by
Joseph Sinel. It will be understood that the author and the editor are bound
to have regard to the possibility of suffering inflicted on any living creature.
Notwithstanding that, they are of opinion that the cutting up of a live
lobster is the better method from the point of view of preparation of the
dishes in question.

Bordelaise (page 17). Cut the tail of the lobster in pieces across, remove the claws, and cut the head in half lengthwise. Remove the little pouch at the top of the head which contains a little grit : keep aside the creamy parts of the head as well as the greenish part known as the coral. Crush the shells of the claws, and add both the claws and the slices of the tail to the mirepoix, and fry until the shell is a bright red and the flesh stiffened. Pour over a glass of good brandy, and set it alight, then moisten with dry white wine and fish fumet, or better still, consommé. Add a few roughly chopped tomatoes, a *bouquet-garni*, a tiny bit of crushed garlic, and cook for twenty minutes. Arrange the slices, claws and the halves of the head in a timbale. Reduce the cooking liquor, bind it with the creamy parts, and the coral from the head crushed on a plate, with a little butter. Thicken with Kneaded Butter, correct the seasoning, and finish with chopped parsley, chervil and tarragon. Pour this sauce over the pieces of lobster.

(NOTE.—With *Lobster à l'Américaine*, a dish of Rice *à l'Indienne* (page 21) is usually handed.)

Homard à l'Américaine Prunier. — This is Prunier's version of the famous dish. Proceed as above, and when the sauce is strained add to it some good Velouté, a tablespoonful for each pint and three-quarters of the sauce. The lobster in this case is extracted from the shell before being served.

Homard à l'Armoricaine.—Proceed as for *Homard à l'Américaine*. Arrange the pieces in a timbale. Strain the sauce, bring it to the boil, and then on the side of the stove bind it with egg-yolks and cream before pouring it over the lobster.

(NOTE.—Add, if you like, as a garnish some mushrooms *à la crème*.)

Homard à la Bordelaise.—Remove the legs and claws from the lobster, and crack the claws. Fry the whole lobster lightly in oil and butter until it is red, then add the claws and the legs. Pour over a glass of brandy and set it alight, moisten with white wine and fish fumet, add a few roughly chopped tomatoes, a *bouquet garni,* a small piece of garlic and a little meat glaze, and cook for a quarter of an hour. Then take out the lobster, with the legs and claws, cut the flesh from the tail in slices, and remove the flesh from the claws and legs. You will have prepared beforehand a *Mirepoix Bordelaise* (page 17) ; now moisten it with the lobster's cooking liquor, add the slices and the flesh from the claws, and bring just to the boil. Keep it just on boiling-point for five minutes, then put the lobster flesh into a timbale. Reduce the cooking liquor and strain it, thicken it with butter, correct the seasoning, pour it over the lobster, and sprinkle finally with a little roughly chopped parsley.

Homard Cardinal.—Cook the lobster in a *court-bouillon.* Cut it in half lengthwise, remove the flesh from each half of the tail, and cut it in slices. Put the two halves of the head on a dish, and spread in the bottom of each a little Cardinal Sauce (page 31). Add the flesh from the claws cut in dice, some minced cooked mushrooms and slices of truffle. Arrange on top the slices of tail flesh, overlapping one another. Cover with Cardinal Sauce, sprinkle with grated cheese, and brown in the oven. On serving, put a few slices of truffle on each lobster-half.

Homard au Champagne.—Fry the lobster in butter, and after the shell has coloured lightly, moisten with very dry champagne, and cook for twenty-five minutes. Then drain the lobster, cut it in slices across, shell these slices, and put the flesh into a timbale. Reduce the cooking liquor, add some, cream, bind it with yolks of eggs, season it with cayenne, and pass it through a sieve. Pour it then over the pieces of lobster.

(NOTE.—A few slices of truffle may be added.)

Homard chez lui.—Take a small live lobster weighing between three-quarters of a pound and a pound, and cook it *whole* according to the method *à l'Américaine* (page 209). When it is cooked, remove the tail, shell without breaking it, wash it and put back into it the tail flesh and the flesh from the claws and legs. Keep warm, sprinkled with a little brandy. Now arrange the lobster, head and shell, on its back on a base of Rice *à la Créole*, and cover the flesh with a rich Sauce Américaine. Add slices of truffles, and chopped chervil and tarragon. Serve very hot, with a Sauce Américaine handed separately.

(NOTE.—The base of rice, while useful for holding the lobster in place, acts also as a garnish to be eaten with it.)

Homard Clarence.—Cook the lobster in a *court-bouillon*. When it is done, halve it lengthways and remove the flesh from the tail, claws and legs. Cut the tail flesh in slices, and that from the claws and legs in half. Remove the flesh and creamy parts from the head, pound it with a little cream, and pass it through a sieve. Mix this with some creamy Béchamel Sauce flavoured with curry powder. Half-fill the two shells with Rice *à l'Indienne* (page 21) with which you have mixed the lobster flesh from the claws and legs. Arrange on it the tail slices, cover them with the sauce, and arrange them on a long dish. Hand the rest of the sauce separately.

Homard en coquilles.—Put a layer of whatever sauce you are using in the bottom of the scallop shells, garnish them with sliced or diced cooked lobster flesh, chopped mushrooms, slices or dice of truffle, tomato, etc. Cover with the sauce, and glaze in the oven or not, as you prefer.

(NOTE.—It is understood that the garnish must be hot when it is put into the shells. If the shells have to be glazed, it is advisable to put a border of *Duchesse* potatoes (page 20) round the edge, so as to prevent the sauce from overflowing.

Homard en coquilles à la Bretonne.—The shells are filled with a mixture of lobster, prawns or shrimps and mushrooms, the sauce used being a White Wine Sauce strongly flavoured with onion. The shells are sprinkled with grated cheese before being browned.

à la Crème.—Slices of lobster in a border of *Duchesse* potatoes. Cover with Cream Sauce, and brown quickly.

à la Nantua.—The shells are garnished with a salpicon of lobster flesh and truffles, and masked with a Sauce Nantua (page 34).

Thermidor.—The shells are garnished with lobster flesh, mushrooms and truffles. Cover with a mustard-flavoured Bercy Sauce (page 31), and brown quickly.

Homard à la Nage (Boiled Lobster).—Make a *nage* or *court-bouillon* as follows : mince a large carrot and two onions, and stew them in butter. Add a pint and three-quarters of white wine and the same of water, with a bouquet of chervil, parsley, thyme and bayleaf tied together. Bring to the boil, and simmer for half an hour. Plunge the lobster in this *nage* as it boils, and for a lobster weighing about a pound let it boil for about twenty minutes. When cooked, it can be served hot or cold just as it is. If cold, it can be left in the *nage* to get cold, and served in it, or with a Mayonnaise. If it is served hot, melted butter is the proper accompaniment.

Homard rôti au Whisky (Roasted Lobster with Whisky).— Cut the lobster in two lengthways, and break the claws. Put it into a baking-dish shell side downwards. Season with salt and pepper, and on each half put two tablespoonfuls of melted butter mixed with Colman's mustard. Then sprinkle over a few white breadcrumbs that have been browned in the oven, and roast the lobster, basting it well, for a quarter of an hour or a very little longer. To serve, dish the lobster, and pour over it the butter from the baking-tin. Add a glass of whisky, set it alight, and finish by basting with the butter. Serve very hot.

Coupe de Homard Polignac.—Make a *court-bouillon* with very dry Pommery, a *bouquet garni* reinforced with a piece of celery, mushroom stalks, a little onion and some very coarsely broken pepper. Salt it moderately. Quickly cut in pieces across three live lobsters weighing about a pound each, take out the little pouch and the creamy parts from the heads, and plunge them and the pieces in the rapidly boiling *court-bouillon*, and boil for twenty minutes. Drain and shell the pieces, cut the flesh in slices, remove the flesh from the claws and legs, and put it all in a timbale or a glass dish. Add some fine grapes, skinned and with their pips removed. Pass the cooking liquor through a cloth, and make with it a fine jelly which should be a light rose in colour, completing it by a little more Pommery. When this jelly is cold, or nearly cold, pour it over the lobster, and keep the dish on ice until it is wanted.

Côtelettes de Homard (Lobster Cutlets).—Make a salpicon in the proper proportions (see Cutlets, under *Hors d'œuvre*, page 55) with lobster flesh, mushroom, truffles and very much reduced Fish Velouté. Shape the mixture when cold into cutlets, egg-and-breadcrumb them, and fry them in the usual manner. Serve separately, whatever sauce is chosen.

Côtelettes de Homard Arkangel.—Cook a lobster, and cut its flesh into dice ; mix this with an equal amount of large-grained caviar, and bind with *Mousse de Homard* (page 217).

When the mixture is set, shape into little cutlets, or, simpler still, put the mixture to set in little cutlet-shaped oiled moulds, and let it set there. Cover them with Chaudfroid Sauce flavoured with a lobster cullis, and cover them with jelly. Arrange on a dish garnished round the edge with slices of jelly, and hand separately a *Sauce Russe* (page 40).

Homard à la crème.—Cut the lobster in pieces across, and fry them in butter. Moisten with thin seasoned cream, and cook for a quarter of an hour. Take out the pieces, shell them, remove the flesh from the claws and legs, and put it all in a timbale. Add to the cooking liquor a certain amount of thick cream, reduce it until it reaches the right thickness, finish with a little good burnt brandy and a few drops of lemon juice, and pour over the lobster.

Homard Diablé ou grillé (Devilled Lobster).—Cut a live lobster in half lengthwise, and lay the two halves shell downwards on a metal dish. Season the flesh, sprinkle it with melted butter flavoured with mustard, sprinkle with browned breadcrumbs, and cook in a hot oven. Serve separately a rather highly seasoned Maître-d'hôtel Butter flavoured with mustard.

Homard à la Française.—Fry in butter some small lobster cut in pieces across and seasoned with salt and cayenne pepper. Moisten with white wine and fish fumet, add some very thin *julienne* strips of onion and carrot stewed in butter, and cook for a quarter of an hour. Arrange the pieces in a timbale, bind the cooking liquor lightly with Kneaded Butter, finish with more butter, and pour over the lobster.

Homard froid en Aspic (Cold Lobster in Aspic).—Line a border mould with white jelly, and decorate it as you will. Put a layer of jelly in the bottom, and on this arrange thin slices of lobster tail cooked in *court-bouillon,* so that they slightly overlap each other. Cover with more jelly, and so in alternate layers until the mould is full, finishing with a layer of jelly. Leave to set, and turn out when wanted.

(NOTE.—If desired, a slice of truffle may be laid between the slices.)

Homard froid en Aspic à la Russe.—Cut the lobster tail into even rounds, put on each a slice of truffle cut with a scalloped cutter, cover with jelly, and let them set. Lightly line a border mould with white jelly. Arrange in it the slices of lobster tails, so that the decorated side touches the side of the mould. Fill up the hollow space inside with a thick *Salade Russe*, cover with a thin layer of jelly, and leave it to set. Turn out only when wanted.

Homard Grammont.—Cook a lobster in *court-bouillon*, and cut it in half lengthways. Take out the flesh from the tail, and cut it in slices. Garnish the halves of the shell with lobster mousse seasoned with paprika pepper, arrange on it the slices (which you have previously covered with jelly), alternating them with some fine poached oysters also covered with jelly. Put the shells on a long dish, and surround them with the oyster shells garnished with a salpicon of oysters and the flesh from the claws and legs of the lobster, bound with Mayonnaise Sauce. Hand separately a Mayonnaise flavoured with lemon juice and finished with whipped cream.

Homard à la Hambourgeoise.—Cook the lobster in *court-bouillon*, remove the flesh from the tail, and cut it in slices. Arrange these slices in a little sauté-pan, add Madeira and meat glaze, bring to the boil and bind with breadcrumbs kneaded with butter. Dilute with a little cream, then finish with chopped parsley and a few drops of lemon juice.   Arrange the slices in a timbale, cover them with the sauce, and serve very hot.

(NOTE.—The sauce should be thick enough to coat the slices.   The centre may be garnished with the flesh from the claws and legs, sprinkled with Lobster Butter or simply with plain melted butter.)

Homard à la Hongroise.—This is made in the same way as *Homard à la crème* (page 215), with the addition of a cullis of onions and a flavouring of paprika pepper.

Homard à la Maconnaise.—Proceed in the same manner as for Matelote of Eel with Red Wine (page 85).   For this method of preparation choose little lobsters weighing round about half a pound, cut them in pieces across, and cook them *à l'étouffée*, that is to say, with butter in a covered pan.   Bind the cooking liquor of the matelote with the coral and the creamy parts mixed with butter.   This dish should be rather highly seasoned.

Mayonnaise de Homard (Lobster Mayonnaise).—Cut the lobster tail flesh in slices, and with this and the flesh from the claws and legs make a Mayonnaise in the same way as described in the recipe for Salmon Mayonnaise (page 139).   The lobster should be cooked in a *court-bouillon*.

Homard Mephisto.—Cut a live lobster in half lengthways, take out the flesh and pound it in a mortar with seasoning, mustard and a little cream.   Garnish the shells with this mixture, sprinkle it with breadcrumbs, sprinkle with melted butter, and cook in the oven.   Serve at the same time a mustard-flavoured Maître-d'hôtel Butter.

Mousse froide de Homard (Cold Mousse of Lobster).— Proceed exactly as under Cold Mousse of Crayfish (page 206).

Homard à la Newburg (Lobster Newburg) (with live

lobster).—Cut the live lobster in pieces across, and fry
these in butter. Swill the pan with Sherry, add enough
cream nearly to cover the pieces. Cook for twenty minutes,
and then arrange the pieces in a timbale. Bind the cooking
liquor with yolks of eggs, and pour it over the pieces.

Homard à la Newburg (with cooked lobster).—Cook the
lobster in *court-bouillon*, and cut the tail flesh in slices.
Arrange them in a sauté-pan, and cook them gently in
butter. Sprinkle them well with Sherry, reduce this, and
then moisten them with enough cream to cover them.
Boil for a few minutes, then bind with cream and egg-
yolks, and pour into a timbale. Add a few slices of truffles.

Homard à la Palestine.—Cut the lobster in pieces across,
and fry it in butter with a Mirepoix (page 16). Pour over
a glass of brandy, set it alight, then moisten with white
wine and fish fumet. Cook for a quarter of an hour, then
take the flesh from the pieces, and keep it warm in a
covered sauté-pan. Now pound up the head and the tail
shells, fry them lightly in oil with an ordinary mirepoix,
moisten with the cooking liquor of the lobster, and cook
for another quarter of an hour. Now add a little Fish
Velouté, the creamy parts and the coral of the lobster
crushed with a little butter and a pinch of curry powder.
Cook on for a few seconds longer, then pass through a
sieve, and finish with cream and butter. You will have
had ready on a dish a moulded border of Rice *à l'Indienne*
(page 21). Put the pieces of lobster in the middle of this,
cover them with some of the sauce, and hand the rest of it
in a sauceboat.

Homard à la Parisienne. See *Langouste (Crawfish) à la
Parisienne* (page 203).

Homard Phocéenne.—Prepare the lobster as if for *à*

l'Américaine (page 209), increasing the amount of garlic,
and adding a seasoning of saffron. Add to the sauce a
iulienne of red sweet peppers, and serve on a dish bordered
with saffron-flavoured Rice *à l'Indienne*.

Homard au Porto.—For this you will want a lobster of
about a pound in weight, which must be stewed in butter
whole, seasoned with salt and paprika pepper. Moisten it
liberally with Port wine, cook for thirty minutes, and drain
it. Strain the cooking liquor, and reduce it by three-
quarters. Bind it with two egg-yolks and a few spoonfuls
of cream, and finish off the fire with a few drops of Port.
Keep hot in the *bain-marie*. Meanwhile shell the lobster,
cut the tail in slices, and leave the flesh of the claws whole.
Arrange in a timbale, and cover with the sauce.

Homard à la Russe. See *Langouste* (*Crawfish*) *à la Russe*
(page 203).

Homard Saint-Honorat.—Cut in half lengthways a lobster
weighing about a pound. Prepare it in the same way as
Homard à l'Américaine (page 209). When it is cooked, take
it out, remove the tail flesh, and cut it in slices. Half-fill
the shells with Pilaff rice, lay the slices on this, and cover
them with the sauce. Garnish with mussels *à la crème*
(served in sea-urchins' shells if you can get them, the spikes
of which have been flattened), with fried oysters on top.

Salade de Homard (Lobster Salad).—This is made with
the same ingredients as Lobster Mayonnaise, but they are
seasoned with an ordinary salad dressing, oil, vinegar,
salt and pepper.

Soufflé de Homard (Lobster Soufflé).—(1) Half cook a
lobster in a *nage* (see page 17), and cut it in half lengthways.
Take out the flesh and pound it with the necessary seasoning.
Pass it through a tammy, and add to it some Béchamel

Sauce to which two raw egg-yolks have been added. Bring to the boil, take off the fire, and let the mixture get cold slowly, adding a little white of egg stiffly whisked. Garnish the half-shells with this mixture, sprinkle them with a little grated cheese, and cook them for twenty minutes in a moderate oven. Serve separately some sauce or other—Américaine, Newburg, White Wine, Bercy, and so on.

(NOTE.—You can add to the mixture, if you like, some thin slices of the lobster tail, or truffle in dice, or poached soft roes, shelled shrimps, minced cooked mushrooms, etc.)

Soufflé de Homard (Lobster Soufflé).—(2) Cut a live lobster in half lengthways, remove the flesh, pound it with the necessary seasonings and a little breadcrumbs soaked in milk and then pressed dry. Pass it through a tammy, put it into a bowl over ice, and work into it a reasonable amount of thick cream. Meanwhile cook the shells in water, being careful not to break them. See that they are well drained. Now garnish them with the soufflé mixture and sprinkle the surface with breadcrumbs. Cook on a baking-sheet in a moderate oven for fifteen to twenty minutes, and serve them on a napkin. Serve at the same time, if you like, one of the sauces mentioned in the previous recipe, all the more if the soufflé mixture contains any of the sauce's ingredients.

Homard Thermidor.—Cut the lobster in half lengthways after it has been cooked. Remove, and cut in slices, the flesh from the tail. Cover the bottom of each half-shell with mustard-flavoured Bercy Sauce mixed with Béchamel Sauce. Arrange the slices on top, and cover them with the same sauce. Brown lightly.

(NOTE.—The lobster slices may be alternated with mushrooms cooked in butter.)

Homard Tourville.—Make a rizotto (page 21). Cut in large dice a cooked lobster tail, mix with them some mushroom dice cooked in butter and some poached mussels and oysters. The lobster flesh should make quite half of this salpicon. Bind with a Fish Velouté flavoured with a fumet of shellfish, heat it up, and serve it in the middle of the rizotto. The lobster, etc., is then covered with Mornay Sauce, sprinkled with grated cheese, and quickly browned.

(NOTE.—The rizotto border can be moulded or simply arranged on the dish with a spoon.)

Homard Vanderbilt.—Cut a live lobster in half lengthways, and prepare it *à l'Américaine.* Remove the flesh from the tail, and cut it in slices. Mask the bottom of the half-shells with a creamy *Sauce Américaine,* and add crayfish tails and truffle dice, or you can mix these with the sauce itself. Arrange on this bed the lobster slices, putting a slice of truffle between them. Cover with *Sauce Américaine* thickened with yolks of eggs, and brown lightly in the oven.

Homard Winthertur.—The same as *Homard Cardinal* (page 211), save that the salpicon of lobster is replaced by shelled shrimps. Mask with Cardinal Sauce, and sprinkle with chopped truffles.

Demoiselles de Caen chez elles.—Cook some very small lobsters, weighing about half a pound each, in *court-bouillon.* Remove the claws and legs, and empty the tails without breaking the top shell. Cut this flesh in slices. Cut some mushrooms in thin slices, and cook them slowly in butter. When they are done, take them out and keep them warm on a plate. In the same butter put the slices of lobster. Cover the pan, and heat them through gently. Then swill the pan with a small glass of brandy (*fine Champagne*).

Prepare a light and unctuous Cardinal Sauce (page 31). Heighten the seasoning with a touch of cayenne, and finish the sauce with a few drops of brandy. Make a base of Pilaff rice (which will serve as a garnish as well), and on it arrange the lobsters on their backs. Mask the bottom of their shells with the Cardinal Sauce, and then arrange in them, overlapping each other, the slices of lobster and slices of truffle. Cover with the same sauce, and brown lightly. Some slices of truffle should be placed on each lobster as they come from the oven, and the dish should be served at once.

Paëlla de Homard.—Toss in butter, as if you were making a pilaff, some chopped onion, a touch of garlic, and Carolina rice. Add peeled, pressed and roughly chopped tomatoes, some sweet red pepper cut in little dice, some small green peas (*petits pois*) and a pinch of saffron. Moisten the rice to half its height again with fish fumet or white stock, add a *bouquet garni* and the usual seasoning, and cook for a quarter of an hour. When the rice is cooked, separate it with a fork, and mix with it slices of lobster or langouste as the principal ingredient, accompanied by shelled mussels ; crab flesh or crayfish tails are auxiliaries. Moisten again very slightly, give it another seven or eight minutes in the oven, and send it to table in a timbale.

(NOTE.—If the rice is put into an earthenware casserole for serving at table, the mixture with the fish can be done in that. It is then only necessary to add the moistening, cover the casserole, put it into the oven for the final heating, and serve it as it is.)

Pâté de Homard.—Cut up a live lobster : keep aside the creamy parts, the coral and the eggs, if there are any. Season the pieces, fry them in butter long enough to stiffen the

flesh, pour in a glass of brandy and set it alight, and then
add as much tarragon vinegar and a little cream. After a
few minutes' cooking, take out the pieces of lobster, and
put into the cooking liquor as much breadcrumbs as will
completely absorb it. Meanwhile take the meat out of the
pieces of the tail, leaving it intact, and especially the flesh
from the claws. Pound the creamy parts, the coral and the
eggs, add the same amount of fresh butter, the soaked breadcrumbs, a little Anchovy Essence and the yolks of several
hard-boiled eggs. Pass through a tammy, correct the seasoning, and heighten it with a little cayenne. Now roll out
some short-crust, put it on a long buttered dish, and raise
the edges with a band of paste about three-quarters of an
inch high. Mask the middle of the pastry with a layer of
the forcemeat, and on this arrange the pieces of lobster, so
as to reconstitute its shape, putting the claws on each side.
Cover with the rest of the forcemeat, and then with a cover
of pastry which must be well joined on to the bottom layer.
Gild with egg, and put it into a hot oven just long enough
to cook the pastry.   Serve at once.

(NOTE.—The lobster must be soft to eat, and the consistence of the forcemeat should be that of a purée, neither
too firm nor too soft. Indeed this dish should be unlike
any other.)

MUSSELS (*MOULES*)

To whatever use they are to be put, the mussels, scraped
and brushed in several waters, must first be "opened" with
a little white wine, chopped onion and shallot and freshly
ground pepper. To serve them, one of the shells is usually
discarded. To " open " them, you proceed as follows : for
three and a half pints of mussels, add a medium-sized onion

and a shallot finely chopped, five or six parsley stalks, a sprig of thyme, the third of a bayleaf, a pinch of freshly ground pepper and eight tablespoonfuls of white wine. Cover the pan tightly, put it on a quick fire, and at the end of two minutes shake the mussels. Do this two or three times more during their cooking, which should only take five or six minutes in all. The mussels should then be cooked, and their shells wide open.

Brochettes de Moules Amiral.—Egg-and-breadcrumb some poached and wiped mussels, and skewer them a dozen on a skewer. Wrap each skewer in a very thin rasher of bacon, sprinkle with butter, cook them for a few minutes in the oven, and serve them with a Tomato Sauce handed separately.

Moules Bonne Femme.—" Open " the mussels in the manner described above, adding a thin *julienne* of mushrooms and the white part of celery. Put the mussels in the serving-dish, reduce the cooking liquor by half, add some Kneaded Butter and a little cream, and pour this over the mussels.

Coquilles de Moules au Currie (Curried Mussels).—" Open " the mussels as for *Moules Bonne Femme*, but with the mushrooms and celery cut in large dice instead of in *julienne* strips. Add, too, a pinch of curry powder. When they are cooked, remove them from their shells. Reduce the cooking liquor by three-quarters, add, off the fire, yolks of eggs and cream, and mix the mussels with this sauce. Garnish scallop shells with it, sprinkle with coarse browned breadcrumbs, and brown in the oven.

Moules à la Dinardaise.—" Open " the mussels, and remove one shell. Arrange them in a shallow fireproof dish, and cover them with a creamy Gratin Sauce rather highly seasoned and with chopped chives added to it. Brown at the last moment.

Moules frites (Fried Mussels).—Take large mussels, poach them, shell them, and wipe them dry. Season them lightly, dip them in fritter batter, and plunge them into very hot fat. Serve on a napkin with fried parsley. Hand separately the sauce chosen.

(NOTE.—Instead of being coated with batter, the mussels may be egg-and-breadcrumbed.)

Moules à la Marinière.—(1) "Open" the mussels in the usual way (page 223), adding an ounce and a half of butter for each three-and-a-half pints of mussels. Serve as they are.

Moules à la Marinière.—(2) "Open" the mussels as above, and put them into a timbale after taking off one of the shells. Reduce the cooking liquor by half, bind it lightly with Kneaded Butter or a little Fish Velouté, and pour it over the mussels.

Moules Pêcheur.—Prepare the mussels as for *Marinière*, adding the heart of a head of celery finely chopped.

Moules en Pilaff (Pilaff of Mussels).—Bind the poached and shelled mussels with a sauce of some kind, for example Curry, Américaine, and so on. Butter a bowl or a timbale and line it with a fairly thick layer of Pilaff rice (page 21). Garnish the middle with the ragout of mussels, cover the top with rice, unmould on to a round dish, and surround the pilaff with some of the sauce used to bind the mussels.

Moules à la Poulette.—Prepare them as for *Marinière* (2), and put them in a timbale. Reduce the cooking liquor to half, bind it with Velouté, yolks of eggs and cream, and finish with a few drops of lemon juice. Pour over the mussels, and scatter over it a little roughly chopped parsley.

Moules à la Provençale.—" Open " the mussels, take off one of the shells, and put them in a dish. Sprinkle them with melted Snail Butter (*Beurre d'escargots*), sprinkle them with breadcrumbs, and brown the top in the oven.

(NOTE.—Snail Butter (*Beurre d'escargots*) is made by mixing and well kneading a pound of butter, two ounces of finely chopped shallot, two cloves of garlic crushed to a paste, a good dessertspoonful of chopped parsley, salt, pepper and mixed spice.

Moules à la Rochelaise.—"Open" some large mussels with white wine, shallot, celery, chives and mushrooms all chopped. Add butter, pepper and a touch of nutmeg. Arrange them on a dish, having removed one shell. Reduce the cooking liquor by three-quarters, bind it with fresh breadcrumbs, and pour it over the mussels. Brown lightly at the last minute.

Moules Saint-Michel.—Prepare the mussels as for *Marinière* (2) (page 225). Finish the sauce, at the last minute, with chopped parsley and chervil, and a spot of mustard.

(NOTE.—If mussels have to be kept until the next day, it is better to take them from their shells and keep them in a cool place wrapped in a napkin. The cooking liquor may be decanted, and kept in a cool place in a porcelain bowl, uncovered. It can be used for a Velouté or a Mussel Soup (*Soupe aux moules*, page 71).)

OYSTERS (*HUÎTRES*)

There is no doubt that the best way of eating oysters is *au naturel*, that is to say, raw from their shells. Nevertheless, there are certain ways of cooking them in demand. These preparations are usually served in the deep shells, which are of course well cleaned beforehand.

Huîtres à l'Américaine.—Take the oysters from their

shells and wipe them. Put in the bottom of the deep
shells a little coarsely ground pepper and a pinch of fried
breadcrumbs. Add the oysters, sprinkle them with grated
Gruyère and a little breadcrumb, put a dab of butter on
each, and brown quickly in the oven.

Anges à Cheval (Angels on Horseback).—The best
savoury in the world ; it is sometimes called *Brochettes
d'Huîtres*. Wrap the raw oysters in a thin rasher of bacon,
and skewer them in half-dozens on little skewers. Grill
them, and arrange them on pieces of toast which have
been sprinkled with fried breadcrumbs seasoned with a
little cayenne.

Bouchées aux Huîtres (Oyster Bouchées).—Poach the
oysters in their own liquor, drain them and remove their
beards. Mix them with a Béchamel Sauce to which have
been added some Anchovy Butter, the reduced liquor of the
oysters, a touch of cayenne and a binding of yolks of eggs.
Garnish small bouchées with these oysters.

Coquilles d'Huîtres au Currie (Curried Oysters).—Poach
the oysters, drain them, and remove their beards. Make
a light sauce with the liquor from the oysters and some
cream flavoured with curry powder. Put the oysters in
the scallop shells, cover them with this sauce, sprinkle with
fine browned breadcrumbs, and put in the oven for five
or six minutes before serving.

Cromesquis d'Huîtres.—Make a mixture as described below
for *Croquettes*. Divide it into pieces about the size of a
pigeon's egg, and roll them into balls. Wrap up each in
a very thin piece of unsweetened pancake, dip them in
frying-batter, and fry them in deep fat. Serve them on a
napkin with fried parsley.

Croquettes d'Huîtres.—Poach the oysters, drain them, and

cut them in dice. Mix them with a Béchamel Sauce to which you have added the reduced liquor from the oysters and bound with yolks of eggs. The final sauce should be very thick, that is to say, eight tablespoonfuls would be enough to bind half a pound of shelled oysters. Spread this mixture on a dish, and let it get cold. Divide it then into whatever sized pieces you want for your croquettes, shape them as you will, egg-and-breadcrumb them, and at the last moment fry them in very hot fat. Serve them on a napkin with fried parsley.

Huîtres en Brochettes (Oysters on Skewers).—Open the oysters, drain them, dry them, and season them. Put them on skewers and into a dish with a little butter. Stiffen them quickly in the oven, and finish them on the grill at the last moment. Serve with them either Maître-d'Hôtel Butter, or a raw Bercy Butter, that is, a Maître-d'Hôtel with lemon juice and shallots cut up very finely.

Huîtres sur Croûtons (Oyster Croûtons).—Shell some oysters and wipe them. Cook some butter in a frying-pan until it is a light brown and smells of nuts, then fry the oysters in this. Arrange them on little round croûtons of fried bread, and sprinkle them with the *beurre noisette*.

Croustades d'Huîtres Montglas.—Line some little brioche or dariole moulds with short-crust and bake them " blind." Fill them with the same garnish as that suggested for Bouchées (page 227), put on each a slice of truffle, and cover with a circle of puff-paste.

(NOTE.—The cooking of croustades " blind," or *à blanc*, is done thus. When they have been lined, you must again line the inside of the paste with greaseproof or thin kitchen paper and fill this with rice or dried peas. After the croustades have been baked, this filling is taken out, and the croustades are kept at the mouth of the oven for a few minutes to dry them.)

Huîtres à la Diable (Devilled Oysters).—Poach several dozen oysters in their own liquor, drain them, and remove their beards. With the oyster liquor and some fresh cream make a Béchamel Sauce ; season it with salt, grated nutmeg and a suspicion of paprika pepper. Mix the oysters with this sauce, and garnish the hollow shells with the mixture. Sprinkle with a little fried breadcrumbs, arrange the shells on a baking-sheet, and put them in the oven for a few minutes before serving them. Be careful not to let them boil.

Huîtres à la Florentine.—Put in the bottom of scallop shells some leaf spinach stewed in butter. Add the oysters, cover with Mornay Sauce, and sprinkle with grated cheese before browning in the oven.

Huîtres frites, ou *à l'Orly* (Fried Oysters, or Oysters à l'Orly).—Wipe some raw oysters and egg-and-breadcrumb them. Cook them in clarified butter, serve them on a napkin, and accompany them by a sauceboat of Tomato Sauce.

Huîtres frites à la Villeroy.—Poach the oysters, remove their beards, and wipe them. Dip them in a nearly cold Sauce Villeroy (page 37) so that they are thickly coated with it. Put them on a dish as you do them, and let them get cold. Then egg-and-breadcrumb them, and fry them in deep fat just before you want them. Serve on a napkin with fried parsley.

Huîtres Maréchal.—Poach the oysters, wipe them, dip them in fritter batter, and fry them in deep fat. Arrange them in threes on a slice of lemon, and surround them with a little fried parsley.

Huîtres Mornay.—Proceed exactly as for *Oysters à la Florentine,* suppressing the spinach.

Pannequets d'Huîtres (Oyster Pancakes).—Make some very thin pancakes with unsweetened batter. Spread on each a layer of the mixture for Croquettes (page 227), roll them up, cut them in lozenge-shape, and put them in the oven for a few minutes before serving.

Petits Pâtés d'Huîtres (Oyster Patties).—Roll out some puff-paste, and cut out of it with a plain or fluted cutter as many rounds as you want patties. Put these out on a baking-dish or tin, and put in the middle of each a piece of the Croquette Mixture (page 227) as big as a small nut. Wet the edges, cover with another round of paste of the same size but a little thicker, join well together, gild with egg, and bake in a hot oven for twelve minutes.

Huîtres Prunier, ou *Croustades Prunier.*—Poach some oysters and remove their beards ; cook also some mush-rooms. Mix these with a fish fumet flavoured with oysters and mixed with an equal amount of Hollandaise Sauce. Garnish the croustades with this mixture, and put a slice of truffle on top of each.

Rissoles d'Huîtres.—With a salpicon of oysters, or oysters coated with Villeroy Sauce, proceed as directed for Crab Rissoles (page 202). Egg-and-breadcrumb these rissoles, and fry them in deep fat. Serve on a napkin with fried parsley.

Soufflé aux Huîtres (Oyster Soufflé).—Poach three dozen oysters ; remove their beards, and cut them in two or three according to their size. Meanwhile make a white *roux* with three dessertspoonfuls of flour, moisten it with the liquor from the oysters and with milk, season it with salt, pepper and a touch of cayenne, bring it to the boil, and boil for a few minutes. It should have the appearance of a thick mash. Add two ounces of butter, three yolks of eggs, the oysters and six stiffly whisked whites of eggs. Butter a soufflé-dish thickly, put in the mixture, and cook in a slow oven for twenty minutes.

(NOTE.—With the same mixture you can make little soufflés in small fluted cases.)

Huîtres à la Tartare.—Take the best hollow shells, as nearly as possible of the same size, and in the bottom of each put some watercress leaves. On these put a few cold poached oysters, with their beards removed, and cover them with a Sauce Tartare seasoned with a little paprika pepper.

Variété à la Prunier—

Huître Saintongeaise.—Oyster poached in its own juice, drained and replaced in its shell, which has been well cleaned. Bercy Sauce, decorated with slice of sausage, lightly browned.

Huître Rochellaise.—Uncooked oyster, served in its shell, with a butter composed of very finely chopped parsley, shallot, onion, chervil, breadcrumbs and lemon juice. The whole is warmed very slightly before serving.

Huître Curry.—Oyster poached, placed on rice mould with a thin, light Curry Sauce.

Huître sautée Tomate.—Cover oyster with crushed cracker biscuits, and lightly fry in butter. Place a spoonful of tomato ketchup in the shell, warm, and place oyster on top.

Huître Mornay.—Poached oyster with Mornay Sauce, covered with grated cheese and lightly baked.

Huître au Poivre rose.—Poached oyster. Boston Sauce made with the cooking liquor and coloured slightly with paprika.

Huître Poulette.—Oyster poached in stock seasoned with onion and shallot. Reduce cooking liquor, add double cream and a little Hollandaise Sauce, minced parsley and minced mushroom.

PRAWNS (*CREVETTES ROSES*)

It has been stated before (under Hors-d'œuvre) that prawns and shrimps are best when boiled in sea-water. If this is impossible, the next best thing is strongly salted water to which have been added thyme, bayleaf, peppercorns and a *bouquet garni*. Bring the water to the boil, and throw in the prawns alive. Cook for two or three minutes according to their size. Let them get cold, but do not hasten their cooling by plunging them in cold water.

Crevettes en Aspic (Prawns in Aspic).—Bind with thick jellied Mayonnaise some small prawns or large ones cut in small dice. Make some little balls of this mixture, and keep them on ice until they are set. Line a border mould with white fish jelly, decorate the bottom as you like, and set the decoration with a little jelly. When it has set, add more jelly to form a thin layer. When this has set, arrange on it the prawn balls, alternating them with small black truffles, and between each a fine prawn placed upside down, so that it will be the right way up when the mould is turned out, Finish by filling up the mould with these three ingredients and the jelly. Leave it to set, and turn out when wanted.

Crevettes en Barquettes.—Garnish the barquettes with shrimps or little prawns bound with the sauce indicated by the title of the dish, for example, *Crevettes en Barquettes à l'Américaine* with *Sauce Américaine*, with *Sauce au Currie*, or *Cardinal, Hollandaise, Nantua, Normande, Soubise,*

Vénitienne, White Wine, and so on. You can add to the shrimps a salpicon of truffles and mushrooms, or you can surmount the barquettes by a slice of truffle, a fried mussel, and so on.

Croquettes de Crevettes (Prawn Coquettes).—Make a salpicon with prawns or shrimps, mushrooms, and truffles bound with the sauce chosen. Proceed as in all other Croquettes.

Pilaff de Crevettes.—The preparation of this Pilaff is always the same. It consists of an outside of Pilaff rice (page 21) with an inside of prawns or shrimps bound with some sauce or other. You prepare it by lining the bottom and sides of a buttered pudding-basin or timbale with a fairly thick layer of Pilaff rice ; the garnish is put in the middle, it is covered in with rice, and turned out on the serving-dish. It is surrounded by some of the same sauce which has been used in the garnish. Here, briefly, are a few different kinds of Pilaff :

Américaine.—Prawns bound with Sauce Américaine in an ordinary Pilaff rice.

Currie.—Prawns bound with Curry Sauce, and the rice flavoured with curry powder.

Cardinal.—Prawns bound with Cardinal Sauce, and diced truffles added to the rice.

Joinville.—Prawns bound with Sauce Joinville, and a *julienne* of mushrooms added to the rice.

Nantua.—Prawns bound with Nantua Sauce, and plain Pilaff rice.

Newburg.—Prawns bound with Newburg Sauce, ordinary Pilaff rice, and prawns stuck over the Pilaff after it has been unmoulded.

Hongroise.—Prawns bound with a White Wine Sauce

flavoured with paprika pepper, and the Pilaff rice flavoured also with paprika.

Orientale.—Prawns bound with White Wine Sauce flavoured with saffron, and dice of tomatoes added to the Pilaff rice.

Valenciennes.—Prawns bound with Creamy Sauce Américaine, and dice of sweet red peppers added to the Pilaff rice.

SCALLOP—ESCALLOP

(*COQUILLES SAINT-JACQUES*)

The Scallop, which was worn by pilgrims to the shrine of Saint James of Compostella, owes its French name, *Coquille Saint-Jacques*, to the following legend :

" When the body of Saint James was being miraculously conveyed in a ship without sails, or oars, from Joppa to Galicia, it passed the village of Bonzas, on the coast of Portugal, on the day that a marriage had been celebrated there. The bridegroom with his friends were amusing themselves on horseback on the sands, when his horse became unmanageable, and plunged into the sea ; whereupon the miraculous ship stopped in its voyage, and presently the bridegroom emerged, horse and man, close beside it. A conversation ensued between the knight and the saint's disciples on board, in which they apprised him that it was the saint who saved him from a watery grave, and explained the Christian religion to him. He believed and was baptized there and then, and immediately the ship resumed its voyage, and the knight came galloping back over the sea to rejoin his astonished friends. He told them all what had happened, and they too were converted, and the knight baptized his bride with his own hand. Now, when the knight emerged from the sea, both his dress and the trappings of his horse were covered with scallop shells ; and therefore the Galicians took the scallop shell as the sign of St. James."

These are the simpler fashions of preparing this delicious shellfish. It must be remembered that in the first place the scallops should be (1) placed on the top of a stove to make them open ; when the top shell rises slightly, take it off with the help of a knife. (2) Slip under the scallop the end of a palette knife, so as to remove it from the shell with the coral and the beard. (3) Wash and brush the hollow scallop shell, as it will be used not only for serving the scallops themselves, but for other purposes afterwards.

In fairness to English fishmongers, it must be stated that these operations will be performed for you without the asking. This reminds me of a dictum I saw recently, and a very true one : " In a fishmonger's shop more is done, after the purchase is made, to save the customer trouble than is done in any other food shop."

Coquille Saint-Jacques à l'Américaine.—Stew the scallops lightly in butter, pour over a glass of brandy, and set it alight. Moisten with the cooking liquor of *Homard à l'Américaine* (page 209), cook for ten minutes, and take out the scallops. Thicken the cooking liquor with butter, and put the scallops back. Serve separately some Rice *à l'Indienne* (page 21).

Coquille Saint-James à l'Armoricaine.—Lightly fry the scallops with a fine *Mirepoix Bordelaise* (page 17), moisten with white wine, add roughly chopped tomatoes, a *bouquet garni*, the usual seasoning, and cook for ten minutes. Remove the scallops, strain the cooking liquor and reduce it by half, add a little cream, and finish it with chopped chervil and tarragon.

Coquille Saint-Jacques à la Bordelaise.—Fry lightly in butter a *Mirepoix Bordelaise* (page 17). Add the white and the red parts of the scallops, put on the lid and let them stew very gently, then pour in a glass of brandy, and set it alight. Moisten with white wine, add some roughly chopped tomatoes, and cook for ten minutes. Remove the scallops, reduce the cooking liquor, thicken it with butter, and correct the seasoning.

(Note.—The process translated above as " stewing gently " is in the original French *faire suer*, or in plain English, " let them sweat," which is what they really should do. The phrase is really untranslatable, but the process will be familiar to all cooks who constantly use it in the preliminaries to braising.)

Coquilles Saint-Jacques à la Bretonne.—Fry lightly in butter the white and red part of the scallops cut in dice, with chopped onion and shallot. Moisten lightly with white wine, add a little chopped parsley and some bread-crumbs, and boil for seven or eight minutes. By then the mixture should have the appearance of a light sauce. Remove the pan from the fire, butter the mixture slightly, and put it into the scallop shells. Sprinkle with coarsely grated browned breadcrumbs, then with melted butter, and brown quickly.

Coquilles Saint-Jacques en Brochettes (Scallops on Skewers). —Poach some scallops and cut the white part in rounds. Wrap each of these in a very thin piece of bacon rasher, and stick them on skewers alternately with the red part egg-and-breadcrumbed. Grill them slowly, and serve with the sauce chosen, handed separately.

Coquilles Saint-Jacques au Currie (Curried Scallops).—Stew the scallops gently (*faire suer*: see page 236) with chopped onion in butter ; moisten with white wine, add a *bouquet garni*, a pinch of curry powder, and cook for a few minutes. Take out the scallops, reduce the cooking liquor, strain it, and add a little cream. Rice *à l'Indienne* (page 21) should be handed with this.

Coquilles Saint-Jacques au Gratin.—Cook the scallops with white wine and Duxelles (see page 13). Reduce the cooking liquor, and add it to a Gratin Sauce (page 33). Put some of the sauce in the bottom of the shells, lay the scallops on it, cover with more sauce, sprinkle with browned bread-crumbs, and brown in the oven.

Coquilles Saint-Jacques frites (Fried Scallops).—Cut the white part of the scallops, raw, in rounds. Season them, egg-and-breadcrumb them, and fry them in clarified butter. The red parts, whole, should be treated in the same way. Hand a Tomato Sauce.

Coquilles Saint-Jacques Marinière.—Using both the red and the white parts, proceed exactly as for *Moules Marinière* (2) (page 225).

Coquilles Saint-Jacques à la Meunière.—Cut up the white parts in fairly thick slices, season them with salt and pepper, dip them in milk and then in flour, and fry them in clarified butter. Arrange on a dish, sprinkle them with nut-brown butter (*beurre noisette*), and scatter a little chopped parsley over them.

Coquilles Saint-Jacques Mornay.—Cut the white part in rounds, season them, and poach them and the red parts with white wine. Cover the bottom of the scallop shells with Mornay Sauce (page 34), and lay on it the well-drained pieces of scallop. Cover with more sauce, sprinkle with grated cheese, and brown lightly.

Coquilles Saint-Jacques à la Nantaise.—Cut the white part in rounds, and poach them with the red part with a little white wine. Arrange them on the serving-dish, surround them with slices of cooked mushrooms, cover them with a fine *Vin blanc* Sauce (page 37), and brown lightly.

Coquilles Saint-Jacques Newburg.—Toss the white and the red parts in butter, add enough Sherry to cover them, and cook for ten minutes. Arrange them in a timbale, and add a few spoonfuls of cream. Reduce the sauce and bind it with a little Béchamel Sauce, finish with Lobster Butter, and pour over the scallops in the timbale.

Coquilles Saint-Jacques à la Poulette.—Poach the scallops, white and red parts, with mushroom cooking liquor (page 20) and white wine. Drain them. Reduce the cooking liquor and add the necessary amount of Fish Velouté. Bind with yolks of egg and cream, butter lightly, and add a few drops of lemon juice. Mix the scallops with this sauce, and serve them in a timbale sprinkled with chopped parsley.

Coquilles Saint-Jacques Prunier.—Poach the white and red parts with white wine and a *bouquet garni*. Reduce the cooking liquor, add the proper amount of Fish Velouté, bind with egg-yolks, and thicken with butter. Cover the bottoms of the shells with some of this sauce, add the white parts cut in slices and the red parts minced up with some cooked mushrooms, cover with more sauce, and brown lightly.

Coquilles Saint-Jacques Provençale.—Fry the white part of the scallops in butter and olive-oil. Slice up a few *cèpes*, or mushrooms, season them, and add them with shallots and garlic. Add also some breadcrumbs and chopped parsley. Serve very hot.

SHRIMPS (*CREVETTES GRISES*)
See PRAWNS (page 232)

Chapter IX

Turtle—Frogs—Snails

I⊤ is unlikely that most of us will ever have to deal with a turtle, or even to cook frogs or snails. But in case we do, here are the ways to prepare them. Frogs' legs are delicious fare, something like very tiny chicken, and we shall help to remove a long-standing and popular reproach that the French eat nothing but frogs, if we come to like them ourselves ! As for snails, they have to be eaten to be believed, and to those who like them they are as ambrosia.

TURTLE (*TORTUE*)

It is not very likely that private houses or indeed many establishments will ever want, or be in a position, to make turtle soup, but for the curious, here are details of the way to make it. They are taken, with acknowledgments, from Escoffier's *Guide to Modern Cookery*.

Potage de Tortue clair (Turtle Soup)—

The Slaughtering of the Turtle.—For soup, take a turtle weighing from 120 to 180 pounds, and let it be very fleshy and full of life. To slaughter it, lay it on its back on a table, with its head hanging over the side. By means of a double butcher's hook, one spike of which is thrust into the turtle's lower jaw, while the other suspends an adequately heavy weight, make the animal hold its head back ; then, with all possible despatch, sever the head from the body. Now immediately hang the body over a receptacle that the blood may be collected, and leave it thus for one and a half to two hours.

Then follows the dismemberment. To begin with, thrust a strong knife between the carapace or upper shell and the plastron or lower shell, exactly where the two meet, and separate the one from the other. The turtle being on its back, cut all the adhering flesh from the plastron and put the latter aside. Now cut off the flippers ; remove the intestines, which throw away, and carefully collect all the green fat. Whereupon cut away the flesh adhering to the carapace ; once more remove all fat, and keep both in reserve.

The Treatment of the Carapace, the Plastron and the Flippers.—The carapace and the plastron, which are the outside bony framework of the turtle, constitute the only portions wherefrom the gelatinous flesh, used as the garnish of the soup, are obtained. Saw the carapace into six or eight pieces, and the plastron into four. Put these pieces with the flippers into boiling water or into steam, to blanch. Withdraw the flippers as soon as they are sufficiently stiff for their skin to be removed, and leave the pieces of carapace and plastron to blanch for five minutes, in order that they may admit of being scraped. Now cool the pieces of carapace and plastron and the flippers, and put them into a stewpan containing enough water to abundantly cover them. Set to boil, garnish with vegetables, as in the case of an ordinary broth, and add a small quantity of turtle herbs (see below). Five or six hours should be allowed for the cooking of the carapace and plastron, but the flippers, which are put to further uses in other culinary preparations, should be withdrawn at the end of five hours. When the pieces are taken from the cooking liquor, remove

all the flesh from the bones, and cool the former ; then trim
it carefully, and cut it into little squares of one and a half
inches wide.   It is these squares, together with the green
fat, poached in salted water and sliced, which constitute
the garnish of the soup.

The Preparation of Turtle Soup.—There are two modes
of procedure, though their respective results are almost
identical.

(1) Make a broth of the flesh of the turtle alone, and then
add a very gelatinous beef consommé to it, in pursuance
of the method employed when the turtle soup is bought
ready-made.   This procedure is practically the best, more
particularly if the soup has to be kept some time.

(2) Make an ordinary broth of shin of beef, using the
same quantity of the latter as of turtle.   Also include half
a calf's foot, and one half-pound of calf's shin per three
pounds of the beef.   Add the flesh of the turtle, or, in the
event of its being thought necessary to clarify—which
operation I do not in the least advise—reserve it for that
purpose.   The condiments and aromatics being the same
for both methods, I shall now describe the procedure for
Method No. 1.

The Ingredients of the Soup.—Put into a stewpan of convenient size the flesh of the turtle, and its head and bones.
Moisten partly with the cooking liquor of the carapace,
and complete the moistening, in the case of a turtle
weighing 120 pounds, with enough water to bring the
whole to 50 quarts.   By this means a soup of about thirty
to thirty-five quarts will be obtained at the end of the
operation.   Add salt in the proportion of one ounce to
every five quarts, set to boil, skim, and garnish with twelve
carrots, a bunch of leeks (about ten bound with a head

of celery), one pound of parsley stalks, eight onions with ten cloves stuck into them, two pounds of shallots, and one head of garlic. Set to boil gently for eight hours. An hour before straining the soup, add to the garnish four strips of lemon-peel, a bunch of herbs for turtle, comprising sweet basil, sweet marjoram, sage, rosemary, savory and thyme, and a bag containing four ounces of coriander and two ounces of peppercorns. Finally, strain the soup through a napkin, add the pieces of flesh from the carapace and plastron which were put aside for the garnish, and keep it until wanted in specially made sandstone jars.

The Serving of the Soup.—When about to serve this soup, heat it, test and rectify its seasoning, and finish it off by means of a Port wine-glass of very old Madeira for every quart. Very often a milk punch is served with turtle soup, the recipe being :

Milk Punch.—Prepare a syrup from half a pint of water and three and a half ounces of sugar, the consistence being 17 (Baumé's Hydrometer). Set to infuse in this syrup two orange and two lemon *zests* (that is, the coloured part only of the peel). Strain at the end of ten minutes, and add half a pint of rum, a fifth of a pint of Kirsch, two-thirds of a pint of milk, and the juice of three oranges and three lemons. Mix thoroughly. Let it stand for three hours ; filter and serve cold.

Potage Tortue lié (Thick Turtle Soup).—This soup is the same as that described above, save that it is thickened either with three ounces of golden *roux* (*roux blond*) or with an ounce of arrowroot mixed with a little cold consommé for every quart of the soup.

Potage à la Tortue avec de Conserve (Preserved Turtle

Soup).—When this is of a good brand, it only needs double its quantity of very strong consommé to make the soup. Seasoning should be corrected, and the final touch of old Madeira added in the proportion and manner given above.

Potage à la Tortue sèche (Dried Turtle Soup).—For the preparation of this soup, the dried turtle must be soaked in cold water for at least twenty-four hours. It is cooked in the same way as the carapace and plastron described above. Once cooked, it is treated in exactly the same manner as fresh turtle. The cooking liquor serves to moisten the meat with which the special consommé is made, very rich and gelatinous, and to which is added, at the last minute, the flesh cut in dice and the old Madeira.

Potage à la Tortue verte de Conserve (Green Turtle Soup).— Put in a little stewpan a very small chicken, first lightly coloured in the oven, half a pound of knuckle of veal cut in rounds, a small onion stuck with half a clove, half a parsley root, half an ounce of mushroom peelings, and a bouquet composed of a leek, a small stick of celery, a small piece of thyme and bayleaf, a touch of mace, and a little basil and marjoram. Moisten with two quarts of ordinary consommé, bring to the boil, and cook gently for two hours. Then strain it through a cloth, add to it half an ounce of arrowroot or potato flour mixed with a little cold consommé, mix quickly with the whisk, season with as much salt as you need, and let it boil gently, skimming it, for a quarter of an hour. Warm in the *bain-marie* enough green turtle to make a pint and three-quarters, drain the pieces, cut them into squares with inch sides, and add them to the soup. Finally season this with a touch of cayenne, and finish it, at the last minute, with a touch of Worcestershire Sauce and four tablespoonfuls of Sherry.

TERRAPIN (*TORTUE TERRAPINE*)

Here, again, is an animal which the ordinary housewife is unlikely to see alive. But this, nevertheless, is how they are served in America.

To Cook the Terrapin.—Plunge the terrapins into boiling water, let them cook for fifty minutes, then plunge them into cold water. Put them now on their backs, remove the intestines, heart and lungs, and skin the legs, removing the claws. Cut up the flesh in pieces, season it with salt and pepper, put it into a stewpan with just enough water to cover the pieces, and let them cook gently for an hour. Then turn them out, and keep them in a cool place until wanted.

Terrapine Club.—Two cooked terrapines, two tablespoonfuls of butter, a cup of cream, a teaspoonful of salt, three yolks of eggs, and a glass of Sherry. Toss the prepared terrapins in the butter, having first drained them well. Add the cream, let it boil and reduce a little, then add, stirring, the beaten egg-yolks, and lastly the Sherry.

Terrapine Maryland.—Two cooked terrapins, two tablespoonfuls of Madeira, half a teaspoonful of salt, one tablespoonful of butter, a cup of cream, two truffles, two egg-yolks, a touch of cayenne. Toss the well-drained terrapin flesh in the butter, and add salt, cayenne, truffles and Madeira. Mix the cream with the beaten yolks of eggs, mix it gently with the other ingredients in the pan, and heat up without allowing to come to the boil.

SNAILS (*ESCARGOTS*)

(Snails are in season from November to March)

Escargots dite de Bourgogne.—Brush the snails in several waters, and remove the chalky partition which closes them. Put them to scour, on the day before they are wanted, in a little water salted with two handfuls of coarse salt for every hundred snails. The next day wash them well again in plenty of water to remove the slime, put them into a stewpan, cover them with plenty of water, and boil them for eight minutes. Drain them, plunge them into cold water, and put them back into the pan with white wine, salt, pepper, a large *bouquet garni*, an onion stuck with four cloves, a head of garlic and a glass of old brandy. Cook gently for three to three and a half hours, according to the size of the snails. Let them get cold in the cooking liquor. Then drain them, take them out of their shells, and remove from each the black end. Put them back in their shells, which you will meanwhile have washed, drained and dried, and finish by filling up the shells with Snail Butter (*Beurre d'Escargots*), which you will find on page 226. To serve them, arrange them on a baking-dish, and put them in the oven for a few minutes before they are wanted. Serve very hot.

(NOTE.—Recognising the difficulties which snail-lovers may encounter in the initial preparation of their favourites, Prunier's can supply them ready-stuffed in their shells. They have then only to be heated up before serving.)

Escargots Petits Gris au vin rouge.—Scour and blanch the snails as described above. When they have been plunged into cold water, take them out of the shells, wash them in several waters, and drain them well. Meanwhile put into an earthenware pan some dice of blanched streaky bacon or pickled pork, button onions, crushed garlic and good red wine in proportion to the number of snails. Then add the snails themselves, salt, pepper and a *bouquet garni*. Bring to the boil, cover and cook in the oven, very slowly, for two hours. When they are cooked and quite tender, finish with a light Kneaded Butter and a liqueur-glassful of old brandy (*Marc*). Serve in the dish they were cooked in, and very hot.

FROGS (*GRENOUILLES*)

Grenouilles à la Bordelaise.—Fry the frogs' legs *à la meunière* (page 5), with chopped shallots and breadcrumbs. Add roughly chopped parsley, and serve.

Grenouilles à l'Espagnole.—Season the frogs' legs with salt, pepper and a touch of mixed spice. Sprinkle them with brandy, and let them marinate for two hours. Then wipe them, and fry them in a little butter, in the frying-pan, until they are golden. At the moment, add thin slices of mushrooms and fresh sweet peppers, chopped parsley and lemon juice.

Grenouilles aux Fines Herbes.—Fry the frogs' legs *à la meunière*, and finish with *fines herbes* (parsley, chervil, chives and tarragon).

Grenouilles frites.—Season the frogs' legs, and let them marinate for an hour with the juice of a lemon, olive-oil, a touch of garlic and chopped parsley. Then dip them in frying-batter, and fry them in deep fat. Serve them on a napkin with fried parsley.

Grenouilles frites, Sauce Américaine.—Egg-and-breadcrumb

the frogs' legs, and fry them in deep oil. Hand a *Sauce Américaine* (page 30) with them.

Grenouilles Parmentier.—Season the frogs' legs, roll them in flour, and fry them in very hot butter. Add to them some little potato dice that have been fried in butter, and toss them together to mix them well. Serve in a timable, sprinkled with chopped parsley.

Pompadour de Nymphes (ou Grenouilles).

(The Editor is not sure whether it was Escoffier, or some-one else, who, in order not to offend the susceptibilities of his *clientèle*, first called frogs *nymphes*. From the evidence of the almost lyrical " Nymphes à l'Aurore," which appears in his *Modern Cookery*, Escoffier is strongly under suspicion!)

(1) Cook the frogs' legs in a light *blanc* (see below), with a *bouquet garni* and lemon. Twenty-five minutes should see them done. Drain them, bone them, and keep the best parts of the meat for the garnish. Add to the rest of the frogs' flesh an equal amount of sole or pike, and make of this a forcemeat in the usual manner (page 14), adding, for each pound of flesh, the same amount of panada (page 17), four ounces of butter, four yolks of eggs and one whole egg, and a seasoning of salt and pepper. At the last, add four dessertspoonfuls of tomato purée, and pass the whole thing through a tammy. With part of this forcemeat make a few small quenelles in the shape of olives, poach them in salted water, plunge them when cooked into cold water, and keep them by.

(2) Make a Velouté with the cooking liquor of the frogs, and prepare a garnish with minced mushrooms, shelled shrimps, the quenelles, the pieces of frogs' flesh already reserved for the purpose, and some slices of truffle. Bind this garnish with part of the Velouté.

(3) Butter a charlotte mould, decorate it with rounds of truffle, and then line the bottom and sides with a layer of the forcemeat about half an inch thick. Fill up the middle with the garnish, cover the top with more forcemeat, and poach the mould in a *bain-marie* for about forty minutes. When it is cooked, take the *Pompadour* from the *bain-marie*, and let it stand for six or seven minutes before you unmould it. At the time of serving unmould it, and surround it with the rest of the Velouté to which you will have added a little truffle juice, mushroom cooking liquor, and cream. Serve very hot.

(NOTE.—An ordinary *blanc*, which is used a great deal in French cookery for boiling white vegetables, is made as follows : put a heaped tablespoonful of flour in a little water, and when it is mixed quite smooth, add to it two quarts of water with two tablespoonfuls of vinegar and a little salt ; stir until it boils, then add whatever has to be cooked in it—in this instance, a *bouquet garni* and the frogs' legs, substituting lemon for vinegar—and finally three table-spoonfuls of clarified veal or beef dripping. This last forms a covering to keep out the air, and the food will cook quite gently underneath and preserve its whiteness and a better flavour.)

Grenouilles à la Poulette.—Poach the frogs' legs with mush-room cooking liquor and white wine : drain them, and mix them with a Poulette Sauce (page 35) to which you have added some cooked button mushrooms. Add the reduced cooking liquor of the frogs to the sauce. Serve in a timbale, sprinkled with chopped parsley.

Grenouilles à la Provençale.—Fry the frogs' legs *à la meunière* (see page 5), with a tiny bit of garlic.

Rizotto de Grenouilles à l'Indienne.—Prepare a Rizotto

(page 21), and mould it in a border mould. Stew the frogs'
legs in butter, sprinkle them with a pinch of curry powder,
moisten with cream, and finish cooking them. Drain the
legs, and after having removed the bones, mix them with
the reduced cooking liquor. Serve them in the rizotto
border.

Grenouilles à la Saintongeaise.—Egg-and-breadcrumb the
frogs' legs, and fry them in clarified butter. On serving,
sprinkle them with a nut-brown butter (*beurre noisette*) with
chopped shallot added to it.

Grenouilles à la Vendéenne.—For four or five people you
will want fifty frogs' legs. Beat up two whole eggs as if
for an omelette, with salt, pepper and grated nutmeg, and
mix in two dessertspoonfuls of cream. Dip the legs in this
mixture, then in fine fresh breadcrumbs. Fry them in very
hot oil so that they are nice and crisp. Serve separately a
light Tomato Sauce rather strongly flavoured with lemon.

Chapter X

Some Prunier Specialities

WHILE this is, strictly speaking, a Fish Book, it has been thought advisable to include in it a few recipes of dishes other than fish which are specialities of Prunier's in London. These are given because guests so often ask for the recipe that it is felt there is some special merit in them for English people. They are all grouped together, therefore, in this chapter.

Omelettes with Fish.—Three eggs, half a pinch of salt, very little pepper, and half an ounce of butter. Break the eggs, season them and beat them very slightly. Put the butter in a very clean frying-pan when it is hot, pour in the eggs, and stir briskly until there is a slight thickening. Now let the eggs spread over the bottom of the pan, and remove the pan from the centre of the fire. Put the garnish in the middle of the omelette, and start rolling the omelette over, beginning with the side nearest to the handle of the pan, tilting the pan as you do so. Omelettes may be garnished with shrimps or prawns, mussels, sea-urchins, the flesh of crab, lobster, Dublin Bay prawns (*langoustines*), smoked haddock, caviar, etc. When using prawns (*langoustines*), mussels, lobsters, etc., toss the meat first in butter, and add two spoonfuls of cream for each person.

Tournedos Boston.—Poach six flat oysters for each tournedos. Reduce their poaching liquor, and add to it half a dessertspoonful of Béchamel Sauce and two of Hollandaise

Sauce. Grill the tournedos, garnish it with the oysters, and coat it thickly with the sauce.

Tournedos grillé, beurre anchois (Grilled Tournedos with Anchovy Butter).—Grill the tournedos carefully, and serve it with a butter made with one ounce of salted anchovy fillets, washed and skinned, an ounce and a half of butter and a pinch of pepper. Pass the butter through a fine sieve. When finished, it should be like creamed butter.

Pieds de Mouton à la Poulette (Sheeps' Trotters with Poulette Sauce).—Make a *blanc*, with two quarts of cold water, two dessertspoonfuls of flour, half an ounce of salt, a large onion stuck with a clove, three dessertspoonfuls of vinegar, and a bouquet of parsley, chervil, thyme and bay-leaf. When the *blanc* is boiling and the sheeps' trotters are ready to go in, add two ounces of finely minced beef kidney suet. Singe the trotters with spirit or on a gas flame, then remove the bone either by disjointing it or by cutting through the skin on the inside of the trotter, and take out a small woolly bit between the two bones. Then scald the trotters again for eight or ten minutes. Put them into the boiling *blanc*, and cook them very gently for about an hour and a half, according to the age of the sheep.

Make a *Poulette Sauce* as follows : melt an ounce of butter, add an ounce of flour, brown it lightly, and moisten with a pint of white stock and three tablespoonfuls of mushroom cooking liquor (page 20). Season with a pinch of white pepper and a pinch of nutmeg, bring to the boil, stirring all the time, then add an ounce of mushroom parings and a small bunch of parsley, and cook gently for twenty-five minutes. Then strain into a saucepan, stir on a brisk fire for a few minutes, add three egg-yolks to thicken it, and finish with two ounces of butter and the juice of half a lemon. A few minutes before serving add to the sauce a dozen small cooked mushrooms and twelve trotters (two for each person). Dress in a timbale or deep dish, and sprinkle with chopped parsley.

Pots de Crème au Chocolat (Chocolate Creams).—Dissolve seventeen ounces of Chocolate in a pint and three-quarters of milk, bring to the boil, and add three and a half ounces of sugar. Let it cool, and add nine yolks of eggs, but do not work the mixture too much. Put the little pots in a dish containing water, and cover them. Put into a gentle oven, and let them cook slowly. Take them out when the cream is not quite firm and still shakes a little, and leave them to cool in the dish.

Mousse au Kirsch.—Mix half a pound of castor sugar with eight yolks of eggs. Heat up a pint of milk with vanilla, and pour in the eggs. Bring almost to the boil, but not quite, or it will spoil. Allow it to cool, stirring frequently, and when it is cold add a pint of double cream. Put the mixture into a freezer, and mix thoroughly. Allow to freeze for about two hours. When it is a good creamy consistence, add a large wine-glassful of Kirsch, and stir again until thoroughly mixed. Serve in deep glasses.

Mousse au Chocolat.—Make a pound of *ganache* by melting a pound of chocolate in a little milk on a slow fire and leaving it to cool. Make also a *pâte à bombe* with a pint and a half of syrup at 30° and eight yolks of eggs. Add the *pâte à bombe* to the *ganache*, and place the container in a *bain-marie*. Whip in half a pound of cream until sufficiently thick, taking care not to let it boil. Take the container out of the *bain-marie*, and let the contents finish thickening off the fire. When quite cold, put in the ice-box.

Crêpes à l'Orange (Orange Pancakes).—Make some batter

as for ordinary pancakes, and cook some. Place in the centre of each pancake the following mixture : grate the rind of an orange, and add this to caramel with a little Curaçao.

M. MICHEL BOUZY'S MENUS
FOR HOLY WEEK

DÉJEUNER (six persons)

Petits Bouchées aux Crevettes
Sole grillée Béarnaise
(Pomme de Terre en Robe)
Pâté de Saumon aux Pistaches
Nouilles fraîches à la Crème
Poires au Rubis

DÉJEUNER (eighteen persons)

Les Huîtres de Belon sur Toast
La Barbue saumonée braisée
(garnie de barquettes d'épinards à la Crème)
Les Homards à la Nage
Pommes de Terre Croquettes
Les Abricots au Riz

DÉJEUNER (twelve persons)

Crevettes—Palourdes—Oursins
Les Merlans au Gratin
Le Homard rôti
Le Bar en Gelée
Les Beignets de Reinettes

DÉJEUNER (sixteen persons)

Les Crevettes Bouquet
Les Moules frites
Le Saumon au Fumet
La Brandade de Morue
Le Haddock au Beurre fondu
Le Rizotto de Clams
Les Poires Figaro

DÎNER (twelve persons)

La Bouillabaisse
Le Turbotin aux Champignons
Le Pilaff de Crabe sauce Currie
Les Écrevisses en Buisson
Les Crêpes au sucre

DÎNER (fifteen persons)

Soupe aux Moules
Les Filets de Sole Carême
Fricandeau d'Esturgeon
(garni de Jardinière)
Le Pâté d'Anguille
Les Céleris at Fonds d'Artichauts
au Velouté
L'Ananas Chantilly

Chapter XI

A Note on Wine and Fish

IF one were to be asked offhand what wines should be drunk with fish, I suppose the answer would be this :

With Caviar	Nothing, or perhaps Vodka.
With Oysters	Chablis, or a good White Burgundy, such as Pouilly, Meursault, etc., or Champagne.
With Fish Soups	A young Hock or Moselle, or a dryish White Burgundy, the choice depending on whether a white or red wine is to follow.
With Turtle Soup	Punch (see page 242). An authority has rightly remarked that Madeira is better *in* the soup than with it.
With Lobsters and other *Crustacés*	Chablis or White Burgundy, or if you are not following with a fine red wine, Champagne.
With Fish in general	White French or German wines, dry or dryish. Some like Sauternes if nothing dryer is to follow.

This list needs some qualifications. Let us begin at the beginning. Caviar speaks for itself. Its strong flavour naturally precludes any wine, which would be killed at once. If anything must be drunk (and this would not be at a serious

meal), the Russian vodka is the only possible thing. With
oysters, a real Chablis is the one and only wine, I think.
Champagne *mousseux* is lost on them, but there is much to be
said for a glass of the still Champagne, which has been
coming into fashion again, with a dozen oysters, and if they
are to be a meal in themselves a word must be said for
stout! Some of the less dry French wines, like Anjou, are
quite good with them too. The advice given above for
fish soups is a sound one, I think, for the days of a universal
glass of Sherry with the soup should be a little *vieux jeu*
nowadays, when our palates are so much more sophisti-
cated. In the same way, lobster and the other *crustacés*
should be treated in much the same way as the *bisques* of
which they are composed, but everyone will agree that if
the lobster is the *clou* of a meal such as an after-the-theatre
supper, nothing could be better than Champagne, and
plenty of it!

We now come to the whole question of drinking wine
with the ordinary fish. In the first place, it is safe to say
that it should always be white. There are a few cases where
red wine may be drunk with fish, but only when the fish
has been cooked in that wine. Red mullet lends itself particularly to red wine, and so to a certain extent does salmon.
In Escoffier's *Guide to Modern Cookery* there will be found a
section on *Soles aux Grands Vins*, where recipes are given
for poaching soles in *Volnay*, *Pommard*, *Romanée*, *Clos-de-
Vougeot*, and so on. But I do not think that these dishes,
or the drinking of red wine with them, will appeal to us
now. When we think of white wine with fish, we think
according to our palates. Fifty or sixty years ago it used
to be popular to drink Sauternes with fish, and there is an
apocryphal story about King Edward VII which is difficult

for us moderns to believe. A certain chef had prepared a
wonderful fish dish for the King, and after the dinner was
over was found to be in an ecstasy of delight. " But," they
said, " the King never said anything about your dish at all ! "
" Didn't you hear ? " asked the chef. " He said that his
Château Yquem had never tasted so delicious. Was not
that a tribute to my dish ? " But then I have never been
able to forgive King Edward for his liking salmon with
curry ! But this is told simply to show that not only a
sweet wine like a Sauterne was drunk with this course, but
even a liqueur-like wine of the type of Château Yquem,
which nowadays no one would dream of drinking before
the sweet.

So when I read here and there that the white wine accompanying fish should always be dry, I sometimes have my
doubts. In the usual way I have what is called a dry palate,
that is, I am inclined to prefer the dryer sorts of wine, but
in the case of fish I find that just a little sweetness is desirable
or the wine may taste a little acid. But as I have said, this
is a matter of taste, and the best way to discover your own
palate is to try it out, preferably at Prunier's !

André Simon, in his *Art of Good Living*, makes the point
that at an informal luncheon it would be as well to serve a
light wine, Graves or Anjou, with a simple dish, whereas
if our meal is more elaborate we can go to the extent of
a good Moselle or a Chablis, and for an even great occasion Champagne or a high-class Hock or White Burgundy,
and there is of course sound common sense in this. If we
suit our wines to our meals, we also suit our meals to our
purses, and this is a wise way of doing it. There are a great
many cheaper and very delicious French wines now to be
found in the English market, and most of these can be

tried at Prunier's. I have already mentioned still Champagne (*Champagne nature*) ; there are also Anjou, Vouvray, Sancerre, and others, which are not only excellent in themselves, but offer an original thought for the hostess planning a luncheon at home and wishing to give a wine which is a little out of the ordinary and impressive as well.

And I must just add a note here, that when I was writing of red wines I had quite forgotten a delicious bottle of *vin rosé* from Anjou which I drank not long ago with a trout cooked a little elaborately *à la meunière*. It was admirable ! But then you cannot call *vin rosé* red wine, nor the divine trout an ordinary fish !

Chapter XII

A Short Glossary of Names and Terms used in Cooking

THIS short glossary has been prepared for the use of those whose knowledge of culinary French is limited.

Ail	Garlic.
Aïoli	A kind of garlicky Mayonnaise popular in the south of France.
Alose	Shad.
Anchois	Anchovy.
Anguille	Eel.
Anguille de mer	Conger.
Attereaux	Skewers.
Bain-marie	A large receptacle containing hot water in which various food can be poached, sauces kept hot, etc.
Bar	Bass.
Barbeau	Barbel.
Barbillon	Small barbel.
Barbue	Brill.
Barquette	A boat-shaped pastry case.
Baudroie	Monk, or angler fish : rockfish.
Beignet	Fritter.
Beurre	Butter.
Bigorneau	Winkle.
Bisque	A rich creamy soup, e.g. *Bisque de Homard.*
Blanc	A special preparation for boiling white meat or vegetables.
Blanchaille	Whitebait.

Blanchailles, en	Fish cut in strips the size of whitebait.
Bleu, au	Fish cooked in a special manner with vinegar and water, so that it is bright blue when done.
Bouchée	A small puff-pastry case.
Bouillabaisse	A savoury stew of fish.
Bouillon	Stock.
Bouquet	Prawns.
Bouquet garni	A bunch of herbs used for flavouring, usually consisting of parsley stalks, thyme and bayleaf.
Brandade	A special dish made with salt cod.
Brochet	Pike.
Brocheton	Small pike, Jack.
Brochette, en	On skewers.
Cabillaud	Cod, fresh.
Cadgéry	Kedgeree.
Canapé	A slice of fried or toasted bread for holding savouries.
Câpres	Capers.
Carpe	Carp.
Carpillon	Small carp.
Carolines	Little savoury éclairs.
Carrelet	Flounder.
Chowder	An American fish soup.
Ciseler	To score before cooking.
Colin	Saithe, coalfish, rockfish.
Congre	Conger eel.
Coquille, en	In a scallop shell.
Coquilles Saint-Jacques	Scallops.

Côtelette	Cutlet.
Coulibiac	A rich Russian pasty made with salmon.
Court-bouillon	A mixture of water, herbs, vegetables and either wine or vinegar used for cooking fish.
Crabe	Crab.
Crêpe	Pancake.
Cresson	Watercress.
Crevettes grises	Shrimps.
Crevettes roses	Prawns.
Cromesquis	A kind of fritter.
Croquettes	A mixture of fish shaped like a cork, rolled in egg-and-breadcrumbs, and fried.
Croûtes	Bread shaped and fried, for containing some garnish or other.
Croûtons	Small dice of fried bread.
Darne	A slice cut across the fish, steak or cutlet of fish.
Daurade	Sea-bream.
Diablé	Devilled.
Duchesses	Little savoury cream buns stuffed with various fillings.
Écrevisse	Crayfish (fresh-water).
Églefin	Haddock.
Églefin fumé	Smoked haddock.
Éperlan	Smelt.
Equille	Sand-eel.
Escabèche	A kind of " souse " for smelts and other fish.
Escalope	A thin slice.
Escargot	Snail.

Espadon	Sword-fish.
Esturgeon	Sturgeon.
Farci, farcie	Stuffed.
Fines herbes	Parsley, chives, chervil and tarragon finely chopped and mixed in equal parts.
Flétan	Halibut.
Four, au	Baked (*lit.* in the oven).
Frit, frite	Fried.
Fritot, en	Fried in batter.
Fruits de mer	Any small shellfish with the exception of oysters.
Fumet	A highly concentrated stock.
Gelée	Jelly.
Glace	Ice.
Glace (de viande, de poisson)	Glaze, meat or fish.
Glacé, glacée	(1) Iced.
	(2) Glazed, with glaze.
	(3) Quickly browned in the oven.
Gratin, au *Gratiné, gratinée*	Generally sprinkled with breadcrumbs and butter, and sometimes cheese, and browned in the oven. But see pages 9-11.
Goujon	Gudgeon.
Goujons, en	Fish cut to the size of gudgeon before cooking.
Grenouilles	Frogs.
Grondin	Gurnet.
Hareng	Herring, fresh.

Hareng fumé	Kipper.
Hareng salé	Bloater.
Hareng saur	Red herring.
Homard	Lobster.
Huîtres	Oysters.
Julienne, en	Cut in thin match-like strips.
Kadgiory	Kedgeree.
Kari	Curry.
Laitance	Soft roe.
Lamproie	Lamprey.
Langouste	Crawfish (sea-water).
Langoustine	Dublin Bay prawn.
Lard	Bacon.
Limande	Lemon sole, sometimes Dab.
Lotte	Eel-pout.
Loup de mer	Bass.
Maquereau	Mackerel.
Marinade	A mixture used for soaking fish before cooking.
Matelote	A savoury fish ragout.
Merlan	Whiting.
Morue	Salt cod.
Moule	Mussel.
Muge } *Mulet* }	Grey mullet.
Nage	A special *court-bouillon* for shellfish.
Nephrops	Dublin Bay prawns.
Nymphes	Frogs.
Oursin	Sea-urchin.

Palourde	Cockle.
Paupiette	A rolled fillet of fish.
Perche	Perch.
Pilaff	A rice dish.
Piroguis	A small fish pasty from Russia.
Poisson	Fish.
Poutargue	An oriental preparation of dried tunny or mullet eggs.
Raie	Skate.
Rastegaïs	A sort of small Coulibiac or Russian fish pasty.
Riz	Rice.
Rizotto	An Italian dish of rice and meat or fish.
Roll-mops	Soused bloater fillets.
Rôti	Roasted.
Rouget	Red mullet.
Roux	The initial preparation of flour and butter, cooked to varying degrees of colouration, used as a thickening agent.
Royan	A kind of sardine.
Saint-Pierre	John Dory.
Salé	Salted.
Salpicon	Dice of any ingredient used for the preparation of a dish, these being about a quarter of an inch sided. If they are cut very finely instead, the preparation becomes a *Brunoise*.
Saumon	Salmon.
Saumon fumé	Smoked salmon.
Suprêmes	The best fillets.

Tanche	Tench.
Thon	Tunny fish.
Tortue	Turtle.
Tourte	Tart.
Truite	Trout.
Truite saumonée	Salmon trout.
Turbotin	Chicken turbot.
Velouté	A thick fish sauce or soup.
Vive	Weever.
Vol-au-vent	A fine puff-pastry case filled with fish or meat.

CLASSIFIED INDEX

FRENCH

PAGE

Poissons de Mer—*Continued*

PAGE

Timbales de Poissons, etc. 196-197

CLASSIFIED INDEX

ENGLISH

INDEX TO AMERICAN FISH SUBSTITUTIONS

A CATALOGUE OF SELECTED DOVER BOOKS
IN ALL FIELDS OF INTEREST

A CATALOGUE OF SELECTED DOVER BOOKS
IN ALL FIELDS OF INTEREST

WHAT IS SCIENCE?, *N. Campbell*
The role of experiment and measurement, the function of mathematics, the nature of scientific laws, the difference between laws and theories, the limitations of science, and many similarly provocative topics are treated clearly and without technicalities by an eminent scientist. "Still an excellent introduction to scientific philosophy," H. Margenau in *Physics Today*. "A first-rate primer . . . deserves a wide audience," *Scientific American*. 192pp. 5⅜ x 8.
60043-2 Paperbound $1.25

THE NATURE OF LIGHT AND COLOUR IN THE OPEN AIR, *M. Minnaert*
Why are shadows sometimes blue, sometimes green, or other colors depending on the light and surroundings? What causes mirages? Why do multiple suns and moons appear in the sky? Professor Minnaert explains these unusual phenomena and hundreds of others in simple, easy-to-understand terms based on optical laws and the properties of light and color. No mathematics is required but artists, scientists, students, and everyone fascinated by these "tricks" of nature will find thousands of useful and amazing pieces of information. Hundreds of observational experiments are suggested which require no special equipment. 200 illustrations; 42 photos. xvi + 362pp. 5⅜ x 8.
20196-1 Paperbound $2.75

THE STRANGE STORY OF THE QUANTUM, AN ACCOUNT FOR THE GENERAL READER OF THE GROWTH OF IDEAS UNDERLYING OUR PRESENT ATOMIC KNOWLEDGE, *B. Hoffmann*
Presents lucidly and expertly, with barest amount of mathematics, the problems and theories which led to modern quantum physics. Dr. Hoffmann begins with the closing years of the 19th century, when certain trifling discrepancies were noticed, and with illuminating analogies and examples takes you through the brilliant concepts of Planck, Einstein, Pauli, Broglie, Bohr, Schroedinger, Heisenberg, Dirac, Sommerfeld, Feynman, etc. This edition includes a new, long postscript carrying the story through 1958. "Of the books attempting an account of the history and contents of our modern atomic physics which have come to my attention, this is the best," H. Margenau, Yale University, in *American Journal of Physics*. 32 tables and line illustrations. Index. 275pp. 5⅜ x 8.
20518-5 Paperbound $2.00

GREAT IDEAS OF MODERN MATHEMATICS: THEIR NATURE AND USE, *Jagjit Singh*
Reader with only high school math will understand main mathematical ideas of modern physics, astronomy, genetics, psychology, evolution, etc. better than many who use them as tools, but comprehend little of their basic structure. Author uses his wide knowledge of non-mathematical fields in brilliant exposition of differential equations, matrices, group theory, logic, statistics, problems of mathematical foundations, imaginary numbers, vectors, etc. Original publication. 2 appendixes. 2 indexes. 65 ills. 322pp. 5⅜ x 8.
20587-8 Paperbound $2.50

THE MUSIC OF THE SPHERES: THE MATERIAL UNIVERSE — FROM ATOM TO QUASAR, SIMPLY EXPLAINED, *Guy Murchie*
Vast compendium of fact, modern concept and theory, observed and calculated data, historical background guides intelligent layman through the material universe. Brilliant exposition of earth's construction, explanations for moon's craters, atmospheric components of Venus and Mars (with data from recent fly-by's), sun spots, sequences of star birth and death, neighboring galaxies, contributions of Galileo, Tycho Brahe, Kepler, etc.; and (Vol. 2) construction of the atom (describing newly discovered sigma and xi subatomic particles), theories of sound, color and light, space and time, including relativity theory, quantum theory, wave theory, probability theory, work of Newton, Maxwell, Faraday, Einstein, de Broglie, etc. "Best presentation yet offered to the intelligent general reader," *Saturday Review*. Revised (1967). Index. 319 illustrations by the author. Total of xx + 644pp. 5⅜ x 8½.
21809-0, 21810-4 Two volume set, paperbound $5.00

FOUR LECTURES ON RELATIVITY AND SPACE, *Charles Proteus Steinmetz*
Lecture series, given by great mathematician and electrical engineer, generally considered one of the best popular-level expositions of special and general relativity theories and related questions. Steinmetz translates complex mathematical reasoning into language accessible to laymen through analogy, example and comparison. Among topics covered are relativity of motion, location, time; of mass; acceleration; 4-dimensional time-space; geometry of the gravitational field; curvature and bending of space; non-Euclidean geometry. Index. 40 illustrations. x + 142pp. 5⅜ x 8½.   61771-8 Paperbound $1.50

HOW TO KNOW THE WILD FLOWERS, *Mrs. William Starr Dana*
Classic nature book that has introduced thousands to wonders of American wild flowers. Color-season principle of organization is easy to use, even by those with no botanical training, and the genial, refreshing discussions of history, folklore, uses of over 1,000 native and escape flowers, foliage plants are informative as well as fun to read. Over 170 full-page plates, collected from several editions, may be colored in to make permanent records of finds. Revised to conform with 1950 edition of Gray's Manual of Botany. xlii + 438pp. 5⅜ x 8½.   20332-8 Paperbound $2.50

MANUAL OF THE TREES OF NORTH AMERICA, *Charles Sprague Sargent*
Still unsurpassed as most comprehensive, reliable study of North American tree characteristics, precise locations and distribution. By dean of American dendrologists. Every tree native to U.S., Canada, Alaska; 185 genera, 717 species, described in detail—leaves, flowers, fruit, winterbuds, bark, wood, growth habits, etc. plus discussion of varieties and local variants, immaturity variations. Over 100 keys, including unusual 11-page analytical key to genera, aid in identification. 783 clear illustrations of flowers, fruit, leaves. An unmatched permanent reference work for all nature lovers. Second enlarged (1926) edition. Synopsis of families. Analytical key to genera. Glossary of technical terms. Index. 783 illustrations, 1 map. Total of 982pp. 5⅜ x 8.
20277-1, 20278-X Two volume set, paperbound $6.00

IT'S FUN TO MAKE THINGS FROM SCRAP MATERIALS,
Evelyn Glantz Hershoff
What use are empty spools, tin cans, bottle tops? What can be made from
rubber bands, clothes pins, paper clips, and buttons? This book provides
simply worded instructions and large diagrams showing you how to make
cookie cutters, toy trucks, paper turkeys, Halloween masks, telephone sets,
aprons, linoleum block- and spatter prints — in all 399 projects! Many are easy
enough for young children to figure out for themselves; some challenging
enough to entertain adults; all are remarkably ingenious ways to make things
from materials that cost pennies or less! Formerly "Scrap Fun for Everyone."
Index. 214 illustrations. 373pp. 5⅜ x 8½.   21251-3 Paperbound $2.00

SYMBOLIC LOGIC and THE GAME OF LOGIC, *Lewis Carroll*
"Symbolic Logic" is not concerned with modern symbolic logic, but is instead
a collection of over 380 problems posed with charm and imagination, using
the syllogism and a fascinating diagrammatic method of drawing conclusions.
In "The Game of Logic" Carroll's whimsical imagination devises a logical game
played with 2 diagrams and counters (included) to manipulate hundreds of
tricky syllogisms. The final section, "Hit or Miss" is a lagniappe of 101 additional puzzles in the delightful Carroll manner. Until this reprint edition,
both of these books were rarities costing up to $15 each. Symbolic Logic:
Index. xxxi + 199pp. The Game of Logic: 96pp. 2 vols. bound as one. 5⅜ x 8.
                                        20492-8 Paperbound $2.50

MATHEMATICAL PUZZLES OF SAM LOYD, PART I
selected and edited by M. Gardner
Choice puzzles by the greatest American puzzle creator and innovator. Selected
from his famous collection, "Cyclopedia of Puzzles," they retain the unique
style and historical flavor of the originals. There are posers based on arithmetic,
algebra, probability, game theory, route tracing, topology, counter and sliding
block, operations research, geometrical dissection. Includes the famous "14-15"
puzzle which was a national craze, and his "Horse of a Different Color" which
sold millions of copies. 117 of his most ingenious puzzles in all. 120 line
drawings and diagrams. Solutions. Selected references. xx + 167pp. 5⅜ x 8.
                                        20498-7 Paperbound $1.35

STRING FIGURES AND HOW TO MAKE THEM, *Caroline Furness Jayne*
107 string figures plus variations selected from the best primitive and modern
examples developed by Navajo, Apache, pygmies of Africa, Eskimo, in Europe,
Australia, China, etc. The most readily understandable, easy-to-follow book in
English on perennially popular recreation. Crystal-clear exposition; step-by-
step diagrams. Everyone from kindergarten children to adults looking for
unusual diversion will be endlessly amused. Index. Bibliography. Introduction
by A. C. Haddon. 17 full-page plates, 960 illustrations. xxiii + 401pp. 5⅜ x 8½.
                                        20152-X Paperbound $2.50

PAPER FOLDING FOR BEGINNERS, *W. D. Murray and F. J. Rigney*
A delightful introduction to the varied and entertaining Japanese art of
origami (paper folding), with a full, crystal-clear text that anticipates every
difficulty; over 275 clearly labeled diagrams of all important stages in creation.
You get results at each stage, since complex figures are logically developed
from simpler ones. 43 different pieces are explained: sailboats, frogs, roosters,
etc. 6 photographic plates. 279 diagrams. 95pp. 5⅜ x 8⅜.
                                        20713-7 Paperbound $1.00

PRINCIPLES OF ART HISTORY,
H. Wölfflin
Analyzing such terms as "baroque," "classic," "neoclassic," "primitive," "picturesque," and 164 different works by artists like Botticelli, van Cleve, Dürer, Hobbema, Holbein, Hals, Rembrandt, Titian, Brueghel, Vermeer, and many others, the author establishes the classifications of art history and style on a firm, concrete basis. This classic of art criticism shows what really occurred between the 14th-century primitives and the sophistication of the 18th century in terms of basic attitudes and philosophies. "A remarkable lesson in the art of seeing," *Sat. Rev. of Literature.* Translated from the 7th German edition. 150 illustrations. 254pp. 6⅛ x 9¼. 20276-3 Paperbound $2.50

PRIMITIVE ART,
Franz Boas
This authoritative and exhaustive work by a great American anthropologist covers the entire gamut of primitive art. Pottery, leatherwork, metal work, stone work, wood, basketry, are treated in detail. Theories of primitive art, historical depth in art history, technical virtuosity, unconscious levels of patterning, symbolism, styles, literature, music, dance, etc. A must book for the interested layman, the anthropologist, artist, handicrafter (hundreds of unusual motifs), and the historian. Over 900 illustrations (50 ceramic vessels, 12 totem poles, etc.). 376pp. 5⅜ x 8. 20025-6 Paperbound $2.50

THE GENTLEMAN AND CABINET MAKER'S DIRECTOR,
Thomas Chippendale
A reprint of the 1762 catalogue of furniture designs that went on to influence generations of English and Colonial and Early Republic American furniture makers. The 200 plates, most of them full-page sized, show Chippendale's designs for French (Louis XV), Gothic, and Chinese-manner chairs, sofas, canopy and dome beds, cornices, chamber organs, cabinets, shaving tables, commodes, picture frames, frets, candle stands, chimney pieces, decorations, etc. The drawings are all elegant and highly detailed; many include construction diagrams and elevations. A supplement of 24 photographs shows surviving pieces of original and Chippendale-style pieces of furniture. Brief biography of Chippendale by N. I. Bienenstock, editor of *Furniture World.* Reproduced from the 1762 edition. 200 plates, plus 19 photographic plates. vi + 249pp. 9⅛ x 12¼. 21601-2 Paperbound $4.00

AMERICAN ANTIQUE FURNITURE: A BOOK FOR AMATEURS,
Edgar G. Miller, Jr.
Standard introduction and practical guide to identification of valuable American antique furniture. 2115 illustrations, mostly photographs taken by the author in 148 private homes, are arranged in chronological order in extensive chapters on chairs, sofas, chests, desks, bedsteads, mirrors, tables, clocks, and other articles. Focus is on furniture accessible to the collector, including simpler pieces and a larger than usual coverage of Empire style. Introductory chapters identify structural elements, characteristics of various styles, how to avoid fakes, etc. "We are frequently asked to name some book on American furniture that will meet the requirements of the novice collector, the beginning dealer, and . . . the general public. . . . We believe Mr. Miller's two volumes more completely satisfy this specification than any other work," *Antiques.* Appendix. Index. Total of vi + 1106pp. 7⅞ x 10¾. 21599-7, 21600-4 Two volume set, paperbound $10.00

THE BAD CHILD'S BOOK OF BEASTS, MORE BEASTS FOR WORSE CHILDREN, and A MORAL ALPHABET, *H. Belloc*
Hardly and anthology of humorous verse has appeared in the last 50 years without at least a couple of these famous nonsense verses. But one must see the entire volumes — with all the delightful original illustrations by Sir Basil Blackwood — to appreciate fully Belloc's charming and witty verses that play so subacidly on the platitudes of life and morals that beset his day — and ours. A great humor classic. Three books in one. Total of 157pp. 5⅜ x 8.
20749-8 Paperbound $1.25

THE DEVIL'S DICTIONARY, *Ambrose Bierce*
Sardonic and irreverent barbs puncturing the pomposities and absurdities of American politics, business, religion, literature, and arts, by the country's greatest satirist in the classic tradition. Epigrammatic as Shaw, piercing as Swift, American as Mark Twain, Will Rogers, and Fred Allen, Bierce will always remain the favorite of a small coterie of enthusiasts, and of writers and speakers whom he supplies with "some of the most gorgeous witticisms of the English language" (H. L. Mencken). Over 1000 entries in alphabetical order. 144pp. 5⅜ x 8.
20487-1 Paperbound $1.25

THE COMPLETE NONSENSE OF EDWARD LEAR.
This is the only complete edition of this master of gentle madness available at a popular price. *A Book of Nonsense, Nonsense Songs, More Nonsense Songs and Stories* in their entirety with all the old favorites that have delighted children and adults for years. The Dong With A Luminous Nose, The Jumblies, The Owl and the Pussycat, and hundreds of other bits of wonderful nonsense. 214 limericks, 3 sets of Nonsense Botany, 5 Nonsense Alphabets, 546 drawings by Lear himself, and much more. 320pp. 5⅜ x 8. 20167-8 Paperbound $1.75

THE WIT AND HUMOR OF OSCAR WILDE, *ed. by Alvin Redman*
Wilde at his most brilliant, in 1000 epigrams exposing weaknesses and hypocrisies of "civilized" society. Divided into 49 categories—sin, wealth, women, America, etc.—to aid writers, speakers. Includes excerpts from his trials, books, plays, criticism. Formerly "The Epigrams of Oscar Wilde." Introduction by Vyvyan Holland, Wilde's only living son. Introductory essay by editor. 260pp. 5⅜ x 8.
20602-5 Paperbound $1.50

A CHILD'S PRIMER OF NATURAL HISTORY, *Oliver Herford*
Scarcely an anthology of whimsy and humor has appeared in the last 50 years without a contribution from Oliver Herford. Yet the works from which these examples are drawn have been almost impossible to obtain! Here at last are Herford's improbable definitions of a menagerie of familiar and weird animals, each verse illustrated by the author's own drawings. 24 drawings in 2 colors; 24 additional drawings. vii + 95pp. 6½ x 6. 21647-0 Paperbound $1.00

THE BROWNIES: THEIR BOOK, *Palmer Cox*
The book that made the Brownies a household word. Generations of readers have enjoyed the antics, predicaments and adventures of these jovial sprites, who emerge from the forest at night to play or to come to the aid of a deserving human. Delightful illustrations by the author decorate nearly every page. 24 short verse tales with 266 illustrations. 155pp. 6⅝ x 9¼.
21265-3 Paperbound $1.50

THE PRINCIPLES OF PSYCHOLOGY,
William James

The full long-course, unabridged, of one of the great classics of Western literature and science. Wonderfully lucid descriptions of human mental activity, the stream of thought, consciousness, time perception, memory, imagination, emotions, reason, abnormal phenomena, and similar topics. Original contributions are integrated with the work of such men as Berkeley, Binet, Mills, Darwin, Hume, Kant, Royce, Schopenhauer, Spinoza, Locke, Descartes, Galton, Wundt, Lotze, Herbart, Fechner, and scores of others. All contrasting interpretations of mental phenomena are examined in detail—introspective analysis, philosophical interpretation, and experimental research. "A classic," *Journal of Consulting Psychology.* "The main lines are as valid as ever," *Psychoanalytical Quarterly.* "Standard reading . . . a classic of interpretation," *Psychiatric Quarterly.* 94 illustrations. 1408pp. 5⅜ x 8.

20381-6, 20382-4 Two volume set, paperbound $6.00

VISUAL ILLUSIONS: THEIR CAUSES, CHARACTERISTICS AND APPLICATIONS,
M. Luckiesh

"Seeing is deceiving," asserts the author of this introduction to virtually every type of optical illusion known. The text both describes and explains the principles involved in color illusions, figure-ground, distance illusions, etc. 100 photographs, drawings and diagrams prove how easy it is to fool the sense: circles that aren't round, parallel lines that seem to bend, stationary figures that seem to move as you stare at them — illustration after illustration strains our credulity at what we see. Fascinating book from many points of view, from applications for artists, in camouflage, etc. to the psychology of vision. New introduction by William Ittleson, Dept. of Psychology, Queens College. Index. Bibliography. xxi + 252pp. 5⅜ x 8½.

21530-X Paperbound $1.75

FADS AND FALLACIES IN THE NAME OF SCIENCE,
Martin Gardner

This is the standard account of various cults, quack systems, and delusions which have masqueraded as science: hollow earth fanatics. Reich and orgone sex energy, dianetics, Atlantis, multiple moons, Forteanism, flying saucers, medical fallacies like iridiagnosis, zone therapy, etc. A new chapter has been added on Bridey Murphy, psionics, and other recent manifestations in this field. This is a fair, reasoned appraisal of eccentric theory which provides excellent inoculation against cleverly masked nonsense. "Should be read by everyone, scientist and non-scientist alike," R. T. Birge, Prof. Emeritus of Physics, Univ. of California; Former President, American Physical Society. Index. x + 365pp. 5⅜ x 8.

20394-8 Paperbound $2.00

ILLUSIONS AND DELUSIONS OF THE SUPERNATURAL AND THE OCCULT,
D. H. Rawcliffe

Holds up to rational examination hundreds of persistent delusions including crystal gazing, automatic writing, table turning, mediumistic trances, mental healing, stigmata, lycanthropy, live burial, the Indian Rope Trick, spiritualism, dowsing, telepathy, clairvoyance, ghosts, ESP, etc. The author explains and exposes the mental and physical deceptions involved, making this not only an exposé of supernatural phenomena, but a valuable exposition of characteristic types of abnormal psychology. Originally titled "The Psychology of the Occult." 14 illustrations. Index. 551pp. 5⅜ x 8. 20503-7 Paperbound $3.50

FAIRY TALE COLLECTIONS, *edited by Andrew Lang*
Andrew Lang's fairy tale collections make up the richest shelf-full of traditional children's stories anywhere available. Lang supervised the translation of stories from all over the world—familiar European tales collected by Grimm, animal stories from Negro Africa, myths of primitive Australia, stories from Russia, Hungary, Iceland, Japan, and many other countries. Lang's selection of translations are unusually high; many authorities consider that the most familiar tales find their best versions in these volumes. All collections are richly decorated and illustrated by H. J. Ford and other artists.

THE BLUE FAIRY BOOK. 37 stories. 138 illustrations. ix + 390pp. 5⅜ x 8½.
21437-0 Paperbound $1.95

THE GREEN FAIRY BOOK. 42 stories. 100 illustrations. xiii + 366pp. 5⅜ x 8½.
21439-7 Paperbound $2.00

THE BROWN FAIRY BOOK. 32 stories. 50 illustrations, 8 in color. xii + 350pp. 5⅜ x 8½.
21438-9 Paperbound $1.95

THE BEST TALES OF HOFFMANN, *edited by E. F. Bleiler*
10 stories by E. T. A. Hoffmann, one of the greatest of all writers of fantasy. The tales include "The Golden Flower Pot," "Automata," "A New Year's Eve Adventure," "Nutcracker and the King of Mice," "Sand-Man," and others. Vigorous characterizations of highly eccentric personalities, remarkably imaginative situations, and intensely fast pacing has made these tales popular all over the world for 150 years. Editor's introduction. 7 drawings by Hoffmann. xxxiii + 419pp. 5⅜ x 8½.
21793-0 Paperbound $2.25

GHOST AND HORROR STORIES OF AMBROSE BIERCE,
edited by E. F. Bleiler
Morbid, eerie, horrifying tales of possessed poets, shabby aristocrats, revived corpses, and haunted malefactors. Widely acknowledged as the best of their kind between Poe and the moderns, reflecting their author's inner torment and bitter view of life. Includes "Damned Thing," "The Middle Toe of the Right Foot," "The Eyes of the Panther," "Visions of the Night," "Moxon's Master," and over a dozen others. Editor's introduction. xxii + 199pp. 5⅜ x 8½.
20767-6 Paperbound $1.50

THREE GOTHIC NOVELS, *edited by E. F. Bleiler*
Originators of the still popular Gothic novel form, influential in ushering in early 19th-century Romanticism. Horace Walpole's *Castle of Otranto*, William Beckford's *Vathek*, John Polidori's *The Vampyre*, and a *Fragment* by Lord Byron are enjoyable as exciting reading or as documents in the history of English literature. Editor's introduction. xi + 291pp. 5⅜ x 8½.
21232-7 Paperbound $2.00

BEST GHOST STORIES OF LEFANU, *edited by E. F. Bleiler*
Though admired by such critics as V. S. Pritchett, Charles Dickens and Henry James, ghost stories by the Irish novelist Joseph Sheridan LeFanu have never become as widely known as his detective fiction. About half of the 16 stories in this collection have never before been available in America. Collection includes "Carmilla" (perhaps the best vampire story ever written), "The Haunted Baronet," "The Fortunes of Sir Robert Ardagh," and the classic "Green Tea." Editor's introduction. 7 contemporary illustrations. Portrait of LeFanu. xii + 467pp. 5⅜ x 8.
20415-4 Paperbound $2.50

EASY-TO-DO ENTERTAINMENTS AND DIVERSIONS WITH COINS, CARDS, STRING, PAPER AND MATCHES, *R. M. Abraham*
Over 300 tricks, games and puzzles will provide young readers with absorbing fun. Sections on card games; paper-folding; tricks with coins, matches and pieces of string; games for the agile; toy-making from common household objects; mathematical recreations; and 50 miscellaneous pastimes. Anyone in charge of groups of youngsters, including hard-pressed parents, and in need of suggestions on how to keep children sensibly amused and quietly content will find this book indispensable. Clear, simple text, copious number of delightful line drawings and illustrative diagrams. Originally titled "Winter Nights' Entertainments." Introduction by Lord Baden Powell. 329 illustrations. v + 186pp. 5⅜ x 8½.   20921-0 Paperbound $1.25

AN INTRODUCTION TO CHESS MOVES AND TACTICS SIMPLY EXPLAINED, *Leonard Barden*
Beginner's introduction to the royal game. Names, possible moves of the pieces, definitions of essential terms, how games are won, etc. explained in 30-odd pages. With this background you'll be able to sit right down and play. Balance of book teaches strategy — openings, middle game, typical endgame play, and suggestions for improving your game. A sample game is fully analyzed. True middle-level introduction, teaching you all the essentials without oversimplifying or losing you in a maze of detail. 58 figures. 102pp. 5⅜ x 8½.   21210-6 Paperbound $1.25

LASKER'S MANUAL OF CHESS, *Dr. Emanuel Lasker*
Probably the greatest chess player of modern times, Dr. Emanuel Lasker held the world championship 28 years, independent of passing schools or fashions. This unmatched study of the game, chiefly for intermediate to skilled players, analyzes basic methods, combinations, position play, the aesthetics of chess, dozens of different openings, etc., with constant reference to great modern games. Contains a brilliant exposition of Steinitz's important theories. Introduction by Fred Reinfeld. Tables of Lasker's tournament record. 3 indices. 308 diagrams. 1 photograph. xxx + 349pp. 5⅜ x 8.20640-8Paperbound $2.50

COMBINATIONS: THE HEART OF CHESS, *Irving Chernev*
Step-by-step from simple combinations to complex, this book, by a well-known chess writer, shows you the intricacies of pins, counter-pins, knight forks, and smothered mates. Other chapters show alternate lines of play to those taken in actual championship games; boomerang combinations; classic examples of brilliant combination play by Nimzovich, Rubinstein, Tarrasch, Botvinnik, Alekhine and Capablanca. Index. 356 diagrams. ix + 245pp. 5⅜ x 8½.   21744-2 Paperbound $2.00

HOW TO SOLVE CHESS PROBLEMS, *K. S. Howard*
Full of practical suggestions for the fan or the beginner — who knows only the moves of the chessmen. Contains preliminary section and 58 two-move, 46 three-move, and 8 four-move problems composed by 27 outstanding American problem creators in the last 30 years. Explanation of all terms and exhaustive index. "Just what is wanted for the student," Brian Harley. 112 problems, solutions. vi + 171pp. 5⅜ x 8.   20748-X Paperbound $1.50

SOCIAL THOUGHT FROM LORE TO SCIENCE,
H. E. Barnes and H. Becker
An immense survey of sociological thought and ways of viewing, studying, planning, and reforming society from earliest times to the present. Includes thought on society of preliterate peoples, ancient non-Western cultures, and every great movement in Europe, America, and modern Japan. Analyzes hundreds of great thinkers: Plato, Augustine, Bodin, Vico, Montesquieu, Herder, Comte, Marx, etc. Weighs the contributions of utopians, sophists, fascists and communists; economists, jurists, philosophers, ecclesiastics, and every 19th and 20th century school of scientific sociology, anthropology, and social psychology throughout the world. Combines topical, chronological, and regional approaches, treating the evolution of social thought as a process rather than as a series of mere topics. "Impressive accuracy, competence, and discrimination . . . easily the best single survey," *Nation.* Thoroughly revised, with new material up to 1960. 2 indexes. Over 2200 bibliographical notes. Three volume set. Total of 1586pp. 5⅜ x 8.
20901-6, 20902-4, 20903-2 Three volume set, paperbound $10.50

A HISTORY OF HISTORICAL WRITING, *Harry Elmer Barnes*
Virtually the only adequate survey of the whole course of historical writing in a single volume. Surveys developments from the beginnings of historiography in the ancient Near East and the Classical World, up through the Cold War. Covers major historians in detail, shows interrelationship with cultural background, makes clear individual contributions, evaluates and estimates importance; also enormously rich upon minor authors and thinkers who are usually passed over. Packed with scholarship and learning, clear, easily written. Indispensable to every student of history. Revised and enlarged up to 1961. Index and bibliography. xv + 442pp. 5⅜ x 8½.
20104-X Paperbound $3.00

JOHANN SEBASTIAN BACH, *Philipp Spitta*
The complete and unabridged text of the definitive study of Bach. Written some 70 years ago, it is still unsurpassed for its coverage of nearly all aspects of Bach's life and work. There could hardly be a finer non-technical introduction to Bach's music than the detailed, lucid analyses which Spitta provides for hundreds of individual pieces. 26 solid pages are devoted to the B minor mass, for example, and 30 pages to the glorious St. Matthew Passion. This monumental set also includes a major analysis of the music of the 18th century: Buxtehude, Pachelbel, etc. "Unchallenged as the last word on one of the supreme geniuses of music," John Barkham, *Saturday Review Syndicate.* Total of 1819pp. Heavy cloth binding. 5⅜ x 8.
22278-0, 22279-9 Two volume set, clothbound $15.00

BEETHOVEN AND HIS NINE SYMPHONIES, *George Grove*
In this modern middle-level classic of musicology Grove not only analyzes all nine of Beethoven's symphonies very thoroughly in terms of their musical structure, but also discusses the circumstances under which they were written, Beethoven's stylistic development, and much other background material. This is an extremely rich book, yet very easily followed; it is highly recommended to anyone seriously interested in music. Over 250 musical passages. Index. viii + 407pp. 5⅜ x 8.
20334-4 Paperbound $2.50

THE TIME STREAM
John Taine
Acknowledged by many as the best SF writer of the 1920's, Taine (under the name Eric Temple Bell) was also a Professor of Mathematics of considerable renown. Reprinted here are *The Time Stream*, generally considered Taine's best, *The Greatest Game*, a biological-fiction novel, and *The Purple Sapphire*, involving a supercivilization of the past. Taine's stories tie fantastic narratives to frameworks of original and logical scientific concepts. Speculation is often profound on such questions as the nature of time, concept of entropy, cyclical universes, etc. 4 contemporary illustrations. v + 532pp. 5⅜ x 8⅜.
21180-0 Paperbound $3.00

SEVEN SCIENCE FICTION NOVELS,
H. G. Wells
Full unabridged texts of 7 science-fiction novels of the master. Ranging from biology, physics, chemistry, astronomy, to sociology and other studies, Mr. Wells extrapolates whole worlds of strange and intriguing character. "One will have to go far to match this for entertainment, excitement, and sheer pleasure . . ."*New York Times*. Contents: The Time Machine, The Island of Dr. Moreau, The First Men in the Moon, The Invisible Man, The War of the Worlds, The Food of the Gods, In The Days of the Comet. 1015pp. 5⅜ x 8.
20264-X Clothbound $5.00

28 SCIENCE FICTION STORIES OF H. G. WELLS.
Two full, unabridged novels, *Men Like Gods* and *Star Begotten*, plus 26 short stories by the master science-fiction writer of all time! Stories of space, time, invention, exploration, futuristic adventure. Partial contents: *The Country of the Blind, In the Abyss, The Crystal Egg, The Man Who Could Work Miracles, A Story of Days to Come, The Empire of the Ants, The Magic Shop, The Valley of the Spiders, A Story of the Stone Age, Under the Knife, Sea Raiders*, etc. An indispensable collection for the library of anyone interested in science fiction adventure. 928pp. 5⅜ x 8.
20265-8 Clothbound $5.00

THREE MARTIAN NOVELS,
Edgar Rice Burroughs
Complete, unabridged reprinting, in one volume, of Thuvia, Maid of Mars; Chessmen of Mars; The Master Mind of Mars. Hours of science-fiction adventure by a modern master storyteller. Reset in large clear type for easy reading. 16 illustrations by J. Allen St. John. vi + 490pp. 5⅜ x 8½.
20039-6. Paperbound $2.50

AN INTELLECTUAL AND CULTURAL HISTORY OF THE WESTERN WORLD,
Harry Elmer Barnes
Monumental 3-volume survey of intellectual development of Europe from primitive cultures to the present day. Every significant product of human intellect traced through history: art, literature, mathematics, physical sciences, medicine, music, technology, social sciences, religions, jurisprudence, education, etc. Presentation is lucid and specific, analyzing in detail specific discoveries, theories, literary works, and so on. Revised (1965) by recognized scholars in specialized fields under the direction of Prof. Barnes. Revised bibliography. Indexes. 24 illustrations. Total of xxix + 1318pp.
21275-0, 21276-9, 21277-7 Three volume set, paperbound $7.75

HEAR ME TALKIN' TO YA, *edited by Nat Shapiro and Nat Hentoff*
In their own words, Louis Armstrong, King Oliver, Fletcher Henderson, Bunk Johnson, Bix Beiderbecke, Billy Holiday, Fats Waller, Jelly Roll Morton, Duke Ellington, and many others comment on the origins of jazz in New Orleans and its growth in Chicago's South Side, Kansas City's jam sessions, Depression Harlem, and the modernism of the West Coast schools. Taken from taped conversations, letters, magazine articles, other first-hand sources. Editors' introduction. xvi + 429pp. 5⅜ x 8½.   21726-4 Paperbound $2.50

THE JOURNAL OF HENRY D. THOREAU
A 25-year record by the great American observer and critic, as complete a record of a great man's inner life as is anywhere available. Thoreau's Journals served him as raw material for his formal pieces, as a place where he could develop his ideas, as an outlet for his interests in wild life and plants, in writing as an art, in classics of literature, Walt Whitman and other contemporaries, in politics, slavery, individual's relation to the State, etc. The Journals present a portrait of a remarkable man, and are an observant social history. Unabridged republication of 1906 edition, Bradford Torrey and Francis H. Allen, editors. Illustrations. Total of 1888pp. 8⅜ x 12¼.
        20312-3, 20313-1 Two volume set, clothbound $30.00

A SHAKESPEARIAN GRAMMAR, *E. A. Abbott*
Basic reference to Shakespeare and his contemporaries, explaining through thousands of quotations from Shakespeare, Jonson, Beaumont and Fletcher, North's *Plutarch* and other sources the grammatical usage differing from the modern. First published in 1870 and written by a scholar who spent much of his life isolating principles of Elizabethan language, the book is unlikely ever to be superseded. Indexes. xxiv + 511pp. 5⅜ x 8½. 21582-2 Paperbound $3.00

FOLK-LORE OF SHAKESPEARE, *T. F. Thistelton Dyer*
Classic study, drawing from Shakespeare a large body of references to supernatural beliefs, terminology of falconry and hunting, games and sports, good luck charms, marriage customs, folk medicines, superstitions about plants, animals, birds, argot of the underworld, sexual slang of London, proverbs, drinking customs, weather lore, and much else. From full compilation comes a mirror of the 17th-century popular mind. Index. ix + 526pp. 5⅜ x 8½.
        21614-4 Paperbound $3.25

THE NEW VARIORUM SHAKESPEARE, *edited by H. H. Furness*
By far the richest editions of the plays ever produced in any country or language. Each volume contains complete text (usually First Folio) of the play, all variants in Quarto and other Folio texts, editorial changes by every major editor to Furness's own time (1900), footnotes to obscure references or language, extensive quotes from literature of Shakespearian criticism, essays on plot sources (often reprinting sources in full), and much more.

HAMLET, *edited by H. H. Furness*
Total of xxvi + 905pp. 5⅜ x 8½.
        21004-9, 21005-7 Two volume set, paperbound $5.50
TWELFTH NIGHT, *edited by H. H. Furness*
Index. xxii + 434pp. 5⅜ x 8½.   21189-4 Paperbound $2.75

La Boheme by Giacomo Puccini,
translated and introduced by Ellen H. Bleiler
Complete handbook for the operagoer, with everything needed for full enjoyment except the musical score itself. Complete Italian libretto, with new,
modern English line-by-line translation—the only libretto printing all repeats;
biography of Puccini; the librettists; background to the opera, Murger's La
Boheme, etc.; circumstances of composition and performances; plot summary;
and pictorial section of 73 illustrations showing Puccini, famous singers and
performances, etc. Large clear type for easy reading. 124pp. 5⅜ x 8½.
20404-9 Paperbound $1.50

Antonio Stradivari: His Life and Work (1644-1737),
W. Henry Hill, Arthur F. Hill, and Alfred E. Hill
Still the only book that really delves into life and art of the incomparable
Italian craftsman, maker of the finest musical instruments in the world today.
The authors, expert violin-makers themselves, discuss Stradivari's ancestry, his
construction and finishing techniques, distinguished characteristics of many
of his instruments and their locations. Included, too, is story of introduction
of his instruments into France, England, first revelation of their supreme
merit, and information on his labels, number of instruments made, prices,
mystery of ingredients of his varnish, tone of pre-1684 Stradivari violin and
changes between 1684 and 1690. An extremely interesting, informative account
for all music lovers, from craftsman to concert-goer. Republication of original
(1902) edition. New introduction by Sydney Beck, Head of Rare Book and
Manuscript Collections, Music Division, New York Public Library. Analytical
index by Rembert Wurlitzer. Appendixes. 68 illustrations. 30 full-page plates.
4 in color. xxvi + 315pp. 5⅜ x 8½. 20425-1 Paperbound $3.00

Musical Autographs from Monteverdi to Hindemith,
Emanuel Winternitz
For beauty, for intrinsic interest, for perspective on the composer's personality,
for subtleties of phrasing, shading, emphasis indicated in the autograph but
suppressed in the printed score, the mss. of musical composition are fascinating
documents which repay close study in many different ways. This 2-volume
work reprints facsimiles of mss. by virtually every major composer, and many
minor figures—196 examples in all. A full text points out what can be learned
from mss., analyzes each sample. Index. Bibliography. 18 figures. 196 plates.
Total of 170pp. of text. 7⅞ x 10¾.
21312-9, 21313-7 Two volume set, paperbound $5.00

J. S. Bach,
Albert Schweitzer
One of the few great full-length studies of Bach's life and work, and the
study upon which Schweitzer's renown as a musicologist rests. On first appearance (1911), revolutionized Bach performance. The only writer on Bach to
be musicologist, performing musician, and student of history, theology and
philosophy, Schweitzer contributes particularly full sections on history of German Protestant church music, theories on motivic pictorial representations
in vocal music, and practical suggestions for performance. Translated by
Ernest Newman. Indexes. 5 illustrations. 650 musical examples. Total of xix
+ 928pp. 5⅜ x 8½. 21631-4, 21632-2 Two volume set, paperbound $5.00

THE METHODS OF ETHICS, *Henry Sidgwick*
Propounding no organized system of its own, study subjects every major
methodological approach to ethics to rigorous, objective analysis. Study discusses and relates ethical thought of Plato, Aristotle, Bentham, Clarke, Butler,
Hobbes, Hume, Mill, Spencer, Kant, and dozens of others. Sidgwick retains
conclusions from each system which follow from ethical premises, rejecting
the faulty. Considered by many in the field to be among the most important
treatises on ethical philosophy. Appendix. Index. xlvii + 528pp. 5⅜ x 8½.
21608-X Paperbound $3.00

TEUTONIC MYTHOLOGY, *Jakob Grimm*
A milestone in Western culture; the work which established on a modern
basis the study of history of religions and comparative religions. 4-volume
work assembles and interprets everything available on religious and folk-
loristic beliefs of Germanic people (including Scandinavians, Anglo-Saxons,
etc.). Assembling material from such sources as Tacitus, surviving Old Norse
and Icelandic texts, archeological remains, folktales, surviving superstitions,
comparative traditions, linguistic analysis, etc. Grimm explores pagan deities,
heroes, folklore of nature, religious practices, and every other area of pagan
German belief. To this day, the unrivaled, definitive, exhaustive study. Translated by J. S. Stallybrass from 4th (1883) German edition. Indexes. Total of
lxxvii + 1887pp. 5⅜ x 8½.
21602-0, 21603-9, 21604-7, 21605-5 Four volume set, paperbound $12.00

THE I CHING, *translated by James Legge*
Called "The Book of Changes" in English, this is one of the Five Classics
edited by Confucius, basic and central to Chinese thought. Explains perhaps
the most complex system of divination known, founded on the theory that all
things happening at any one time have characteristic features which can be
isolated and related. Significant in Oriental studies, in history of religions and
philosophy, and also to Jungian psychoanalysis and other areas of modern
European thought. Index. Appendixes. 6 plates. xxi + 448pp. 5⅜ x 8½.
21062-6 Paperbound $2.75

HISTORY OF ANCIENT PHILOSOPHY, *W. Windelband*
One of the clearest, most accurate comprehensive surveys of Greek and Roman
philosophy. Discusses ancient philosophy in general, intellectual life in Greece
in the 7th and 6th centuries B.C., Thales, Anaximander, Anaximenes, Herac-
litus, the Eleatics, Empedocles, Anaxagoras, Leucippus, the Pythagoreans, the
Sophists, Socrates, Democritus (20 pages), Plato (50 pages), Aristotle (70 pages),
the Peripatetics, Stoics, Epicureans, Sceptics, Neo-platonists, Christian Apolo-
gists, etc. 2nd German edition translated by H. E. Cushman. xv + 393pp.
5⅜ x 8. 20357-3 Paperbound $3.00

THE PALACE OF PLEASURE, *William Painter*
Elizabethan versions of Italian and French novels from *The Decameron*,
Cinthio, Straparola, Queen Margaret of Navarre, and other continental sources
— the very work that provided Shakespeare and dozens of his contemporaries
with many of their plots and sub-plots and, therefore, justly considered one of
the most influential books in all English literature. It is also a book that any
reader will still enjoy. Total of cviii + 1,224pp.
21691-8, 21692-6, 21693-4 Three volume set, paperbound $8.25

THE WONDERFUL WIZARD OF OZ, *L. F. Baum*
All the original W. W. Denslow illustrations in full color—as much a part of "The Wizard" as Tenniel's drawings are of "Alice in Wonderland." "The Wizard" is still America's best-loved fairy tale, in which, as the author expresses it, "The wonderment and joy are retained and the heartaches and nightmares left out." Now today's young readers can enjoy every word and wonderful picture of the original book. New introduction by Martin Gardner. A Baum bibliography. 23 full-page color plates. viii + 268pp. 5⅜ x 8.
20691-2 Paperbound $1.95

THE MARVELOUS LAND OF OZ, *L. F. Baum*
This is the equally enchanting sequel to the "Wizard," continuing the adventures of the Scarecrow and the Tin Woodman. The hero this time is a little boy named Tip, and all the delightful Oz magic is still present. This is the Oz book with the Animated Saw-Horse, the Woggle-Bug, and Jack Pumpkinhead. All the original John R. Neill illustrations, 10 in full color. 287pp. 5⅜ x 8.
20692-0 Paperbound $1.75

ALICE'S ADVENTURES UNDER GROUND, *Lewis Carroll*
The original *Alice in Wonderland*, hand-lettered and illustrated by Carroll himself, and originally presented as a Christmas gift to a child-friend. Adults as well as children will enjoy this charming volume, reproduced faithfully in this Dover edition. While the story is essentially the same, there are slight changes, and Carroll's spritely drawings present an intriguing alternative to the famous Tenniel illustrations. One of the most popular books in Dover's catalogue. Introduction by Martin Gardner. 38 illustrations. 128pp. 5⅜ x 8½.
21482-6 Paperbound $1.00

THE NURSERY "ALICE," *Lewis Carroll*
While most of us consider *Alice in Wonderland* a story for children of all ages, Carroll himself felt it was beyond younger children. He therefore provided this simplified version, illustrated with the famous Tenniel drawings enlarged and colored in delicate tints, for children aged "from Nought to Five." Dover's edition of this now rare classic is a faithful copy of the 1889 printing, including 20 illustrations by Tenniel, and front and back covers reproduced in full color. Introduction by Martin Gardner. xxiii + 67pp. 6⅛ x 9¼.
21610-1 Paperbound $1.75

THE STORY OF KING ARTHUR AND HIS KNIGHTS, *Howard Pyle*
A fast-paced, exciting retelling of the best known Arthurian legends for young readers by one of America's best story tellers and illustrators. The sword Excalibur, wooing of Guinevere, Merlin and his downfall, adventures of Sir Pellias and Gawaine, and others. The pen and ink illustrations are vividly imagined and wonderfully drawn. 41 illustrations. xviii + 313pp. 6⅛ x 9¼.
21445-1 Paperbound $2.00

Prices subject to change without notice.

Available at your book dealer or write for free catalogue to Dept. Adsci, Dover Publications, Inc., 180 Varick St., N.Y., N.Y. 10014. Dover publishes more than 150 books each year on science, elementary and advanced mathematics, biology, music, art, literary history, social sciences and other areas.